'The Beatles are the greatest cultural force
we've ever had.'

Steven Spielberg

'They were like the sun coming up on Easter morning.'

John Updike

'I say in speeches that a plausible mission of artists is to
make people appreciate being alive at least a little bit.
I am then asked if I know of any artists who pulled
that off. I reply, "The Beatles did."'

Kurt Vonnegut

'What The Beatles did can never be replaced or
superseded. They gave art back to the people at a time
when every thinking man had long ago decided that the
people could never have art again.'

Clive James

'The Beatles almost single-handedly rescued
the western musical system.'

Howard Goodall

'When I – a mixed-race boy, brought up in a rough,
lower-middle-class London suburb after the war – dream
of this group of friends and collaborators, The Beatles,
they remind me of everything I love about Britain. That
love is for the exhilarating, dissenting art that comes from
its young people. When I think about The Beatles, which
I do every day – I sit down and play one song all through
in the morning, before starting work, to ignite my mood –
I dream of magic, stardust and variety, of lightness, charm
and joie de vivre. And I often wonder how this sunshine
seemed to break out one fine day in the 1960s.'

Hanif Kureishi

'Totally devoid of talent.'

Noel Coward

'I suppose we'll stay doing this sort of stuff for a couple
of years. I mean, naturally we won't be able to stay at this
level. But we should have another two years at least, I
think.'

George Harrison, backstage, Doncaster 1963

STUART MACONIE

WITH A LITTLE HELP FROM THEIR FRIENDS

The Beatles changed the world.
But who changed theirs?

Harper
North

HarperNorth
Windmill Green
24 Mount Street
Manchester M2 3NX

A division of
HarperCollins*Publishers*
1 London Bridge Street
London SE1 9GF

www.harpercollins.co.uk

HarperCollins*Publishers*
Macken House, 39/40 Mayor Street Upper
Dublin 1, D01 C9W8, Ireland

First published by HarperNorth 2025

1

A catalogue record for this book is
available from the British Library

HB ISBN: 978-0-00870586-2

Printed and bound in the UK using 100%
Renewable Electricity by CPI Group (UK) Ltd

To Alice Maconie

INTRODUCTION

One afternoon in 2007, I was sitting in a dressing room at the Roundhouse in London interviewing Paul McCartney who was appearing there that night in a concert for the BBC. I've met Paul McCartney three times now I think, but I can barely remember anything about those meetings, a common syndrome among his many interviewers (Craig Brown notes that the same thing happens to the memories of people who met the late Queen Elizabeth II.) The details that adhere about these encounters are the odd ones; he offered me some chocolate Brazil nuts backstage in Manchester and was mildly, charmingly flirtatious with my co-presenter Elizabeth. The second occasion was in a studio in Broadcasting House and the only thing I remember is that he signed my copy of his new album without being asked, which I thought was both briskly efficient and genuinely sweet. Everyone's going to ask aren't they, and it saves all present an 'eggy' moment.

But on that particular North London afternoon in 2007, it was all going so well that I decided to risk a few curveball questions working on the principle that every avenue of enquiry about The Beatles and their music, their friendships, feuds, songs, drums, hair, shoes and so on had been fastidiously and perhaps tediously (for him) trodden over a thousand times before by a thousand different, excitable and nervous interviewers.

This is how I came to ask Paul McCartney if he'd ever thought he'd rather have been in Gerry and The Pacemakers?

Let me try and explain what I meant by this. I was essaying the notion that maybe, just maybe, Paul could have enjoyed a lifetime of playing music, having hits, making a nice living, being loved far beyond their native Liverpool; all without the hassle, scrutiny and tragedy that has come with the territory of being a Beatle.

I guess I was trying to be smart. I failed.

Paul McCartney, one of the most musical human beings who has ever lived, one of the most significant cultural figures in history, looked at me as if I was demented – which I did feel a little – and said with a baffled but kindly smile 'Stuart, you do know that I was in The Beatles, don't you?' I answered that I was well aware of that and somehow managed to steer the interview back on to saner, safer ground.

I suppose, in part, this book is my way of saying sorry.

When I mentioned to Hunter Davies, the only official Beatles biographer, that I was thinking of writing a 'Beatles book', he replied 'Oh you absolutely should. There hasn't been one for a good half hour.'

There are over two thousand books about The Beatles. As well as the ones you might reasonably expect – the ones about their singles, albums, films and concerts – there are serious, scholarly books about their haircuts, their amplifiers, their use of language and grammar, book length accounts of their visits to Scandinavia, Ireland, Wales, Scotland, Bournemouth and Hull (among many other places) and, of course, the secret Soviet mind-control programme they were involved in.* You can find Beatle books and films and essays to suit

___
* They weren't.

every taste; from brilliant, forensic histories like Mark Lewisohn's *The Beatles: All These Years: Tune In* to parodies such as *Paul is Undead: The British Zombie Invasion* to the downright unhinged claiming The Beatles never existed. There is even a book about the books about The Beatles. It's called *The Beatles and the Historians* by Erin Torkelson Weber and it's really very good.

So why another? It's a good question.

The honest, nearly complete answer is that, essentially, I really wanted to write a book about The Beatles. In early 2022, the year after both my parents passed away and the Covid pandemic had closed down our daily lives completely while the country and the world seemed to be circling downwards to Hades in a kind of death spiral of political chaos and chicanery and sleaze, Peter Jackson's documentary series, *Get Back*, came along and made everything all right again.

This is an exaggeration for effect, but not much. On the release of Jackson's epic revisiting of the sessions and unused footage for what became the *Let It Be* album and Michael Lindsay-Hogg's 1970 movie, millions of people all over the world seemed to let out an exhalation of relief, reminded joyously of the love and hope and burst of colour that The Beatles had gifted to the world. Jackson even rushed out a little 'sneak peek' montage at the height of the pandemic 'to hopefully put a smile on your face in these rather bleak times'. I disagree with many of the biographer Philip Norman's opinions, as expressed in his many Beatles books. But when he described them as 'the most powerful engine for creating human happiness that the entertainment world has ever seen', I think for once he got it about right.

Rich and fulsome though all the quoted praise at the start of this book from those celebrated fans is, it might not go far enough. There is a strong case for saying that The Beatles re-shaped the world. Communism was doomed from the moment teenagers in Moscow, Prague and Budapest heard 'She Loves You'. If this seems hyperbolic, maybe trust former Soviet president Mikhail Gorbachev: 'More than any ideology, more than any religion, more than Vietnam or any war or nuclear bomb, the single most important reason for the diffusion of the Cold War was … The Beatles.' Or perhaps this from one of his successors: 'The Beatles brought a taste of freedom, a window on the world' said one Vladimir Putin. What a pity he didn't pay more attention to them.

They changed the whole nature of masculinity and kept on changing it. Before The Beatles, men had never looked the way they did or sounded the way they did or spoke or sang about the things they did. As Jonathan Freedland pointed out when reviewing the Apple rooftop concert footage, 'They look so current, so fresh – John wearing trainers, George in baseball boots – they seem like visitors from the future, emissaries from 2021 who have somehow landed in the world of Bedford vans, Charles Hawtrey and *The Daily Sketch*.' They elevated popular culture as the pre-eminent mode of artistic endeavour, helping invent the modern world we live in. As the writer Peter Paphides put it, 'For me, it's like the greatest story ever told … We know it has everything in it. We know it has friendship, love, incredible music. The whole human condition is just encased in the story of The Beatles.'

They did all this in many ways, and of course one important way was by making some great records. But The Beatles' story is not just about music, imperishably great though that music is. It goes far beyond the famous songs and albums. It is a great British story, an absorbing epic replete with valour and tragedy, triumph and disaster that we talk about as we might World War II or the Canterbury Tales or the storied history of battles and royal houses. The Beatles' narrative has both shaped and reflected the country and the world we live in today. Alongside Shakespeare they are the great British cultural export to the world, a world they changed and re-made in their own image in a blaze of creativity. But the four dominant personalities changed the world not in isolation but with a little help from their friends, the many and varied individuals that are the heart and spine of this story. This book tells The Beatles' story, our story, through one hundred characters that comprise their dramatis personae.

The Beatles' story feels Shakespearean too in scope and range, a story with all the most compelling elements of the bard's great narratives. Ambition, power, triumph, disaster, heartbreak, tragedy, drama, intrigue, lust and, above all, love. Here, then, you will find the Iagos, the Lady Macbeths, the Rosencrantz and Guildensterns, the Beatrice and Benedicks, and the four Autolycuses exiting, pursued by fans and flashbulbs and destiny.

This book tells of the world that made them and the new world they made, via the kaleidoscopic cast of 'supporting players' and the varied lives that fell within their orbit, sometimes intimately and powerfully, sometimes tangentially but tantalisingly. Some of the major players and their stories offer real insights into the nature of politics, fame, class, sexuality, religion, race and more. Others are just endlessly, quirkily absorbing. As Jason Arkeny said of Ivor Arbiter, one of the many characters you will encounter in the next few hundred pages, he 'was one of the enormous cast of characters who made a small but vital and enduring contribution to the saga of The Beatles'. And so, by extension, a contribution to the shape and history of the modern world. Music geeks who love intensive discussion of finger picking, tape loops, piccolo trumpets, even those infamous 'aeolian cadences' (and I am one of them) may find this short on musicological details. All of the above are discussed. But this book is really about art, class, sex, fashion, gender roles, politics, war, economics, race and more, because The Beatles' story encompasses all of this.

Paul McCartney has a song called 'Early Days' on his 2013 album, *New*, which speaks of his memories of just that – his teenage friendships with the other Beatles and the times they shared back then. It was inspired by a real incident as he has explained. 'I was on holiday once and there was this little American girl on the beach. She says "Hi there. I've just been doing a Beatles appreciation class in school." I said "Wow that's great" and I think "I'll be really cool here. I'll tell her a little inside story." So, I go on about how something happened and it was a fun story. And she looks at me, she says: "No, that's not true. We covered that in The Beatles appreciation class." I'm going: "Oh fuck! There's no way out, man! They're teaching this stuff now!"'

When I mentioned Ian MacDonald's magisterial analysis of The Beatles' recorded canon, *Revolution in the Head*, to Paul McCartney that October day at the Roundhouse, even though it is generous and celebratory, especially towards him, he replied a little steely 'He isn't right about everything, you know.' Similarly, George Harrison once dismissed a statement from the pre-eminent Beatle historian of our time, Mark Lewisohn, with a curt 'You weren't there.' These are daunting admonitions for anyone who has the nerve, the chutzpah to write about The Beatles.

So, let me say now that this is not, cannot be and is not intended to be, a definitive archaeological Beatle history. Clearly, I hope I've not got anything completely and utterly wrong. But what follows is personal, subjective and impressionistic (although I acknowledge that this might be what the combative Leeds United stalwart Billy Bremner called 'getting your retaliation in first').

Anyone looking for a debunking, Albert Goldman style, or a contrarian 'hot take' should look elsewhere. This is unashamedly a celebration of what, for me, is the greatest, most joyous and transcendent cultural force of the modern world and the people around them. But it is personal and idiosyncratic. It is not a canonical addition to the field of Beatle scholarship; not an academic text as much as a reflective, anecdotal one. It isn't a work of reference. There are already fine examples of those. Neither is it exhaustive. There just wasn't room, and I've never been one for completism for its own sake. If I could use one entry to make observations about another – Royston Ellis leading me to discussions of other poets in

The Beatles' story – then I did. I have only largely included those who were part of this great drama as it was being played out, i.e. between 1957 and 1970. That said, I have included three former Beatle drummers, simply because each of their stories is different and compelling in its own melancholy way, rather like Tolstoy's unhappy families. Some entries included themselves by dint of their looming significance – Epstein, Yoko, George Martin – others because The Beatles connection, however slight, was delicious, like Buddy Dresner. Instead of a Beatles leviathan, I've tried to give a personal impression, some interesting thoughts, and maybe a fact or two, or details or musings that are not so common.

I am roughly contemporary with The Beatles. I was born in the week they first went to Hamburg. Their faces and their music are some of the first things I can remember, at the very awakening of consciousness. Hearing 'Can't Buy Me Love' as a toddler in my cousins Eileen and Elizabeth's bedroom. I was taken to see them at the ABC cinema in Wigan in 1964 by my mum, and amongst a tranche of pictures I've found of that night (two shows, 6.30 and 8.30, we were at the early one as my mum was at the mill in the morning and, well I was just turned 4) I'm convinced I can see me and my mum. When I look at it now, that photograph, blurry little confused and elated me on my mum's knee, her almost hypnotised gaze, the madness and delight from the girls around me, The Beatles on stage before me, it explains a lot.

It explains, among other things, this book.

PROLOGUE

1. Ivan Vaughan, Woolton, 1957

'To this very day, it still is a complete mystery to me that it happened at all. Would John and I have met some other way, if Ivan and I hadn't gone to that fête?'

Ask someone to picture Liverpool and they probably don't imagine Woolton. Unfairly, Liverpool for some conjures either gritty urbanity or the grandly civic and proudly maritime; we think of The Docks and the Dingle, handsome cathedrals or cars ablaze in Toxteth, ocean liners and cheeky comics, a city like no other, feisty, funny, tough, tender. Woolton, though, is Liverpool at its most sweetly, prosaically suburban; leafy, charming, prosperous – at the time of writing, its three councillors are all Liberal Democrats. It was probably much the same in the summer of 1957.

On a warm June day in 2024, as I walked up the gentle rise of Church Road, past the Simon Peter Centre and The Hub, turning left into the lychgate of St Peter's Church, I felt a frisson, you might even call it a chill, as I considered the two schoolboys who had walked up this lane almost exactly sixty-eight years before. Had one of those Liverpool schoolboys, Ivan Vaughan, not been so gregariously likeable, the history of the twentieth century would have been different, and the lives of millions might have played out differently. Though we never knew him, we owe him a huge debt of gratitude.

In his poem, 'Musée De Beaux Arts', W. H. Auden makes the brilliant 'apercu' that even the darkest tragedy plays out while elsewhere others are blithely, indifferently doing other things; Icarus falls from the sky while the farmer ploughs his field and his horse scratches its rump against a tree. As with tragedy, so with joy perhaps. This is how I feel about Woolton Village Fête, 7 July 1957. Pictures reveal it as an endearingly British and very 1950s kind of celebration, the nation then in microcosm. A parade with a lorry full of smiling Girl Guides, a fake blood donor 'float' with a body on a gurney, a rose queen, various Scouts. There was a police dog obedience exhibition, and perhaps some judging of prize marrows and drop scones. Meanwhile, somewhere just out of shot, two teenage Teddy Boys are now turning off Church Road and into the field to watch a local skiffle band. Ivan Vaughan is about to introduce 15-year-old Paul McCartney to 16-year-old John Lennon and the world will begin to shift on its axis.*

Ivan Vaughan was born the same day as Paul McCartney and started Liverpool Institute grammar school with him in September 1953. Vaughan was a pal of one John Lennon from Dovedale primary school and a sometime part of Lennon's skiffle band on tea chest bass, inscribed with 'Jive with Ive, The Ace on the Bass'. Future newsreader Peter Sissons, a classmate at the Institute, said Vaughan

---

* It's a globally significant moment of course but also of personal, practical importance for many of us. The musician Gary Kemp, of huge success with Spandau Ballet and beyond, once said to me that his wife had been surprised at finding him tearful at that point in a Beatles bio when John and Paul meet. When she looked surprised at his emotional state he pointed out, 'If John Lennon and Paul McCartney hadn't met, we wouldn't be living in this house.'

was 'a complete original with an entirely distinctive sense of humour' which perhaps explains how he came to be close friends with both John and Paul, and thus their Pandarus and go-between. As Paul reflected many years on, 'To this very day, it still is a complete mystery to me that it happened at all. Would John and I have met some other way, if Ivan and I hadn't gone to that fête?'

Later, as The Beatles developed and their fame grew, Ivan entered academia – in fact, he warned Paul against going on the Johnny Gentle tour as it would harm his exam grades and future career – teaching psychology at Homerton College, Cambridge. He married a colleague from Homerton, Jan, a French lecturer and moved to London but never lost touch with his old friends, now known to the world as Lennon and McCartney. One night, Jan and Ivan were having supper at the Ashers' when Paul mentioned a problem with a song he was writing: 'He wanted a French first name and an adjective that rhymed with it,' Jan told the Homerton College website in 2018. 'My answer became "Michelle, ma belle, sont les mots qui vont très bien ensemble" … When I was in hospital after the birth of our son, Paul visited and left a pile of bank notes on my bed, much to the surprise of the nurses!'

For a while, Vaughan was on the payroll of Apple, charged with setting up one of the most fascinating but ultimately vainglorious Beatle endeavours; the Apple School, an attempt at a progressive educational establishment heavy on the lively arts, low on discipline and ultimately a non-starter. Vaughan was coaxed out of his job as an educational psychologist for this, but he was wise enough to ask for ten grand in his bank account first. In 1977, he was diagnosed with Parkinson's disease and forced into early retirement. He featured in a BBC documentary in 1984 presented by Jonathan Miller about his search for a cure and a book, *Ivan: Living with Parkinson's Disease*, followed. He died of pneumonia in 1993, his death affecting Paul profoundly. He wrote the poem 'Ivan' about him in McCartney's book, *Blackbird Singing*. One verse refers to 'Cranlock naval/

Cranlock pie', an opaque, Goonish private joke the pair shared which would still reduce them to paroxysms of laughter decades later. It remains a mystery to the rest of us.

Back on that sweltering summer's day in 1957, after watching The Quarrymen's first set at the fête, Ivan took Paul into the Scout hut to meet a boozy Lennon. McCartney eventually plucked up the courage to ask for a go on Lennon's guitar. He tuned it, something Lennon couldn't do, and played Eddie Cochrane's 'Twenty Flight Rock' and 'Be-Bop-A-Lula'. 'It was uncanny' recalled Quarryman Eric Griffiths, 'he had such confidence; he gave a performance. It was so natural.'

John Lennon years later recalled his own reaction: 'I thought if I take him on, what will happen?'

What happened was pretty much everything imaginable, including this book, all thanks to Ivan Vaughan.

Part One

BEFORE THE BEATLES

2. Julia Lennon

'Ocean child, calls me ...'

She played the banjo and the ukulele and did the housework with woollen knickers on her head. She loved pranks and practical jokes and would put tea or other random ingredients in a stew on a whim. McCartney said of her that 'she was beautiful, lively, gay in the old sense of the word'. When she first met Pete Shotton, John's schoolfriend, she stroked his waist and cooed 'Ooh, what lovely slim hips you have.' Julia Lennon, nee Stanley, was many things depending on your point of view – saint, sweetheart, muse, flibbertigibbet – but she was never anything as quotidian and prosaic as a mum, which is why she haunted her only son's psyche all his short, crowded life.

Aside from the fact that they were five not six, the Stanley sisters were the Mitfords of Wavertree, a Scouse counterpart to those famed aristocratic siblings, striking young women alternately imperious, idiosyncratic, beguiling, talented. Julia was their Jessica, rebellious, musical, the 'red sheep' of the family. She was their father George's favourite even when she turned up, defiantly waving a certificate, announcing that she had married an erratically employed 'entertainer' called Freddie Lennon. They'd met in Sefton Park where she told the dapper young five-foot-three scally that he looked silly in his bowler hat, which he reportedly promptly skimmed into the lake. Later, they married, and a little later still, they had a child called John.

This much is certain. But the details of the seventeen years that Julia and John Lennon were together on the earth are both as fixed as scripture and contested as the Apocrypha. John Winston Lennon was not born during an air raid, as is often claimed, but on a rare quiet day in the middle of the Liverpool blitz; Wednesday, 9 October 1940. Julia's sister, Mimi, was present at the birth and fell in love with him immediately. No one was sure where the father was, possibly at sea. He sent money for some year and a half, but that stopped when he jumped ship and spent three months in jail in New York.

During this time, Julia took up with a Welsh soldier and became pregnant. She didn't divorce the absent Freddie, though, although there was understandably a 'scene' when he returned eighteen months later. Her family, not keen to take on a new child, the new baby, Victoria, was adopted. A year later Julia became involved with 41-year-old Bobby Dykins, an elegant wine steward at the (then) classy Adelphi Hotel in town. When it was found that the six-year-old John was sharing a bed with Julia and Dykins in their tiny flat, social services and Aunt Mimi intervened and John was taken to live with his aunt and uncle in 'the Mendips', as the suburban villa on Menlove Avenue was rather grandly known.

John may have thought Dykins 'a little waiter with a nervous cough and thinning margarine coloured hair' dubbing him 'Twitchy', but as he entered his teens he was a regular visitor to their flat, presumably to be with his mother who he was growing close to again. In her turn, Julia would often come around to visit Mimi and John at the Mendips. About 10 p.m. on the night of 15 July 1958, Julia was leaving after passing on the news that, with Dykins having lost his job after an arrest for drunk driving, John might have to spend less time with them and more time at home at Mimi's Mendips.

After saying goodbye to a friend of John's, Nigel Whalley, who'd called by to see John who was out, she walked a little way with him before she seems to have cut through the hedges screening off the old tram tracks and stepped out on to the road. She was struck and killed instantly by a Standard Vanguard saloon driven by a 24-year-old learner driver called Eric Clague. Apart from Clague, Whalley was the only witness to what happened; even then, he saw nothing but heard the thud of impact, running to Julia who lay in the road.

John maintained throughout his life that Clague had been drinking and speeding, but at the inquest he was acquitted of all charges by the jury – unsurprisingly perhaps given that he was an off-duty police officer. At the verdict, Mimi Smith screamed 'Murderer!' adding later, 'The coroner seemed to be bending over backwards to help this man who'd killed Julia.' In time, Clague resigned from the force and became a postman. In 1964, his beat included Forthlin Road, and he regularly delivered sacks of fan mail to the McCartney home. He remained anonymous until a *Sunday Mirror* reporter tracked him down in 1998. 'I have been haunted by this for all these years' he said.

'It was the worst thing that ever happened to me' said John years later. 'I thought, fuck it fuck it fuck it, that's really fucked everything now … Twitchy took it worse than me. Then he said, "Who's going to look after the kids?" and I hated him. Bloody selfishness. We got a taxi over to Sefton General where she was lying dead. I didn't want to see her. I talked hysterically to the taxi driver all the way, ranted on and on, the way you do. The taxi driver just grunted now and again. I refused to go in … I lost her twice … once when I moved in with my auntie. And once again at 17 when she actually physically died. That was very traumatic for me. It made me very, very bitter.'

In the coming years, as they moved away from conventional pop structures and subject matters, and conscious perhaps that their own lives and stories were becoming the stuff of myth, both McCartney and Lennon wrote beautiful late period paeans to their mothers. But it's not quite that straightforward in John's case. 'Ocean Child', one of the dreamy epithets he applies to Julia in the 1968 song, is the Kanji translation of Yoko. For the adult Lennon, lost mother and new lover were becoming one.

Lennon wrote several songs about his Julia. Critical consensus tends to have it that the best, by which they mean the rawest, starkest and thus supposedly most 'authentic', are 'Mother' and 'My Mummy's Dead' from his *Plastic Ono Band* album. For me, 'Julia', written during the Rishikesh retreat in India where Donovan taught them to finger pick, is vastly superior. The chordal movement is delicately lovely and mysterious – I remember playing it continually in my bedroom in Wigan, my cheap Woolworths guitar and battered *Complete Beatles* songbook on my knee – but the vocal melody, as in 'I Am the Walrus' and many Lennon songs, is monotone and largely unchanging. Here though, this merely serves to heighten the mood of forlorn sweetness and loss. It is the only Beatles song that features just John and was the last track recorded for *The Beatles White Album* of 1968, perhaps the strangest, most dazzling tour de force in the history of pop.

In a parallel world, one of the ones that many physicists think exist in multiplicity, Eric Clague swerves to avoid Julia Lennon that summer evening in suburban Liverpool, and on the same kind of night in New York, Mark Chapman abandons his dreadful mission to hunt down her son. Both grow old, mother and child, through the long decades.

But had the first not come to pass, would the second? The world where Julia Lennon makes it safely to the other side of Menlove Avenue is perhaps a world where The Beatles never happened.

3. Mimi Smith

'My dear boy, you are not the second Messiah.'

If Julia was Jessica, then Mary Elizabeth Stanley, 'Aunt Mimi', was Deborah 'Debo' Mitford perhaps, the least shocking, most straightforward of those famed sisters, with something of the Duchess about her, though in Mimi's case not literally. Both were also devoted to the upkeep and propriety of their respective homes. The Mendips was no Chatsworth House, but it was a solid, respectable middleclass home and, despite his later cynicism, a strong, moulding influence on the young John Lennon.

Like all the Stanley sisters, the eldest, Mimi, was striking looking 'with fine cheekbones like a Cherokee,' as Philip Norman put it in Beatles biography *Shout*, a little weirdly. She was surprisingly sympathetic to her flighty younger sister's dilemma when Julia decided she couldn't handle both her seven-year-old son and a new relationship: 'Julia had met someone else with whom she had a chance of happiness and no man wants another man's child.* That's when I said I wanted to bring John to Menlove Avenue to live with George and me. I wouldn't even let him risk being hurt or feeling he was in the way. I made up my mind that I would be the one to give him what every child has a right to, a safe and happy home life.'

You arrive at that home today via a minibus that picks you up at Liverpool's South Parkway station courtesy of the National Trust who now own it. The first time I made the trip, perhaps more attuned to the nuances of British housing than the Argentinian couple and the earnestly studious German girl with notebook and Lennon 'NHS' glasses, it was immediately obvious that 251 Menlove Avenue was a much more affluent residence than Paul's neat little

---

* Even by the standards of the 1940s, this seems revealingly biblical.

council house, and certainly far posher than the Harrisons' terrace in Speke with a chicken run by the front door, or Ringo's in the notorious 'Welsh streets' of the Dingle. Built in 1933, it was a relatively new, smart mock Tudor villa with seven rooms including a 'morning room' and bells in the kitchen to summon any 'live in' servants. Here, John became close to his Uncle George, an unassuming dairy farmer who would often quietly support him against the diatribes of Mimi. George taught him to ride a bike, put him to bed with kisses and bought him a mouth organ which he carried everywhere. Not long after George's devastating sudden death from a haemorrhage, John obtained his first guitar, after some 'soft soaping', as she put it – the Gallotone Champion famously 'guaranteed not to split'. It was a turning point for Mimi, for John, and for the rest of us.

When she met the other young Beatles-to-be, Mimi disliked George for his thick Scouse accent and Teddy Boy stylings and she patronised Paul, announcing with a sneer on his every arrival 'Your little friend is here.' For his part though, Paul seems to have admired her: 'She struck me as being an honest woman who looked after John's interests and would take the mickey but … I never minded it … in fact I think she quite liked me.' Though they would often harmonise in the Mendips porch area with its tiled floor, leaded glass and grand acoustics, only 'I'll Get You' and 'Please Please Me' were actually written there, which was why the National Trust initially felt it not as historically significant as Paul's home on Forthlin Road.

Mimi always seemed less elated by the band's success than, for instance, the Harrisons. But she did join them on the Australian and Far East section of the 1964 tour, where the enormous crowds treated Mimi to her own bijou Beatlemania. In Hong Kong, she was mobbed and police had to clear a path for her shouting 'John Mama! John Mama!' But after the chaos and crowds of Adelaide and New Zealand, she was happy to fly home to Woolton.

When life at Mendips, with its constant, besieging stream of invasive and light-fingered 'fans' became unbearable, she moved south to a six-bedroomed bungalow, Harbour View, that John had bought on the Dorset peninsula Sandbanks, home to some of the world's most expensive residences as well as, at different times, Liam Gallagher, Rick Stein, J. R. R. Tolkien and the founder of Topps Tiles. John would sometimes escape there when the pressures of London and The Beatles grew too great, visiting incognito and according to Mimi he'd 'turn cartwheels on the beach'. When the Sandbanks ferryman recognised him and tipped off the press to Mimi's annoyance, John was sanguine, 'Ah, he probably got a fiver for it.'

After the dissolution of the band, in 1971 a freelance writer called Alana Nash from Kentucky, whose 'entrée' was a solitary postcard reply from Mimi received at the height of Beatlemania, turned up unannounced on her doorstep directed there by a mechanic from the corner garage. She told the 'Meet The Beatles For Real' blog of her meeting with Mimi, 'She peered around the door the way women in Hitchcock films do just before they become victims. I quickly dredged up the ancient postcard.' This, remarkably, was enough to gain her access to Mrs Smith's home for the next few hours, during which some revealing moments emerged. Mimi pooh-poohed John's repeated claims of a desperately unhappy childhood as 'fantastic stories ... it's true that his mother wasn't there and there was no father around but my husband and I gave him a wonderful home'. She also disparaged his credentials as an urban guerrilla, despite the Che Guevara look he was then sporting. 'Don't talk to me of such things! I know that boy. He doesn't know what he's saying. It's all an act. If there was a revolution John would be first in the queue to run! Why, he's scared to death of things like that. That's Yoko talking not John.'

In his post-Beatles thirties, John's still-strong relationship with Mimi was largely conducted via phone. He would ring once or twice a week, talk current affairs and be chastised for whatever controversial new utterance or activity he was involved in. She told Nash, 'Every time John does something bad and gets his picture in the papers, he rings me up to smooth me over. See that new colour television? It was a Christmas present, but he had it delivered early. A big present arrives every time he's been naughty.' He also became surprisingly nostalgic for his youth and old haunts, asking for trinkets, photos and school reports and anything bearing the motto of his Quarry Bank alma mater 'Ex hoc metallo virtutem' ('From this metal, virtue').

In response to one such communication from John containing a request about some family genealogy, Mimi seems to have seen red, replying in the form of a taped message 'Now, you needn't, for a start, send any B.S. genealogist down here, giving him a fine old holiday tramping around graveyards. What a good old time he must have had! This thing must have cost you a fortune ...' She goes on to berate him about his politics – 'What's this rubbish you're talking about? You wouldn't mind donating your money to a real socialist government? For heaven's sake. Use Your Nut. There's no such thing.' She also disparaged his sour attitude towards his band mates, 'And you say The Beatles were dumb. They may have been ... but in many respects, they could've taught you a thing or two. The first thing they did was to make their parents secure. Forever.' There is a section about his self-regard that recalls *The Life of Brian*; 'My dear boy, you are not the second Messiah. You are never likely to be. And that's the way you're behaving these last few years. Would you please understand that you are a speck in the ocean.'

Perhaps in the end, this was Mimi's uniquely bracing take; one that might have become more profound and useful had Lennon lived longer. She 'knew that boy' and saw through the protective superstructure of arrogance and sarcasm to see a bewildered five-year-old whose mummy abandoned him, a complicated teenager whose mother was killed, an angry young man with the world at his feet. For a while.

Mimi was listening to the World Service in bed at Harbour View when she heard her little boy had been shot dead. He had rung her the night before, excited to be coming to Dorset and to see Mimi soon for the first time in ten years. Mimi lived a further eleven years and died in 1991. The next year, Harbour View was demolished and a new house called, almost inevitably, Imagine, developed on the site. It was last sold in 2021 for eight million pounds.

4. Harry Graves

'I learned gentleness from Harry.'

When Ringo Starr was just three, and still Richie Starkey, his parents split up. His father, also named Ritchie, offered little in the way of support, leaving wife and son on the breadline. Then, when the lad from the Dingle was 11, his hard-working mum, Elsie, met a man from Romford called Harry Graves. Though an offcomer from the dark heart of the mistrusted south, neighbours and workmates warmed to this sweet, genial man. He had a good voice, much enjoyed in pub singalongs and he introduced young Ritchie to the jazz songbook of Sarah Vaughan, Billy Eckstine, Cole Porter and Johnny Mercer.

At 13, soon after Elsie and Harry were married, Ringo contracted pleurisy and was to spend most of the next two years in Heswall Children's Hospital. 'He made me laugh, he bought me DC comics, he was great with music, he was a really sweet guy, all animals and children loved him … I learned gentleness from Harry.' To cheer the sickly Ritchie up, Harry enrolled him in the Arsenal supporters club. Harry himself was a fanatical West Ham fan but Arsenal were more famed and successful (Manchester United were the glamour team of the early Fifties but even a man from Essex knew better than to enrol a Scouser into a Manc fan club).

At Christmas 1956, Harry travelled back to Romford to see his parents and while there, his dad James told him that a local dance band were selling a drum kit; long an item of mystical allure to young Ritchie. Harry's offer of ten pounds was accepted and so, via the Central and Circle line, and then steam train to Lime Street, Ringo Starr's first drum kit arrived in the Dingle on Boxing Day 1956, into a freezing cold back bedroom above a row of outside lavatories.

By 1968, when Hunter Davies visited them, the Graves were now ensconced in a posh bungalow in leafy Woolton. They'd been helped to find it by Ringo's old neighbour and early girlfriend Marie Maguire, who taught him to read. The walls, Davies noted, were festooned with gold discs and they were clearly enormously, touchingly proud. Ringo's biological dad was, at the time, a window cleaner in Crewe and wanted nothing to do with his rich and famous son. But Elsie and Harry, like all the Beatle guardians except perhaps John's Aunt Mimi, were delighted with their son's success. Elsie enthused 'I think the biggest thrill was going down to the Palladium that first time sitting in the audience and listening to all the London people cheering. Course the two film premieres were nice and the civic reception in Liverpool. They were all lovely. Everything was.'*

Harry added 'I think I prefer their earlier music best, the rock 'n' roll stuff. But they've got to change, haven't they? You've got to in this business. You've got to listen to the tunes properly now more than once.' Harry gave up his painting job for Liverpool council in 1965 at the age of 51. 'Ritchie was on at me for a long time to retire but I didn't think I should. Then one day one of his mates saw me up a forty-foot ladder in the snow painting a council house and he forced me to give up. Sometimes I go around the corporation sites if I'm passing. I look up at the lads and they all shout down at me. I shout back "that's how it goes lads … keep the brush going!"'

Those of us who've been and are stepdads will take something particularly special from Ringo's origin story. Without Harry's kindness and gentleness, his support and encouragement, we might never have got the Ringo who made the world happy with a toss of his head. Harry Graves was the oldest of the men and women who

---

* That said, Freda Kelly, close friend and Beatles fan club organiser has said, 'of all the parents she found it quite difficult to cope. She could have done without any of the success. Elsie would have preferred Ritchie to be ordinary, to live down the road with four children she could visit every day.'

raised The Beatles. He was born the year before the Great War broke out. As he lugged those drums from Romford to Liverpool, he cannot have imagined what it would lead to.

5. Jim McCartney

'Couldn't you sing "She loves you, yes, yes, yes?"'

Thirty-nine was late for a working man to be still a bachelor back in 1941. Perhaps it was the Depression, then the threat of war, or the precarious work situation; perhaps his glamorous role as leader of the Jim Mac Jazz Band brought enough female attention to keep him occupied. Whatever the reason, cotton salesman Jim McCartney was almost 40 when he proposed to Mary Mohin, a pretty nurse who he'd met at his sister's house in Huyton. Neighbour Bella Johnson said of her, 'She was a beautiful person; it came from something deep inside her ... Jim adored her.' She thought him 'utterly charming and uncomplicated'.

When not selling cotton, Jim loved to play music. Despite setbacks, such as smashing an ear falling off a wall at the age of 10 and then having to abandon the trumpet when he lost his teeth, he was a decent, enthusiastic piano player. When the McCartneys ended up at Forthlin Road, in a council house that came with Mary's job as a midwife, his son Paul learned his first chords on the living room piano, bought from the North End Music Stores (NEMS) run by Harry Epstein, father of Brian.

At the age of just 46 in 1956, Mary developed breast cancer. The day she was due to have a mastectomy operation, she cleaned the McCartney house and laid her two sons' school clothes out, ready for the next day, saying 'Now everything's ready for them in case I don't come back.' Mary died on 31 October 1956. Her last words to her sister, Dill, were 'I would love to have seen the boys growing up.'

Jim was left a widower in his early fifties on modest wages, having to learn to cook and sew, wash and iron – baffling mysteries for most working-class northern men of the time – and bringing up two boisterous young lads, although with the support of the redoubtable

27

aunties, Millie and Jin,* and the rest of the McCartney clan. Mike, Paul's brother, reflected 'We both owe him a lot. He's a very good man and he's a very stubborn man. It would have been easy for him to have gone off with other birds when Mum died or have gone out getting drunk every night but he didn't. He stayed home and looked after us.' Ian Leslie, in his book *John and Paul*, reflects beautifully on how the boys must have felt: 'Paul lived inside the ordinary miracle of a loving family and like everyone else who does so, took it for granted. Until it was taken away.'

Jim smoothed his sons' passage into adulthood. He wired the downstairs 'radiogram' to their bedrooms so that the boys could have rock and roll 'on tap', early and surely supremely formative exposure to Little Richard, Buddy Holly and Elvis. When Paul became a rock and roller himself, not without Jim's misgivings, he was the first of the Beatle parents to investigate the lunchtime sessions at The Cavern. 'You should have been paid danger money to go down there,' was his verdict. But soon he would drop by regularly in his own lunchtime from Hannay's, dropping off something for Paul and Mike's tea while he was still hard at work. All Jim's support soon paid off. One night at Forthlin Road, Paul and John were completing a song they had begun in a Newcastle hotel room on tour and, as McCartney has often recounted, 'We played it to my dad and he said, "That's very nice, son, but there's enough of these Americanisms around. Couldn't you sing, 'She loves you, yes! yes! yes!'" At which point we collapsed in a heap and said, "No, Dad, you don't quite get it!"'

---

* Jin came to London in 1967 to chastise Paul about his pot use. 'She came down to visit me in Cavendish Avenue, where I'd been living for a while. When your auntie comes to visit, you do some of the old things you did when you were younger. So I was sitting around, playing a bit of piano, having a drink, playing cards, and having a good old chat. It was a very warm atmosphere, and the song arose out of that sense of family.' The song was 'Your Mother Should Know'. She is also, of course, namechecked in 'Let 'Em In'.

That was in 1963 when The Beatles were now approaching escape velocity. The year after, the *Hard Day's Night* premiere fell on the eve of Jim's 61st birthday and at the after-show party at the Dorchester Hotel Paul announced 'Happy Birthday, Dad,' and handed him a painting of a horse prompting Jim to mull, 'It's very nice but couldn't he have done better than that?' Then Paul revealed that the painting was of a racehorse called Drake's Drum which he'd bought for his father for a grand. 'You silly bugger!' said a delighted Jim. The horse went on to win the race before the Grand National at Aintree, later being retired by Paul to High Park Farm, Paul's place on the Mull of Kintyre.

The same year, he married again to Angela Williams,* a young widow twenty-eight years his junior with a five-year-old daughter, Ruth, who he later legally adopted. Jim retired from his £10-a-week job at the Cotton Exchange and he and his new family moved into Rembrandt, a house bought by Paul in Heswall on the Wirral. It was here, playing the piano with Ruth, that Paul found the sheet music to the song, 'Golden Slumbers Kiss Your Eyes', a setting of a 1599 poem by Thomas Dekker. 'I can't read music ... so I just started playing my own tune to it. I liked the words so I kept them, and it fitted with another bit of song I had ... it's very possible that I'd been feeling down in London. I was back in the solace of family and Liverpool, and what with The Beatles' troubles down south, I was likely thinking, "Wouldn't it be nice to get home and have that comfortable feeling again?"'

Jim passed away in 1976 while Paul was on tour with Wings in Europe. Angie told Mike McCartney that just before he died, he said 'I'll be with Mary soon.' Their old home, 20 Forthlin Road, Allerton, is now also a National Trust property. Every time I visit, there comes a point, in the tiny kitchen perhaps, or in the boys' bedrooms where

---

* At time of writing, 94-year-old Angie has just published a book of Liverpool limericks.

they listened to Elvis on the headphones Jim wired up, where I feel overcome. It's not just the historical significance of the modest house. It's the emotional heft. This is one of the most important houses in Britain, and it is a neat, compact council house, not a castle built for a baron or an earl, but for working-class people, public servants and their families, so clearly full of love and laughter, good times and sad times, and music.

Above the front door, the wooden plaque makes no mention of The Beatles. It simply states 'the proud family home of the McCartney family; Jim, Mary, Paul and Mike'.

6. Mike McCartney

'It's like if Rembrandt's kid brother was in the corner.'

I have met many people (in Liverpool pubs, usually) who've claimed to be related to a Beatle; folk who have assured me that their dad is Ringo's second cousin or that their wife is John's step-niece. Mike McCartney is that rarity though; someone who deliberately tried to hide that he had a Beatle for a brother.

Mike McCartney's first love was art and photography but thwarted in his ambition to go to art school he became first a tailor then a hairdresser. And also The Beatles' earliest photographer. He told the *Guardian*'s Henry Yates in 2021, 'I didn't intend to pick up a camera. I'd been practising on drums that had fallen off the back of a lorry into our house ... But when I was 13, I broke my arm at Scout camp, so Pete Best got the job in our kid's group. That's when I started taking photos on the family box camera ... I would go everywhere with The Beatles. I was part of the act. It's like if Rembrandt's kid brother was in the corner with a pad and paper, sketching his older brother. I was lucky – you couldn't have had a better group to practise on, could you?' Brian Epstein called him Flash Harry for his constant snapping, and his moody monochrome shots of Paul and John at Forthlin Road have become 'iconic', to use that poor abused word correctly.*

In 1962, just after The Beatles released their first single, the younger McCartney appeared in a sketch at the Merseyside Arts Festival with Roger McGough, teacher and nascent poet, and a Post

---

* The famous shot of Paul playing the guitar in the little back garden, sitting in a deckchair and shot through a washing line, became the cover of Paul's album, *Memory Almost Full*. I tried to recreate this on a TV documentary I made about The Beatles and fell straight through, tearing the canvas and having to be extricated by the uproariously amused crew.

Office engineer called John Gorman. The sketch was a hit and the three decided to stick together as a quirky comedic/poetic trio called The Scaffold, turning professional the following year. By now, Mike's little brother Paul was so well known that Mike did not want to appear to be trading on his sibling's newfound fame and so he changed his name to, a sly nod here, Mike McGear.

The Scaffold became an entertainment fixture of the late 1960s and early 1970s. They were TV regulars, usually in their trademark white suits, and provided the theme tune to the hit Scouse TV comedy, *The Liver Birds*. Their debut single (produced by one George Martin) was 1966's 'Two Days Monday' but their first hit was Mike's own 'Thank You Very Much', inspired by the refrain he had chanted down the phone to 'Our Kid' after the latter had bought him a Nikon camera. In 1968, they had the Christmas UK Number 1 with 'Lily The Pink', inescapable on radio and TV, although many of the audience who watched and heard and bought may have been unaware that the tall long-haired one was Paul McCartney's brother. (They may though have recognised him the next year when he was Paul's best man at Marylebone Register Office, very delayed on the train from Liverpool and having to fight through the enormous crowd.)

Paul produced the McGough and McGear album as well as the 1974 Scaffold reunion hit, 'Liverpool Lou'. Their closeness (and that of the McCartneys in general) was sometimes mocked by John ('Paul liked it with daddy and the brother … and obviously missed his mother') but this would seem to speak more to Lennon's own inner issues and insecurities. Perhaps he was jealous of the warmth of 20 Forthlin Road, where he was a constant visitor, a home that Mike has done much to help in the restoration of, including sourcing exactly the right brick-effect wallpaper from Sanderson's of Loughborough.

Appearing on *Saturday Superstore* in 1982, a caller asks Mike if he has ever played on a Beatle recording session and he remembers delightedly, 'Yes … somebody must have it on camera, maybe Mike Lindsay-Hogg … they were filming at Savile Row … and I came in … I had a new leather coat on, I was showing it off … and I was playing the piano with the lid closed (I thought this is satirical … this is funny) and the camera came round to me and Billy Preston … and someone must have that somewhere.'

Someone did have it. Half a century later, this shot was seen for the first time in Peter Jackson's *Get Back*. It's a great jacket.

7. Harry Harrison

'There he was, was a miniature version of me.'

The pale green Liverpool corporation buses of the 1950s and 1960s trundle through The Beatles' story. Indeed, there may not even have been a Beatles story if George and Paul hadn't taken the same bus from Speke to the Liverpool Institute or 'Inny', discovering on the smoky top deck a shared love of guitars and rock and roll. In the days before working-class people routinely had cars – and well before The Beatles had E types and Rollers – buses were a daily fixture of life and the man on the Clapham (or Speke) omnibus was a cypher for the everyman. The Beatles would take a bus across town to track down the kid who could teach them a new chord. The elaborate gatefold design of the *Sgt. Pepper* sleeve was intended by Paul as 'something I could read on the back of the bus ... because that's what I used to do ... I'd read some albums for half an hour. We wanted to pack [*Sgt. Pepper*] with goodies.'

Then there are the songs. 'Magical Mystery Tour' is about a bus excursion of sorts and the interlude of 'A Day In The Life' finds Paul taking a bus 'trip' in the acrid blue fug of the 1960s upstairs deck, 'having a smoke' and going into a dream. One significant route, the No 5, inspired both 'In My Life' – a discarded line ran 'past the tram sheds with no trams/On the 5 bus into town' – and 'Penny Lane', 'a big bus terminal which we all knew very well' Paul recalled in 1980, later adding: 'When I was going to John's house in Liverpool, I would change buses at the Penny Lane roundabout, where Church Road meets Smithdown Road.' Contrary as ever though, in 1963 George told teen magazine *Romeo* in an article titled 'These Beatles Aren't Bugging Anybody!' that his pet hates were getting his hair cut and 'travelling on buses'. Perhaps this had something to do with being locally famous pre-Beatles for being a well-known driver's son who spent thirty-one years 'on the buses'.

Harold Hargreaves Harrison was born in 1909 and, like John's biological dad, Freddie, was attracted by the gritty glamour of the Liverpool waterfront, going to sea with the White Star Line at 17. In 1929, he encountered grocer's assistant Lou French in the street and was instantly smitten. After a year of postal courtship – he sailed to Africa the day after they met with a promise to send her perfume, which he kept – they were married. Times were hard though and after two years of casual work and the dole, he finally landed a steady job as a tram conductor then bus driver, a job he would hold for the next three decades.

During that time, they would live initially in a little mid-terrace 'two up, two down' in Arnold Grove, Wavertree with a tiny flower bed, chickens and an outside loo.* George spent his first seven years there before they relocated to 25 Upton Green, Speke in 1950. Largely untouched by the tragedies and sickness that clouded the lives of the other Beatle families, the Harrisons were ostensibly the happiest, although daughter Lou's eloping to Gloucester with a married man twelve years her senior with five children did strain the domestic equilibrium for a while. George's older brother Harry said, 'We always knew the comfort and security of a very close-knit home life.' Mum and Dad, Lou and Harry, embraced with gusto the new life and attention that came with their son's stratospheric rise to fame. Hunter Davies said that Lou 'turned being a Beatle mum into a full-time job' becoming a matriarchal figure to the hordes of teenage girls who besieged their little home.

In early 1964 she told *The Beatles Are Back* magazine: 'They come from all over the country … Usually, I ask them in for a cup of tea

---

* Now privately owned in an unprepossessing bit of Liverpool with no National Trust patronage nor blue plaque, chiming with George's typically testy description of himself as the 'economy class Beatle'.

and a biscuit. It's the least I can do after all … The fans are really nice. Along with George's fan mail, Mr. Harrison and I are constantly getting little gifts of chocolates and things from all the fans who called. And sometimes we're up until two in the morning writing replies to all the lovely letters we get – but we don't mind.'

Harry Harrison became a legend among the 'Inny' kids for an incident that stuck with McCartney. On the Michael Parkinson chat show in the mid 1980s, he recalled 'George got done once, and the teacher missed him and got him here on the wrist. So he had a couple of big wheals, you know those rash things, and he went home, and he is having his tea with his dad, and they're all chatting about how it went at school, and he says "What's that?", they saw these things, and George told him, you know, "teacher did it". So, the next day we were in class, and somebody pops the head around the door and said "mister", you know, whoever the teacher was and said "George, come out for a moment please." He came out, and it was George's dad there, he said, "Did you do that to my son?" and the teacher said "Yes", and he goes "Whack".' Macca was filled with both admiration and envy. 'I used to tell my dad, "I've got caned," and he said, "Well, you probably did something wrong."'

Harry could be similarly forceful both as a shop steward and tire-less promoter of his son's music. He bought George his first guitars, a Dutch Egmond flat top acoustic and a Hofner President, and arranged for lessons with a musical bus driver pal, Len Horton, above a local off-licence on Wednesday evenings. He booked The Quarrymen and early Beatle variants for gigs at the Picton Busmen's Club where he and Lou taught ballroom dancing. His is one of the six signatures on the contract between The Beatles and Brian Epstein signed in October 1962. He even took some credit for George's fulsome barnet in *The Beatles Are Back* magazine interview: 'I'm the one to blame for George being The Beatle with the longest hair … I used to cut it for him when he was little, and I always gave him a really short back and sides. George hated it, and he always said he would never have his hair cut when he grew up. Well, he certainly kept his word, didn't he!'

Though drivers and 'clippies' were often minor local celebrities, Harry's fame obviously rocketed with the explosion of Beatlemania. *The Beatles Are Back* reported 'Dad Harrison is probably Liverpool Corporation's most popular driver of school buses. He had a Ford Anglia of his own which George bought him, and tells a funny story about that: "One morning I took the car to the bus depot at five A.M. It was still dark, and it wasn't till I finished work in the afternoon that I noticed it was covered in lipstick-scrawled messages to George. What a laugh that was!"'

The work was steady but the wages meagre. When George learned, amazed, that his dad had never earned more than £10 a week, he offered him £50 a week if he'd retire early and bought them a bungalow in three acres of land in the village of Appleton near Warrington. He was a regular visitor to George's Friar Park mansion. Always a heavy smoker like his son, he died of emphysema in 1978.

In later life, Harry often hung out with George, touring the States with him in 1974. From this period, there's a fabulous photo of George and Harry. Father and son stand side by side smiling for the camera, both clad in matching black satin floral 'cosmic cowboy'-style shirts à la The Byrds circa 'Sweetheart of the Rodeo' and both, strikingly, boast flowing locks, greying in Harry's case. When George was born in February 1943, Harry dashed upstairs to see the new arrival and said, 'There he was, was a miniature version of me.' By the time of his death, Harry had become a miniature version of George.

8. Louise Harrison

*'I remember looking at him and thinking
I'll always be there for you.'*

America's first encounter with the onstage magnetism of The Beatles is generally dated to 9 February 1964, the night they dazzled millions on *The Ed Sullivan Show*. But the lucky folks of Benton, Illinois (population 6,700) experienced their own intoxicating taste five months before when George Harrison joined The Four Vests on stage at the VFW Club, Benton. In 150 days, Harrison would be one of the most famous faces on Earth and the object of hysteria across America. But for now, he was just Louise Harrison's limey kid brother with the weird hair, ripped jeans and cool guitar chops. It's one of the most charming and fascinating tales in the whole Beatle epic, and we have Louise to thank.

George was the baby of the tight, raucous Harrison family. Eleven-year-old Louise cradled him when he was hours old, bathed him in the tin bath in front of the fire and taught him his first words. 'I remember looking at him' she would say in later life 'and thinking I'll always be there for you.' Until her little brother's meteoric rise to global fame, Lou Harrison's was the more eventful, interesting life. She trained as a teacher in Newcastle before switching her ambitions to journalism and being accepted as a BBC trainee, despite having no degree and a Scouse accent in the period before her brother made it fashionable. But her parents forbade her to pursue this, regarding it as a poor second to teaching. Perhaps as a reaction, after a spell as a dental nurse, she eloped with her first husband, Scottish mining engineer Gordon Caldwell (already married with five kids) and, after a brief estrangement and then reconciliation with her family, moved with his job to Ontario, thence to Peru and in 1963 to Benton, where she was living when Beatlemania broke like a wave over Britain.

This then was the perfect place for George to escape from the incipient madness overtaking Britain in September 1963, in the wake of the huge success of their first three singles, 'Love Me Do', 'From Me To You' and 'She Loves You'. Though their records had been released in the States, they had done nothing, despite Louise's best efforts at sisterly promotion; she had forced local radio station WFRX to play 'From Me To You' in June 1963, their first airplay in America, but to little attention.* Thus George, arriving at 133 McCann Street with brother, Peter, for a fortnight's vacation, was completely unknown to the small midwestern township.

George immediately loved small-town America. Louise later astutely remarked that 'It was the only experience any one of The Beatles ever had of living in this country as a normal human being.' He enjoyed his first drive-in ('they have, like, parking meters but really they're speakers!') and burgers and root beer at the A&W Diner. He hopped on stage with local band The Four Vests at the VFW (Veterans of Foreign Wars) Club in Benton's even smaller neighbour, El Dorado, and, having been introduced as The Elvis Of England, stole the show with renditions of Carl Perkins, Hank Williams and Chuck Berry. One audience member said 'You should hire that guy if he's trying out for you.' George became especially friendly with bass player Gabe McCarty – a spooky echo this – and gifted him a sheaf of songs either never shown to The Beatles and George Martin or possibly rejected by them. Sadly, every one of these early Harrison originals were later lost in a trailer fire.

Benton was charmed and intrigued by this unusual young man with 'the real nice disposition'. When someone found his lost wallet, the fact that the kid with torn jeans and shaggy hair was carrying $400 amazed and impressed the townsfolk. Two members of The Four Vests took him to buy a Rickenbacker 420 for $400, which

---

* The turntable on which it was played now has pride of place in the Franklin Jail Museum, Benton.

Lou paid for as an early 21st gift for George.* He also bought a single by James Ray, 'I Got My Mind Set On You', which he would take to the top of the US charts twenty-four years later when he covered it.

When George returned with the other Beatles five months later for their all-conquering *Ed Sullivan Show* appearances, Lou dashed to his side to nurse his strep throat at the Plaza Hotel. After the break-up of both The Beatles and Lou's second marriage, George gifted her a monthly $2,000 pension with the injunction, 'Don't go get married again. You don't seem to choose the right people very well. Let me fix you something to live on.'

Sad then, that in the mid-Nineties when Lou was involved in the promotion of her old Benton home into a B&B called A Hard Days Nite [sic], George took umbrage and the two were estranged for years. They were reunited at the end, though. Louise drove to visit him in Staten Island where he was receiving cancer treatment and they were alone for a ninety-minute reconciliation. 'We were able to look into each other's eyes again with love … It was a very, very positive and loving meeting … George was pretty frail, yet he was also still vibrant … His eyes were still bright. He was still George. He must have been in pain, but he didn't show it. We reminisced about our childhood, and his sense of humour was the same as ever. People always teased him about his sticky-out ears; now his oxygen tubes were hanging over them. He laughed and said: "My ears finally came in useful for something." It was distressing, but also I knew that he was on his way, back to where he belonged.' Louise made her own journey in 2023.

---

* It sold at auction in 2014 for $617,000 more.

9. Pete Shotton

'If John hadn't come along then I might
have ended up a crook.'

John Lennon's constant quest for a companion and guide, leading him variously to the Maharishi, Arthur Janov, Allen Klein, Magic Alex, Yoko, Paul and more, has occupied amateur Beatle psychologists for years. But one near constant presence in his life was Pete Shotton. Like Ivor Arbiter, The Beatles' logo designer, who enjoyed an unexpected post-Beatles second act we shall come to in due course, Shotton became a wealthy man for entirely non-Beatles related business innovations long after the band had dissolved.

Lennon and Shotton met aged three and became inseparable at Quarry Bank school, to the extent that teachers referred to them as Shennon and Lotton.* Shotton was an original Quarryman, given a washboard to rub by Lennon, but included in the line-up principally because he was John's mate. Shotton was thus present at the epochal Woolton Fête performance. He joined the police and lost touch with John during Beatlemania, but in 1965 the now jobless and unmoored Shotton bumped into John by chance in Liverpool and they resumed their friendship. John offered to back Pete in any business schemes he might devise. 'I was on holiday in Hampshire when I noticed this supermarket on Hayling Island. I liked the look of it, so John bought it for me to run.' It cost £20,000, but Shotton made such a lucrative success of the venture, he could eventually pay John back in full, saying 'If John hadn't come along then I might have ended up a crook ... I had no money at all. I was getting into lots of shady deals and meeting bad people.'

---

* A Beatlesy psychedelic band from Valencia are called Shennon And Lotton.

In 1967, he handed over the supermarket to his mother to become, briefly and like many other Beatle associates, an Apple employee, first managing the boutique then becoming CEO of Apple Corps. When this foundered, he went back to the Hayling Island supermarket till the late Seventies when, in a curveball move, he created the successful Fatty Arbuckle's diner chain which made him a multi-millionaire and a Dublin tax exile. He died at his home in Knutsford, Cheshire of a heart attack in 2017 at the age of 75. His Wikipedia entry refers to him firstly as a 'British businessman' and relegates his Beatle connection to a later sentence.

10. Alan Durband

'We can't all be Tommy Steele, you know.'

Six years after he'd left the Liverpool Institute, when Paul McCartney revealed in the song, 'Getting Better' that he used to get mad at his school, and that, furthermore, the teachers who taught him weren't cool, it was, like much else on the *Sgt. Pepper* album, partly fantastical. Alan 'Dusty' Durband, the teacher who had most influence on the young McCartney's lyrical imagination, and therefore the imaginative landscape of the world, was certainly cool, and Macca knew it.

The Beatles' relationship with the British education system was variously complicated. His many childhood illnesses and hospital stays meant that Ringo was barely schooled at all, though honourable mention should be made of Dingle neighbour Mary Maguire who taught him to read. John and George both cultivated a surly, willed uncooperativeness that they carried into adulthood. George was an underachieving rebel, while Lennon bridled at every perceived educational burden even in the relaxed environs of art college. Both he and Stu Sutcliffe, though, were encouraged by the formidable Arthur Ballard. Ballard was something of a legend at Liverpool Art School. A former heavyweight boxer and hard drinking lothario, he spotted some spark of inchoate talent in the pair. In his Beatles biography, Bob Spitz maintains 'No one outside of The Beatles took more interest in John's welfare until three years later when Brian Epstein materialised.' Ballard held court in the backroom of Ye Cracke pub on Rice Street, which he called The War Office, where John was a cheeky acolyte. He even came to see the fledgling Beatles play at an art school dance but told colleagues he was 'troubled' by his prize student's 'distraction'. The prize student being Stuart Sutcliffe.

Alan Durband was, like Ringo, a working-class Dingle lad but his academic career was rather more exalted. He studied under the formidable critic F. R. Leavis at Cambridge before returning home to teach at his alma mater, the Liverpool Institute, eventually becoming head of English. One of his eager young charges was Paul McCartney. Under his strict but benign tutelage, McCartney's interest in literature blossomed. He told Radio 4's *This Cultural Life* podcast 'I had a brilliant English literature teacher who was called Alan Durband … I owe him. I had great respect for Mr Durband because he managed to get us to read books. He taught Chaucer and to this day I know where all the naughty bits are.' Durband also noticed that McCartney was at school seemingly unaffected on the day after his mother had died. But he sensed his pain; 'I think it shattered him.' He wrote to all Paul's other teachers asking them to be sensitive and tolerant of any changes in his behaviour.

Later, inspired by Durband and as befitting the young intellectual, Macca affected a pipe which he puffed on thoughtfully as he read Wilde, Sheridan and Tennessee Williams. Any thespian dreams were short lived though, at least until *A Hard Day's Night*. Durband didn't think he was a good enough actor for a speaking part so cast him as a nodding and murmuring background monk in the school production of Shaw's *St Joan* while classmate Peter Sissons scooped the plum role of the Earl of Warwick by virtue of his 'great booming voice'.

In 1960, McCartney approached Durband for some career's guidance. In a 1965 interview with Australian TV, Durband recalled, 'At the age of 18, about a week before he left school, he came to me and asked me for my advice. He wanted to know if he should carry on playing the guitar professionally because he'd been offered a job in Hamburg playing the guitar at £20 a week, or whether he should carry on and become a teacher as he'd always intended to be.' Durband gave him the 'schoolmaster's advice' and suggested that he go to Teacher Training College 'because we can't all be Tommy

Steele, you know'. A few years later, when Macca popped round to see him 'in a lovely Aston Martin', Durband noted ruefully, 'He wouldn't have had an Aston Martin if he'd been a schoolteacher, I can assure you.'

In that same TV interview with ABC, Durband praised The Beatles for their ever-growing rebelliousness against conservatism, stuffiness and the English status quo. 'I'm glad they're critical,' he said. 'They typify a kind of English North country attitude, a particular brand of wit which is all the time, as they say, taking the mickey out of people in authority. They would never recognise that there was anyone better than them.'

Watch the interview on YouTube and you will glimpse the glint of steel beneath Durband's undoubted grace and politesse. Something of the real man is coming to the fore here. Durband got his nickname, Dusty, when he was sent down the mines as a conscientious objector in World War II. He was a committed atheist, nuclear disarmer and socialist, but like his bright young pupil, he also relished good food, wine, clothes, cars, houses and conversation. He helped found Liverpool's radical and brilliant Everyman Theatre which fostered talent like Jonathan Pryce, Bill Nighy, Julie Walters and Willie Russell (in fact, Russell wrote *Educating Rita* in Durband's Welsh cottage).

Even at the end of The Beatles, via Durband's influence, the bard was sneaking into Paul's lyrics. 'While I was studying English literature at the Liverpool Institute High School for Boys with my favourite teacher, Alan Durband, I read Hamlet ... There are a couple of lines from late in the play: "O, I could tell you – But let it be ..." I suspect those lines had subconsciously planted themselves in my memory.'

The classroom where 'Dusty' Durband taught Paul is now The Alan Durband Room at LIPA, The Liverpool Institute of Performing Arts, co-founded by Paul McCartney.

11. Bill Harry

'Bloody hell, there's a Teddy Boy!'

Even in a city full of quirky and characterful boozers, Ye Cracke is one of the most storied and eccentric. Tucked away on tiny Rice Street in the city centre ('Cracke' is old Scouse for an alley), I enter beneath the vintage Bass and Marston's ales signs and push my way through the garrulous Saturday teatime crowds – students, hipsters, elderly rogues, shoppers, glamorous girls, Evertonians celebrating a home win and more – and sip my Shipyard IPA at the bar before noticing a sign that says, bluntly, 'If we're busy, when you've got your drink at the bar, f**k off!'

Other signage confirms that this is no Wetherspoons or Moon Under Water, no corporate leisure chain. 'Free Palestine', 'Justice for Grenfell', 'Don't Buy The Sun', 'Merseyside Anti-Fascist Network' and, inscribed on a huge plaque in the back bar, a tribute to four regulars from an earlier age who called themselves The Dissenters. In a tiny snug by the side door with room for just one table partitioned by glazed wooden screens, sit four old men quaffing stouts. This is 'The War Office' where, seven decades before, when these drinkers were young men, four other young lads would talk politics and philosophy over nursed pints. These were the aforementioned Dissenters; Rod Murray, Stuart Sutcliffe, John Lennon and Bill Harry. Bill Harry has been called the 'Zelig' of The Beatles' story. But unlike Woody Allen's accidental witness to history, Harry had, to use the modish phrase, 'agency'. He was, certainly during the group's fledgling or pupal phase, a catalyst, there from the start, before the start in fact; friend, peer, spur.

'Bloody hell, there's a Teddy Boy!' exclaimed Harry when he first spotted the bequiffed John Lennon in the canteen of Liverpool College of Art in September 1957. With his oily pompadour and greaser outfit, Lennon was conspicuous among the uniform polo necks and duffle coats affected by the rest of the student intake. Harry decided 'I've got to get to know him.' He, Lennon, Stuart Sutcliffe and flatmate Rod Murray would soon take to holding their boozy salons in Ye Cracke's War Room beneath a reproduction of *The Death Of Nelson*.

'We used to talk about art and literature and read books by the San Francisco poets and the Olympia press in Paris', Harry told the BBC news website in 2014. A sci-fi buff, he wrote stories by candle-light – his spartan household had no electricity – and produced a magazine called *Biped*, becoming a penfriend of the science-fiction writer, Michael Moorcock. Later he founded the art college magazine *Premier*. But the literary endeavour Harry is best known for emanated from a room above a wine merchant at 81 Renshaw Street, now a groovy independent record shop,* then the headquarters of *Mersey Beat*, launched by Harry and girlfriend Virginia with fifty pounds of borrowed money in June 1961. The intention was to cover the music of the region that gave the mag its name, with a double meaning as in a policeman's beat or patch.

The Beatles were prominent from the start. Issue 2's front page was emblazoned 'Beatles Sign Recording Contract', and soon jealous rivals sarcastically dubbed the mag 'Merseybeatle'. The band would drop by the Renshaw Street office, take calls, help with the typing and generally 'goof off'. Lennon contributed zany Beachcomber-style columns including one in which he advanced the famously daft explanation of their name. 'It came in a vision – a man appeared on a flaming pie and said unto them "From this day on you are Beatles with an 'A'." The most iconic cover was Issue 13, 4 January 1962, with the front page announcing, 'Beatles Top Poll!', one of the last

---

* Owner Neil told me that, thanks to a misprint in a Liverpool Council Beatle tour leaflet, people from all around the world queue up to get a picture outside the Indian restaurant next door.

images of them sporting their 'rocker look' and still with Pete Best in the fold.*

Mersey Beat was perhaps a fascinating evolutionary stage between the 'trades' like *Melody Maker* and the counter-cultural stylings of *Village Voice, Rolling Stone* and the 1970s *NME*; a magazine written enthusiastically but not uncritically by fans 'on the ground'. It was an instant success, selling out at twenty-eight newsagents and venues. The pace was tough as Harry told *Shortlisted* online magazine: 'I'd be working around the clock and until about four o'clock in the morning when I'd go to the Pier Head for a cup of tea and a pie.' Brian Epstein ordered twelve copies of the first issue and Harry claims that it was him, and not NEMS customer Raymond Jones, who first persuaded him to visit The Cavern and see for himself what the fuss was about. This would seem in character; pugnacious and opinionated, Harry has never been shy of offering combative opinions on everything from disputatious Beatle history (was Allan Williams their first manager? Harry thinks not) to the quality of John and Yoko's experimental albums (he doesn't like them).

In September 1964, Harry merged *Mersey Beat* into a new Epstein-backed title, *Music Echo*, but later resigned over editorial issues. He went on to an illustrious career in PR representing Pink Floyd, Jethro Tull, David Bowie, Led Zeppelin, The Beach Boys, Hot Chocolate, Suzi Quattro, Kim Wilde and others. He is the author of both *The Encyclopaedia of Beatles People* and the monumental *The Beatles Encyclopaedia*, a book you could stun an ox with, should the need arise. He does not include an entry for himself in either.

---

* And famously misspelling their bass player as Paul McArtrey.

12. Cynthia Lennon

'Postman, Postman, don't be slow.
I'm in love with Cyn, so go man, go!'

On my shelf is a book called *Men, Masculinity and The Beatles*, an academic text by Martin King of Manchester Metropolitan University. It's an absorbing read, even if readers unused to sociological prose may be daunted by sentences such as 'It is argued that many men live in some tension with or distance from hegemonic masculinity and that hegemonic masculinity is supported by the collusion of dominant forms of femininity.' If not always in touch with their feminine sides (they were working-class Northerners of the 1950s, lest we forget) The Beatles were acutely emotionally sympatico with their female fans.

In the terrific *Love and Let Die*, John Higgs examines how The Beatles differ radically from their cultural twin, James Bond, and how these Sixties British soft power siblings born on the same day, 6 October 1962,* represent utterly opposing notions of masculinity and Britishness. Bond, in whatever actor's incarnation, looks exactly like what he is; a posh, emotionally stunted, ultra-conformist reactionary. The Beatles both looked and acted like no men had ever looked or behaved before. After The Beatles, men would never look or act the same again. As Alan Bleasdale has said, 'Because of The Beatles we were going to be different from our dads.'

So far, so progressive. But then consider 'Cyn'. Her relationship with John was the longest romantic relationship any of them had within the lifetime of the group, from autumn 1958 to the terrible moment in 1968 when she arrived home from a Greek holiday John

---

* On this day, the first Beatles single, 'Love Me Do', was released and the first Bond movie, *Dr No*.

had insisted she take, to find him and Yoko partly dressed in their home. But back in the late Fifties, her and John's initial attraction seems mutual, genuine and passionate. He carved her name on a church tower in Hamburg, sent her loving and ardent letters when he was away containing vivid if unromantic exhortations like 'I love you Cyn Powell and I wish I was on the way to your flat with the Sunday papers and cherries and a throbber! Oh Yes!' On the envelopes he would write: 'Postman, Postman, don't be slow. I'm in love with Cyn, so go man, go!' and 'SWALK' [Sealed With A Loving Kiss]. Pete Best remembered 'John and I would go and have a couple of quiet beers, just to sit down and chew the fat. And he'd talk about Cynthia and how much he missed her.'

But he could also be distant, and worse. On the night of their wedding, which Aunt Mimi had resolutely opposed, The Beatles had a gig in Chester and John was clearly ill at ease, haranguing the support act and arguing with his bandmates; Ringo didn't even know that Lennon had married that afternoon. During their marriage he was, by his own admission, often violent. 'I was a hitter. I couldn't express myself and I hit. I fought men and I hit women.' In an interview published after his death, he admitted 'occasionally hitting my dear wife in the early days'.* In her 2005 memoir, Cynthia remembers an incident in a club where 'he raised his arm and hit me across the face, knocking my head into the pipes that ran down the wall behind me'.

At the height of Beatlemania, she and son Julian lived in a five-pound-a-week-bedsit in Liverpool and was portrayed, as she puts it, as a 'dim little girlfriend in a headscarf' in the film *Backbeat*. All

---

* Different attitudes to difficulties with women often emerge in Lennon and McCartney's individual songs. Paul's often come from a place of apology, regret and bewilderment ('The Night Before', 'Yesterday', 'You Won't See Me') while many of John's boil down to 'I feel wronged by you and thus am going to kill you and all your future boyfriends' ('You Can't Do That', 'Baby's In Black', 'Run For Your Life'.)

through her life with him, she felt compelled, was compelled, to morph into whatever John needed or wanted her to be at that time. After her seduction at Gambier Terrace following a night of boozing in Ye Cracke in which he had largely ignored her, she transformed herself from demure Hoylake student to a Wirral bottle-blonde in tight sweaters to please him, in the same way that she compliantly downed Preludin in Hamburg and dropped acid in swinging London, both of which she hated. She donned the requisite flowers and kaftans for the sojourn to Rishikesh and did find meditation there calming and beneficial, or might have done had she not been increasingly aware of John's infatuation with Yoko Ono, who he was writing to daily. In the end, becoming an enigmatic Japanese avant-garde conceptual artist was an impossible transformation too far. In all her interviews, she uses the same rote, anodyne clichés to describe him; 'non-conformist', 'rough diamond', 'rebel', as if she had begun to accept the received wisdom, the official story, rather than interrogate her own lived experience. Perhaps it was easier that way.

In a 1984 interview with Tony Wilson, boss of Factory Records (but known to Northerners as a teatime news anchor), she exudes that air of quiet, elegant, sadness that characterised most of her TV appearances. When Wilson suggests he was not an easy man to be with, she defends him: 'He was wonderful with me for many years … I mean, it's impossible for somebody to be wonderful all the time.'

When Wilson asks her to choose a song that sums up everything about her and John's complex, sometimes painful, story, she chooses 'The Long and Winding Road'. A lovely song, but one written by Paul McCartney.

13. Mona Best

*'It's jealousy ... because Peter is the
one with the terrific following.'*

West Derby, three miles east of the bustle of downtown Liverpool, is
looking its best on a gleaming sunny winter Saturday after a sparkling
shower. The only sounds are bells pealing and bird song as I turn left
at the church, two churches in fact, just by the trattoria and the dog
grooming parlour and into Haymans Green. There's money here, and
there always has been it seems. Number 8 stands back from the road,
a large, handsome Victorian villa built circa 1860 that, but for a faded
wooden sign that reads 'The Casbah Club' you would never suspect
was what the BBC World Service once described, in a moment of
mildly unhinged hyperbole, as 'popular music's Sistine chapel'. Almost
exactly a century after it was built, Number 8 Haymans Green, home
of the Best family, became the first real home of The Beatles.

'Small, dark-haired, voluptuous, very strong and determined,' as
Hunter Davies found her, it's no surprise that Mona Best had a
potent effect on the young men – one in particular – that orbited
within and around The Quarrymen as they metamorphosed into
The Beatles. In *Anthology*, Paul describes her, with the classic
McCartney penchant for understatement and discretion, as 'a very
nice woman'. 'Nice' would seem too small and wan a word for her.

Her impact on the fledgling Beatles was profound, not least on
their friend and later road manager, Neil Aspinall, who became her
lover. But while indisputable, this is to trivialise her significance. Her
son, Pete, was their drummer at a formative time, but more importantly her club, The Casbah, was the birthplace of The Beatles, long
before The Cavern could ever claim as much. Moreover, Mona Best
was not just the first Beatles 'agent'; she was arguably the world's first
ever female rock promoter.

'Born in India in 1924' profiled David Leafe in the *Daily Mail*, 'she was of Irish parentage and her father was a colonel serving in the Bengal Lancers. A free spirit, with olive skin and amazing long jet-black hair, she broke many hearts. But it was Johnny Best, a major posted to India during World War II, who wooed and won her.' Mark Lewisohn is similarly minded: '(she) sailed into Liverpool in 1945, the war bride of Johnny Best, the city's well-known boxing promoter ... exuding a beauty that bewitched men of all ages, she was full of life and in love with fun'.

She arrived from Madras with four-year-old son Peter and made an instant impression with her exotic looks, style and aesthetic. Highly individual, she tried in vain to persuade her husband to move into, first, a lighthouse in Formby, then a windmill in St Helens (surely the only one) and a distinctive circular abode in Southport. Overruled on all of these by Johnny, and, as Lewisohn put it, being 'a perpetual can-do woman, a human hurricane to whom anything was possible', she took matters into her own hands. According to Best family legend, in 1954, she pawned all her jewellery and put the resulting cash on a rank outsider called Never Say Die in the Derby. Ridden by an unknown teenager called Lester Piggott, it romped home at 33-1 and with her winnings she bought a derelict former Conservative Club in the well-to-do Liverpool suburb of West Derby. Mark Lewisohn strongly contests this story as an invention of her adoring sons but what is in no doubt is that, inspired by a TV item about the 2i's club in Soho, she converted the capacious cellar into a coffee bar-cum-club, decorated in oriental style by some local likely lads including John Lennon, his girlfriend Cyn and George Harrison. Their band The Quarrymen, then consisting of John and George plus Paul McCartney and a guitarist named Ken Brown, opened The Casbah Club, named after a line ('Come with me to The Casbah!') in the film *Algiers* that Charley Boyer never actually says, in August 1959.

The Quarrymen played here thirteen times and The Beatles at least forty. The house above the cellar also became home to Neil

Aspinall who, still a teenager in 1960, moved in with the Bests as a lodger and soon began a relationship with the 36-year-old Mona. It was a secret affair that produced a child (whose parentage was attributed to Johnny Best to avoid scandal) and seems to have even, for a while at least, survived The Beatles sacking of his friend, Pete.

In a TV interview recorded soon after this rupture, Mona and Pete (but effectively just Mona), rails against this dismissal. 'It's jealousy … because Peter is the one who has the terrific following … I think it was for that reason that Peter had to be got rid of at that stage because if it wasn't and they went national and international Peter would have become the main Beatle with the others just props …'

This may be understandable, admirable even. But it was as preposterous then as it is now. The short clip makes for mildly uncomfortable viewing; Mona forceful while Pete looks on sheepishly with the mixture of inscrutability and vacuity that was surely what compromised his suitability as a Beatle as much as any musical shortcomings. She adds though 'we haven't come here to throw sticks and stones at the boys' and, from what we can gather, she remained cordial enough towards 'the boys' to lend John her father's military medals that John wears on the *Sgt. Pepper* sleeve (though this was disputed by Aspinall according to Mark Lewisohn) and receive the 'All You Need Is Love' doll from said cover as a thank you.

As I stroll back from what was once The Casbah to the main road and my Uber, I bump into a nice middle-aged Scouse couple who recognise me, tell me that The Beatles also played at The Pillar Club based a few doors down at 'Lowlands' and offer to show me Pete Best's current house around the corner. 'We live in the same street. He never comes out.' As for The Casbah, the former coal cellar was made a Listed Building in 2006. In 2024, it was turned into an Airbnb run by Roag Best, son of Neil and Mona, and half-brother of Pete. There are Lennon, McCartney and Harrison suites for rent but, significantly, none named after Ringo.

Part Two

WITH THE BEATLES

1960

14. Larry Parnes

'Your name is Johnny and you're quiet ...
how about Johnny Gentle?'

Or Mr Parnes, Shillings and Pence as the UK press of the late 1950s dubbed him. Or the manipulative, avaricious Major Rafe Ralph as played by Peter Sellers in a Muir and Norden skit on *Songs For Swingin' Sellers*. Or Laurie London as he became in Colin McInnes *Absolute Beginners*, played in the 1986 movie with appalling relish by Lionel Blair.

Laurence Maurice Parnes was the 'beat svengali', the benevolent(ish) dictator who dominated pre-Beatle pop with his anodyne roster of young men of variable talent. George Melly in his pioneering pop culture survey, Revolt into Style, speculated that Parnes rechristened them all to suggest something of their sexual character: Billy Fury, Marty Wilde, Tommy Steele, Vince Eager, Johnny Gentle, Duffy Power, Dickie Pride. Understandably, future hitmaker Joe Brown refused to become Elmer Twitch.

We will never know what lubricious sobriquets Parnes might have foisted on John, Paul, George and Ringo as he was not sufficiently impressed to sign up The Silver Beetles to his stable when he initially auditioned them in 1960. But he did book them as backing band for fellow Scouser and Parnes protégé Johnny Gentle's upcoming tour of Scotland, infamous for its sub-zero conditions and the car crash in which hapless stand-in drummer Tommy Moore was hospitalised.

John Askew was born on Scotland Road, Liverpool in 1936. He worked the local clubs and cruise liners and entered a talent show at Butlin's under the name George Baker, losing out to a young comic called Jimmy Tarbuck. After that he changed his name again to Rick Damone. He laboured on London building sites while striving for that elusive break in the recording industry which came when he approached Larry Parnes. Parnes initially suggested he call himself Tim McGee before suggesting 'Your name is Johnny and you're quiet … how about Johnny Gentle?'

Gentle/Askew seems to have bonded well with his fellow Scousers on that formative Scottish jaunt, repeatedly asking Parnes to come up and see their set as 'they're doing better than me'. Soon, that would be obvious to all. After the tour, as The Beatles soared in popularity, Gentle joined a band called The Vikings before calling it a day around the same time as his former backing band did in 1970, quitting the business to become a joiner in Jersey and eventually retiring to Kent.

In 1983, Parnes filed a suit against Paul McCartney and the BBC over a flippant aside from Paul on his *Desert Island Discs* appearance the previous year when he claimed they'd never been paid for the Gentle tour. Presenter Roy Plomley later made a formal apology, while wearily pointing out that Paul had meant it as a joke. Presumably Muir and Norden's Major Rafe Ralph was less actionable if clearly Parnesian. This is how the Major/Parnes described the ideal teen crooner of his stable: 'A good specimen, he's about seventeen or eighteen years old, about five foot ten fully extended, sagging to about five foot four in the singing position. Points to look for are: forehead – well, there shouldn't be more than about half an inch of that. Plenty of mouth, the lower lip permanently slack, and beware of possible fallen arches. They save a lot of trouble in mid-career, you know.'

Parnes died in 1986 from meningitis. As the obituaries were wont to say, he never married.

15. Johnny Hutchinson

'I wouldn't join The Beatles for a big clock.'

My favourite moments of the joint interviews filmed for the *Anthology* series are not the discussions of recording techniques, celebrated gigs and such, but the quick, impromptu resurfaced memories of the 'Threetles' collective past, the fascinating everyday of their Liverpool youth. For one, all of them amusedly remembering that Ringo's first car was bought from 'Johnny Hutch ... seventy-five quid ... hand painted ... red and white ...' Ringo adored his Standard Vanguard and drove illegally for nearly a year before even attempting to take his driver's test in November 1960. He failed. But he did possess the great good sense to join The Beatles, which is more than can be said for the vendor Johnny, at least the way he tells it.

'Hutch' was a meaty drummer well known around town, having served his percussive apprenticeship with the tremendously named skiffle outfit Cass and The Casanovas. Boldly, indeed treacherously, ousting Cass himself, the remaining trio continued as The Big Three with Hutch as that rarity, the drumming frontman.* The Big Three were famed for their aggressive performances, a power trio long before Cream, Jimi Hendrix Experience and others made that a rock trope. But in the brief interim between Pete Best's departure and Ringo joining The Beatles, Hutch, also managed by Brian Epstein, stepped in for a couple of shows including the famous Larry Parnes audition. After a show in Chester, Hutch claims 'We sat down, and

---

* The Big Three's bassist John Gustafson had a rich and varied career, playing with Kevin Ayers, Ian Gillan and most famously Roxy Music in the mid-Seventies, contributing the notable bass line to 'Love Is The Drug'. Guitarist Adrian Barber went on to engineer and produce The Allman Brothers, Aretha Franklin and the first Aerosmith album.

Brian Epstein and Bob Wooler were just looking at me. So I said, "What the fuck do you two want?" And they looked at each other, and Brian said to Bob, "What do you think?" Bob said, "Well, Brian, I think John would suit The Beatles down to the ground." Then Brian said, "I do, too. John, I want you to be The Beatles' drummer." I told him that "I wouldn't join The Beatles for a big clock", a fabulous expression beloved of Scousers of a certain vintage.'

According to Hutchinson, he then suggested that Epstein 'go and get Ringo. He's a bum, he'll join anyone for a few bob.' Other sources though, perhaps more impartial ones, suggest that Hutchinson's belligerent temperament (which does seem to manifest itself in most interviews) made him a poor fit for the band. He continued with The Big Three, of whom Rock historian Pete Frame wrote, 'Dynamite live, they were thwarted by Epstein's and Decca's efforts to mould them into a "nice" group. They toured Britain, did the TV shows but their records belie their wall-shaking, sweaty, roaring, on-stage magnificence.'

After the band's split in 1966, Hutch became a builder and property developer. He has always maintained that he has never once regretted his decision not to join The Beatles.

And if you believe this, you will believe anything.

16. Tommy Moore

'You can piss off. He's not playing with youse anymore.'

There are any number of Beatles nearly men. Individuals whose lives became defined by their tangential brush with eternal fame, twisted out of shape by that warping magnetic field of talent and stardom, that gravitational pull of destiny. Some later made careers or roles of sorts from it all, emanating various residual emotions; bruised hurt (Pete Best), rueful chirpiness (Allan Williams) or a kind of PTSD (Jimmie Nicol). But no tale is glummer than that of Tommy Moore, who history will record as the man who gave up The Beatles for a shift on the forklifts at Garston Bottle works.

Moore was their first professional drummer, a technically solid jazz player resident at The Temple Club on Dale Street when he answered a newspaper ad for a drummer placed by Paul and George. Allan Williams had arranged an audition at The Blue Angel on Seel Street with the impresario Larry Parnes, seeking a backing band for Billy Fury, then the biggest thing in UK pop and a fellow Scouser. Moore, though, had a day job at Garston Bottle works and arrived late and dishevelled. Perhaps because of this, and Moore's advanced years – he was 28 – Parnes passed on the fledgling Fabs.

Later though, Parnes needed a back-up group for a short notice Scottish tour by Johnny Gentle, a gig Gerry and The Pacemakers, Rory Storm and Cass and The Casanovas had all turned down. Perhaps because of this, Moore was not keen. He was almost a decade older than the other Silver Beetles and more the lugubrious Scouse everyman than the sarky, bright grammar school lads in the band. Also, as his formidable girlfriend Veronica Hughes often forcibly reminded him, he had steady if unglamorous work at the aforementioned glassworks. The Beatles were persuasive though.

Fifteen quid was more than his wage from the factory. His girlfriend still said he was a fool.

On 23 May, after a boozy visit to a local pig farmer friend of the Scottish promoter (no, really), Johnny Gentle himself was driving the van from Inverness to Fraserborough when it rear-ended a stationary Ford Poplar just outside Banff.* Two elderly ladies were hurt but nothing like as badly as the hapless Moore who was struck in the face by a flying guitar which left him concussed and minus his front teeth. A few hours later he would come round, heavily sedated, to find himself being dragged from his hospital bed by one John Lennon and the manager of the Dalrymple Hall in Fraserborough, venue for the night's gig. Dazed and in pain, Moore drummed while the gleefully malevolent Lennon would turn around and mock Moore's bandaged and inflamed face, and toothless visage. Moore was, not unreasonably, beginning to tire of all this.

Back from Scotland, on Saturday, 11 June, Moore failed to show up for a Beatles show – they had dropped the Silver and the other E by now – at The Grosvenor Ballroom, Wallasey where they had a residency. It was a rough gig. 'The Grosvenor Ballroom in Wallasey was one of the worst places' according to Paul, 'there would be a hundred Wallasey lads squaring up to a hundred lads from Seacombe and all hell would break loose.' On this summer Saturday though, Moore was nowhere to be seen. Williams and The Beatles drove in the former's flash 'Jag' to Moore's house in nearby Fern Grove. Here the feisty Veronica, in a speech she might later have had cause to regret, shouted from an upstairs window 'You can piss off. He's not playing with youse anymore. He's had enough. He's down at the bottle factory.' Driving on down to the Window Lane works, they found Tommy, unmoved, staying fast to his forklift in his overalls.

---

* While they waited for the ambulance, The Beatles signed some scraps of paper for local teenage girls who had spotted gig posters in the van. These are thought to be the earliest surviving Beatle autographs.

Thus ended Tommy Moore's brief but eventful stint with The Beatles.

In the early Seventies the BBC's Bernard Falk returned to his native Liverpool to make a documentary about The Cavern's tenth anniversary. Tommy Moore appears in it, looking the dictionary definition of the expression 'hangdog' and introduced by Falk, a little harshly some would say, as 'a walking tragedy'. He stayed in Liverpool and died in 1981 of a brain haemorrhage aged just 50, having outlived his erstwhile tormentor by less than a year.

17. Royston Ellis

'We didn't have any leather but I had my oilskins and we had
some black polythene bags from somewhere.'

Sexual intercourse began in 1963 for Philip Larkin ('between the
end of the Chatterley ban and The Beatles' first LP') which was of
course considerably later than for the four young Liverpudlians who
rocked and rolled on Hamburg's infamous Reeperbahn. But that
poem of Larkin's 'Annus Mirabilis' from which his famed observation comes was just one of the many occasions where poets and
poetry intersect with The Beatle narrative.

Roger McGough, who, along with Adrian Henri and Brian
Patten, published the enormously successful collection, *The Mersey
Sound*, a kind of verse Beatles album, was later in The Scaffold with
Mike McCartney: 'I didn't have many cool clothes because I'd been
living on teachers' wages. So Mike gave me his brother's old stage
clothes – two pairs of trousers, a shirt and a suit – which Paul didn't
need and had given to him. About four years ago, I found the trousers and the shirt in my attic. Sadly, the moths had gotten to the
trousers, all around the crotch. I had the trousers put on a canvas
and I wrote a poem called Macca's Trousers ... if I ever get really
hard-up, I could sell them.' He later, uncredited and for a minimal
fee, 'scoused up' the dialogue on 'Yellow Submarine' which he said
initially read 'like Woody Allen talking to Steve Martin'. Adrian
Henri himself wrote quite a bad poem six years after Lennon's death
that ends 'at the dark end of the street waits the inevitable stranger',
as tendentious as it is meaningless. Another Adrian, Mitchell,
beloved of the Hampstead left but clearly not averse to the *Daily
Mail* shilling, wrote in that paper in 1963 that 'Please Please Me' was
'almost incoherent except for its solid battering beat', proof if it were
needed that you should never trust posh poets about pop music.

The Irish poet, Paul Muldoon, was McCartney's choice as collaborator on his collected *Lyrics* books. Another Irish poet, Sinead Morrissey, has written a superb poem called 'Perfume' in her collection, *On Balance*, about the sheer and all-consuming power and lustre of the early Beatles. Candidly, the worst of the poets to stray into The Beatles' ken was probably Royston Ellis. Yet he adds a little something to our narrative, particularly for fans of The Beatles' early drug experiments and the *Abbey Road* Side 2 medley.

'Hard on the heels of the American "Beat Generation" comes an 18-year-old from Hatch End, and in his own circles he has caused a minor revolution,' ran a 1959 profile of Ellis in that underground bible *The Harrow Observer and Gazette*. 'Indicative of the young people in the world today … he seeks to capture their restless, unsettled imaginations.' By the turn of the 1960s, he was a familiar face and voice around British culture; 'The King of The Beatniks' as he was dubbed, chatting on arts shows, tartan shirted and bearded, reciting his poetry live over the music of The Shadows (who look faintly sheepish about it in the existing clips), an artistic merger of arguable quality he called 'rocketry'.

In the spring of 1960, he came to Liverpool to read his poems at the University to little response, but while in town dropped into The Jacaranda, and 'got talking to a boy, George, in a striped matelot T-shirt and black leather jacket who told me his friends played music'. He went back to Gambier Terrace where he met the rest of the Silver Beetles* and instigated what seems to have been The Beatles' first drug experience, showing them how to crack open a nasal inhaler and to chew the Benzedrine-soaked strip to achieve an amphetamine high. 'We cracked up the Vicks inhaler, ate it and sat up all night till nine the next morning rapping and burping up the taste' remembered George, affectionately.

---

* Ellis maintained he suggested the change to 'Beatles', contested by Mark Lewisohn.

Ellis can claim another couple of moments of Beatles significance too. He always said that despite the interest shown in his early books of hip verse, he 'wanted to be a paperback writer', that is, a mass market major seller.* And on 8 August 1963, after The Beatles' two shows at the Candie Park Auditorium, Guernsey, John had dinner with Royston Ellis (who was working there as a ferryboat engineer) and his girlfriend Stephanie at their hotel. After much drink had been taken, Ellis, Stephanie, John and Suzanne Sellers, who was working at the hotel that summer, repaired to Ellis' flat. Interviewed in Martin Creasy's *Spend 1963 With The Beatles*, Sellers recalled: 'It was quite strange, because when we got there, Royston and his girl-friend went off and made fried egg sandwiches. I'd never had a fried egg sandwich before, so that's why that sticks in my mind!'

'After we ate the fried egg sandwiches, Royston and his girlfriend went off again, and then came back wearing these black plastic bags! John and myself kind of looked at one another, and they said, "Do you want to join in?" and we said, "Join in with what?", and they said, "Well we kind of play games with these plastic bags then end up having sex." They offered John and I a plastic bag each, I said, "No, thank you very much." I didn't want anything to do with that sort of thing, and as far as I can remember, neither did John. I recall afterwards that I decided to go, and John came down the stairs with me and gave me money for a cab to get home ... As a result of that, he wrote the song called "Polythene Pam". I certainly wasn't involved, and "Polythene Pam" certainly wasn't me!'

After much globetrotting, and in the wake of his hillside log cabin in Dominica being blown down by Hurricane David, Ellis settled in Sri Lanka, where he lived for more than forty years, writing travel books, novels and memoirs, until his death at the age of 82, a long way from Pinner.

---

* He later achieved this with the exploitative and, to modern readers, shocking MA Bond-master novels, written as Richard Tresillian.

18. Rod Murray

'The Beatnik Horror.'

On a damp early summer's evening, while Liverpool's nearby city centre buzzes with life and noise, Gambier Terrace is serene in a gauzy mist of shy rain. Giles Gilbert Scott's imposing Anglican Cathedral towers above this hidden, private lane just off the city's handsome Georgian quarter. At number 3, a nurse delivering a prescription is chatting to the resident via the intercom. A couple under an umbrella stroll by. The mood is placid. But in the summer of 1960, Number 3 Gambier Terrace was a scene of horror, at least according to the *Sunday People*.

Rod Murray met Stuart Sutcliffe on registration day for Liverpool Art College and they bonded over a mutual love of art and hatred for their common Christian Brother's education.* They shared several flats and studios, including one in Percy Street rented to them by Mrs Plant. One day, however, when she made an impromptu visit for the rent, she found 'a table leg burning in the grate in my room … and then when she went upstairs to Stuart's room she found that all the furniture was painted … black and white and circles … so she evicted us served with a month's notice.'

Their next abode was the large first-floor unfurnished flat at 3 Hilary Mansions, Gambier Terrace with a kitchen, a bathroom and three bedrooms, one of which was perfect as an art studio. All of this came for what became an affordable three pounds when joined by girlfriends Margaret Morrison ('Diz') and Margaret Duxbury ('Ducky') and, fairly soon, John Lennon. At first, the flat seemed grand, luxurious even but, as anyone who's experienced shared student lodgings will attest, standards soon began to slide.

---

* I also had one. And hated it too.

Around the same time, the nascent Beatles needed a bass player, a position Stuart and Rod were both keen to fill. However, both were bassless and financially embarrassed. Rod decided, boldly, to make one but when Stuart managed to acquire a bona fide version after selling a painting to local pools tycoon, John Moores, Rod's carpentry project was abandoned. Several early sessions here were taped by Rod and he remembers Tommy Moore practising with them on the eve of the Johnny Gentle tour.

Gambier Terrace was decidedly, to use a word The Beatles would usher into the vernacular, 'grotty'. Bare floorboards, unshaded bulbs, camp beds and squeezed paint tubes. But it was hardly as grisly as it was denounced to the nation one Sunday in 1960 when it became a cause célèbre in the tabloid press. The Beatles' manager Allan Williams turned up at Ye Cracke pub one afternoon with a journalistic contingent in tow ostensibly from the middle-brow *Empire News* researching a piece on the paucity of student grants. Egged on by the never publicity-averse Williams, Stu Sutcliffe and pals told how they would, as above, burn pieces of furniture to stay warm and scavenge food from friends and relatives. Eventually they took the reporter, photographer and several bottles of beer and whisky back to Gambier Terrace. But when it failed to live up to squalid expectations, the pressmen – actually from the racy and downmarket *Sunday People* – haphazardly tossed empty beer bottles and rubbish everywhere to create some very mild dilapidation and excess.

The subsequent 'exposé' and picture appeared on 24 July 1960 under lurid headlines about 'The Beatnik Horror … The Cult of Despair That Is Driving Teenagers To Violence'. The piece is worth seeking out as much for its superb insight into the (now disappearing) world of the Sunday 'scandal sheet' as for any Beatle connections. The guilty men behind this sick cult are named and shamed; Allen Ginsberg 'The Hate Merchant', Jack Kerouac 'The Hobo Prophet' and William Burroughs the ex-drug addict who 'lived in Tangiers for a year without taking a bath or changing his clothes'. Not surprisingly, when the resident's association saw the piece, the students were soon in search of new accommodation. Murray ended up with some of John's notebooks and his self-penned *Daily Howl* comic as well as a lighter and a pewter tankard, all of which have fetched several thousand pounds at Sotheby's.

John and Stu are not, as claimed and asserted by Wikipedia, in that infamous *Sunday People* picture; they were probably away visiting Royston Ellis. Allan Williams, Rod Murray and unnamed others are though, and though the scene is mildly grubby, Gambier Terrace looks no worse, indeed marginally better, than Nolan Street, Southport, my very own student hovel. On the wall is a torn poster for Gerry and The Pacemakers. Support act … The Silver Beetles.

19. Allan Williams

'No Allan Williams, no Hamburg. No Hamburg, no Beatles.'

Growing up in what we romantically termed 'Granadaland' (named after the North West's excellent and radical regional TV franchise) a regular televisual visitor to my childhood living room was a rotund, cherubic, bushy-haired fellow with a piping voice, often called upon to pass comment on matters musical pertaining to Liverpool and, in particular, its most famous pop export. Later, at some point, Tony Wilson or Bob Greaves would remark wryly, 'Allan Williams there … the man who gave The Beatles away.'

It's a good line. Williams himself used it as the title for his memoir. But like much else in that book – it's perhaps best described as an entertaining work of historical fiction a la – it isn't really true. He didn't give them away simply because they were never really his, or so it's alleged. Williams always claimed to have been their first manager, and eminent Beatleologists like Mark Lewisohn agree, but some argue he was merely their booking agent. What is not in doubt is that he was crucial in the early gestation of the band. As Lewisohn puts it 'No Allan Williams, no Hamburg. No Hamburg, no Beatles.'

After trying his hand as a plumber, jeweller and door-to-door salesman, Welsh Scouser, jazz devotee, bearded beatnik and would-be impresario Williams opened a coffee bar on Slater Street near Chinatown called The Jacaranda and run by Williams and his Chinese wife Beryl. These days, the 'Jac' is a lively downtown bar with live music downstairs (and a plaque unveiled in 2024 by Julian Lennon and his dad's former lover May Pang) and a hipster vinyl shop upstairs where I sipped my pint while flipping through the Japanese jazz imports. Back in 1960, it attracted a not dissimilar crowd. Under Allan Williams' gimlet eye, the 'Jac' soon became a popular hangout with penurious art students like John Lennon and

71

Stuart Sutcliffe, 'right layabouts' as he viewed them. Nevertheless, he became involved in promoting their fledgling rock and roll band, Johnny and The Moondogs or The Silver Beetles or Beatles or whatever they were called now.

He picked up a German student hitchhiking from Chester to Liverpool and his interest was piqued by tales of the Hamburg rock and club scene. Ever entrepreneurial, he soon established contacts in the German port and so, on 17 August 1960, he drove five weary, travel-sick young Beatles the 630 miles to Hamburg via the Harwich ferry in his cream and green Morris van, hugely and dangerously overloaded, sometimes reading his teenage charges *The Wind in the Willows* en route.

Thirty-nine months later, they were, as Mark Lewisohn put it in his social media obituary of Williams 'catapulted to a measure of mass fame unknown in our civilisation'. In the meantime, they had argued over Williams' commission on the second Hamburg visit and parted company acrimoniously and with recourse to lawyers (the first of many in The Beatles' tale). Williams was left to curse and, apparently, throw cushions at the television as he watched their gilded rise to global domination, an upward accession that would have made him a very rich man.

They seem to have later buried the hatchet at least partially. The Beatles would hang out at his Blue Angel club in Liverpool even after they were famous and, much later, he would be instrumental in organising the first UK Beatle fan conventions. Paul did refer to him as their first manager in *Anthology* and John loved his rambunctious and unreliable memoir, giving it a lovely 'blurb' in the mid-Seventies. Only George seems to have borne a grudge, sniping and gainsaying Williams in several 1970s interviews. Via George's influence, one imagines, Williams becomes Arthur Scouse in The Rutles, their first manager who they acquire through a bet, 'a bet they lost'.

Williams never appeared bitter, though, in those regular TV appearances of my youth. There are worse things to be than the man who found and lost The Beatles. As Lewisohn's obituary concludes, 'You could buy him a pint in the bars of his beloved Liverpool, watch him lose as many friends as he made, and witness a character … his place in history is written because … without his eccentric enterprise we'd never have known them.'

20. Lord Woodbine

'Their name liveth for evermore.'

When the SS *Empire Windrush* docked at a grey, chilly Tilbury Docks in 1948, its 492 trepidatious, expectant yet exuberant passengers from Jamaica cannot have known or even speculated the effect they would have on 'the mother country' as many of them touchingly viewed it. They could not have guessed how they would change the way Britain dressed and ate, the way its young people spoke and the music it danced to. Many of the passengers were pioneers in their different ways. Euton Christian would become Britain's first black magistrate, Sam King a future black mayor of Southwark. Lord Beginner and Lord Kitchener would bring calypso to Britain. Another passenger would play a crucial part in the origin story of one of the 'mother country's' greatest cultural exports to the wider world.

Trinidadian Harold Adolphus Phillips lied about his age to join the RAF aged 14. After the war, he returned to his home islands and began to sing calypso. After arriving in England with the other hopeful Windrush immigrants, he lived in Clapham then Wellington in Shropshire before eventually fetching up in Liverpool playing steel drums as Lord Woodbine (nicknamed for the totemic cheap British cigarettes he smoked). As a member of The Royal Caribbean Steel Band, he had a residency at Allan Williams' Jacaranda Club while also running some of Toxteth's wilder nights and shebeens. He booked The Silver Beetles for his own New Colony Club and later, Williams and Woodbine opened the New Cabaret Artists Club where the boys would play the Harry Lime Cha Cha for the resident Mancunian stripper, Janice.

Several people of colour are integral or of significance in the early Beatles' story. In the early days, Derry Wilkie of Derry and The

Seniors was a friend and inspiration who smoothed their progress in Hamburg. Hanging out with black musicians in Liverpool added grit, raunch and drive to their songs. It also more generally informed their outlook on the world as McCartney explained to Samira Ahmed at the Southbank launch of his *Lyrics* book. 'Liverpool [included] the first Caribbean community [in the UK], so it was just a given. Nobody thought anything of it. A lot of the guys in the groups were black, so we didn't think much of it. We just thought they were mates, we just thought they were equal – because they were ... When we went to America, there was this time when we were going to play Jacksonville or somewhere ... the promoter said, "OK, get ready because tomorrow night [when] you're going to be playing, the black people will sit over there and the white people will sit over there." We said, "Excuse me?" He said, "Yeah, that's how we do it down here." So we said, "Oh no, no, no, no! You can't do that."'

'Woody' and his wife Helen died in a fire in their Toxteth home in 2010.* Lord Woodbine has been described as the 'forgotten sixth Beatle' which is well meaning but absurd on several levels. Nonetheless, he was certainly significant, part of that inchoate cast list of early friends, promoters and supporters. He was there on Williams' overloaded minibus to Hamburg when, en route, they stopped at Arnhem War Cemetery and, at Williams' rather touching insistence, paid their respects to the fallen. There's a picture of the moment and Woodbine is there in the photo, in the group to the left with a Beatniky Allan Williams, his wife Beryl and an impossibly cool looking Stu Sutcliffe. With eerie prescience, the inscription behind them reads 'Their Name Liveth For Evermore.'

---

* Their daughter Barbara is a dramatist who has written for *Brookside* and *Doctors*.

21. Stuart Sutcliffe

'Everything he did crackled with excitement.'

The former house of the Kirchherr family at 45a Elmsbutteler Strasse in Hamburg's affluent Altona district is grand and elegant yet, with its proud though unshowy frontage an air of inscrutable German propriety. Inevitably, for those who know though, the eye is drawn to that upper storey. This is where Stuart Sutcliffe, known with varying accuracy and undiminished romance as the fifth Beatle, the lost Beatle, the coolest Beatle, the Beatle that never was, spent the last two years of his young life, absorbed in love and art, and where he died in the arms of his beloved.

For a phenomenon that brought the world so much joy, the Beatles story is blighted by tragedy, particularly that of premature death; Julia Lennon, Mary McCartney, Brian Epstein, Lennon himself of course. But the case of Stu Sutcliffe is as poignant as is imaginable, dead at 21 having helped shape the band that would reshape the world and destined, it appeared, for a glittering career on the international art scene. His former teachers were convinced of it. Arthur Ballard said 'Stu was a revolutionary. Everything he did crackled with excitement.' His teacher Eduardo Paolozzi, the pop art pioneer, reflected in 1968, 'If he'd lived, he could easily have been *the* Beatle. He was imaginative, ultra-intelligent, and he was open to everything, not just to painting or pop but to every media and experience possible … He had so much energy and was so very inventive. The feeling of potential just splashed out from him. He had the right kind of sensibility and arrogance to succeed.'

Stuart's father came south from Edinburgh to Liverpool to work in the Camel Laird shipyards and was often away at sea, an echo of George Harrison and John Lennon's fathers. 'We young artists are like young sailors,' wrote Stu in an early notebook. 'Unless we encounter rough seas and are buffeted by the winds, we'll not become real sailors', a detail that for someone who would cross the North Sea by boat never to return is spookily resonant. His early loves were painting and music. He was head chorister at Prescott Grammar School but soon fell hard for the look and energy of rock and roll. As befits someone who was blazingly talented at art, the lure of being in a band was as aesthetic as it was musical for Sutcliffe. When he moved to art college, his style grew unique and distinctive; high-sided winkle pickers, chiffon shirts, pink striped jeans. It was here that he met John Lennon, at this point essentially a boozy greaser with fairly primitive tastes, 'a big Ted' in George's words. Lennon became enamoured though with the artistic and bohemian demi-monde that Stuart offered and represented, Sutcliffe being a year older, more sophisticated and an avid reader of Kierkegaard and Sartre. Stu became the first of John's many and various guides and gurus.

Lennon soon became resident in Sutcliffe and Rod Murray's squalid Gambier Terrace flat and though eviction soon followed for Stu, so did a new life as a Beatle to be. Lennon, slightly besotted, wanted him in his band as much for his unimpeachable cool and daring style as for his musical abilities, which at this point were negligible. Sutcliffe entered a large Abstract Expressionist painting in the prestigious biennial John Moores' Exhibition at the Walker Art Gallery, which Pools magnate Moores bought for sixty pounds.* One night at The Casbah Club, Paul and John badgered Sutcliffe until he agreed to spend the money on a bass guitar, a Hofner President from Hessy's Music Store. He was unconvinced though about the band's then moniker of Johnny and The Moondogs. Stuart

-----

* Or rather he bought half a painting. So large and unwieldy was the canvas that only half of it ever made it to the Walker; Stu and Rod Murray never delivering the second half.

suggested Beetles, after the female biker gang in Brando's *Wild Ones* movie, and then Beatals. They toured Scotland with Johnny Gentle as The Silver Beetles with Sutcliffe rechristened Stuart De Stael after his favourite Expressionist painter, Nicolas De Stael. Eventually, and to the undying gratitude of future generations, they settled on The Beatles.

A few months after arranging this tour with Larry Parnes, the ever-resourceful Williams dispatched The Beatles to their date with destiny in Hamburg, and Sutcliffe was soon spending hours of his life on stage at the Indra and the Kaiserkeller, looking as spectacular as his playing was debatable. Opinions still differ on just how competent or otherwise a musician Stu actually was. Johnny Gentle thought him 'inept'. George Harrison largely agreed but felt 'it didn't matter. He looked so cool.' Unsurprisingly, Paul McCartney had the most 'complicated' relationship with Stu; one can imagine the driven and gifted Macca finding Sutcliffe's musical shortcomings vexing as well as maybe being irked by Stuart being so clearly John's new favourite. Nonetheless, Stu's regular solo spot of 'Love Me Tender' always went down enthusiastically with the crowd. This may have contributed to the tensions that erupted on the infamous night Paul and Stuart came to blows mid-number.

If Stuart's bass technique was sketchy, his popularity was obvious. He wrote home to his sister Pauline that 'I've become very popular both with girls and homosexuals who tell me I'm the sweetest, most beautiful boy. Imagine it, me the one who had such a complex because I was small and thought I was ugly. It appears that people refer to me as the James Dean of Hamburg.' Voormann, one of their new German friends, recalls a female audience member who seemed to be having an orgasm 'just looking at the way Stuart was standing'. But soon it would be only Astrid Kirchherr's opinion that mattered. Her mother, a widow who had rather fallen for the boys and sourced them their 'prellies' (Preludin) from a pharmacist friend, invited him to live and paint on the top floor of their handsome house in

Altona.* Clearly, his days as a Beatle were numbered. In April 1961, he won a scholarship to study at the Hamburg School of Art under the aforementioned Eduardo Paolozzi, and left The Beatles to devote himself to his painting. Another pivotal moment. Had he not quit the band for art and Astrid, Paul McCartney would never have been forced to reluctantly pick up the bass and so revolutionise the way that instrument was used in popular music.

While his former bandmates continued to nightly 'mach schau' on the Reeperbahn, Stu devoted himself to his painting and his (now) fiancée while making the occasional appearance with them or other visiting Merseybeaters like Howie Casey. Sutcliffe had never been a robust youth, but now his health was starting to give real concern. He began to suffer from headaches of increasing pain and intensity, and acute light sensitivity. This gave rise to sleeplessness, temporary blindness, blackouts and periods of agitation where he would write lengthy, tormented letters and diary entries. On 10 April 1962, Astrid's mother called her home from work worried about Stuart who had spent most of the last two weeks in bed but had collapsed again. Astrid Kirchherr rushed home to accompany him in the ambulance, but the now unconscious Sutcliffe died in her arms. He was 21. (In the film *Backbeat* this is travestied into an offensive tableau where Stuart writhes in agony in a garret while Astrid goes to slip into a slinky dress and returns screaming.)

The cause of death was given as a cerebral haemorrhage, specifically a ruptured aneurysm causing severe bleeding into the brain. Some have speculated that this was due to injuries sustained when he was jumped and thrown against a wall by Teddy Boys outside the Lathom Hall, Seaforth in May 1960 and rescued by Pete Best and John Lennon. Alternatively, his sister Pauline Sutcliffe has suggested

---

* So much of this, even down to the top floor flat, seems to echo Paul's relationship with the Ashers, the young working-class autodidact adopted by generous bourgeois liberals.

that Lennon himself kicked Stuart in the head in what she conjectures might have been a lover's jealous rage one night in Hamburg. But death would surely have occurred much sooner in these cases and the post-mortem revealed no injuries to the skull. It seems a rare medical condition, possibly an unnatural swelling of the brain, is a more likely cause.

Three of The Beatles, John, Paul and Pete, were scheduled to return for a new Hamburg stint the day after Sutcliffe died. Astrid was waiting for them at the airport with the dreadful news. They were stunned, ashen, weeping. George, getting over a bout of illness, followed the next day. It was his first ever flight. Onboard was Stuart's grief-stricken mum, Millie. Five years later Lennon told Hunter Davies 'I looked up to Stu. I depended on him to tell me the truth the way I do with Paul today.' He rarely spoke publicly about Stuart after this, but according to Yoko, he would mention him and think about him every day.

Stuart Sutcliffe's effect on the developing Beatles was dramatic and energising. His style and charisma set them apart, got them noticed, won them friends. He gave them a name, a look, a 'cool' that their peers lacked. As a *New Yorker* profile concluded 'The Beatles' creation story is deeply entrenched, and teleological: it is simply inevitable that Lennon will meet McCartney, that their genius will conquer the world. But … without Sutcliffe's arrival, they might never have found their way to the ferry.'

22. Pete Best

'Mean, moody and magnificent.'

We've all been dumped. It's as much a part of growing up as Farley's rusks, as a flatmate of mine once said consolingly. We've all had the sack, or failed an audition, or missed a lucky break somewhere along the line. But imagine that transitory feeling of loss multiplied a millionfold and never ever really going away, because the world won't let you forget. Imagine the entirety of your life being coloured, overshadowed even, by that gig you lost in a scrappy teenage band six decades ago. Imagine being reminded of it, reminded of what your life could have been, every single day, almost every time you turn on the radio, or the TV, or open a magazine or walk the streets of your hometown, of any town.

Imagine being Pete Best.

Thirtieth March 1964; a young man steps on to the set of *I've Got A Secret*, hit US panel show of the day. He's moodily good looking and sharp suited but what you notice first is the hair, a vertiginous, sweeping, bouffant that's already looking out of date, thanks to some old friends of his. Those former pals have washed the grease out of their locks, combed them forward, shaken their lustrous heads a little and, right now, every kid on the planet wants to look like them, rather than him. For, as is worked out with merciful speed and brevity by the panel, the secret of Pete Best (of 'West Derby, Lancashire') is that he used to be a Beatle.

'Two years ago, he made a big career move ... he left his job! Not in itself unusual, but he was Ringo's predecessor in The Beatles!' Host Garry Moore then asks 'Why?' Pete's reply lies somewhere between disingenuous, diplomatic and face-savingly discrete. 'Well, at that time I thought I'd like to start a group of my own and I also thought they weren't going to go as big as they are now.'

'Well, don't worry' chortles Moore, a little meanly, 'nobody's perfect.'

I won't dwell on Pete Best's whole life history, simply because it is really one particular aspect of that life that concerns us here; that one bald, immutable fact that defines his story and his life. Born in Madras to the beautiful and exotic Mona, he came with her and husband Johnny to Merseyside aged four in 1945. An athletic lad, he excelled in sports, but like most boys of his generation, fell hard under the snaring beat and hypnotic spell of rock and roll. He was first a Quarryman and then a Beatle, the seventeenth and penulti- mate of their eighteen drummers. He played with them at The Cavern and around Liverpool, and served the same fervid Hamburg apprenticeship with the band. Yet he seems never to have really been 'one of them' there or elsewhere, noticeably absent from their most infamous scrapes. Nevertheless, he was a fan-fave especially with the girls and his propulsive if unsubtle playing earned the tag 'the atom beat'. In 1962, *Mersey Beat* magazine said of him that he was 'a figure with mystique; darkly good looking and seemingly the one likely to emerge as the most popular Beatle'.

Posterity had other plans. On 16 August 1962, almost exactly two years after he joined them, at 10 a.m. in the NEMS office in Whitechapel Liverpool, Brian Epstein awkwardly terminated Pete Best's contract as a Beatle. In a book he co-authored with Patrick Doncaster (*Beatle! The Pete Best Story*) Best recollected, 'I found Brian in a very uneasy mood when I joined him in his upstairs office. He came out with a lot of pleasantries and talked anything but busi- ness, which was unlike him. These were obviously delaying tactics and something important, I knew, was on his mind. Then he mustered enough courage to drop the bombshell. "The boys want you out and Ringo in." I was stunned and found words difficult. Only one echoed through my mind. Why, why, why?'

Pete Best's sacking is the Kennedy assassination of The Beatles' story, though sadly we have no Zapruder footage to pore over. The fact of it may be indisputable, but the circumstances have spawned a cottage industry of competing narratives and wild theorising. Mona Best thought they were envious of her son's popularity (well, she would, wouldn't she?). Beatle historian David Bedford attributes it to some misunderstanding at Abbey Road with George Martin. When David Letterman asked him why he had been dismissed, Best replied, perhaps even believing it himself, 'In a nutshell, Dave … jealousy.'

Spencer Leigh devotes an entire volume to these speculations in *Drummed Out! The Sacking of Pete Best*, tantalisingly if absurdly subtitled 'The Last Unsolved Beatle Mystery'. For is there really any mystery? The most straightforward if callous explanation is surely the most accurate. He probably wasn't as good a drummer as Ringo and he definitely wasn't as good a Beatle. As Paul recalled 'George (Martin) took us to one side and said "I'm really unhappy with the drummer. Would you consider changing him?" If he wasn't up to the mark slightly in our eyes and definitely in the producer's eyes then there was no choice. But it was still very difficult. It was one of the most difficult things we ever had to do … It was a personality thing. We knew he wasn't that good a player. He was slightly different to the rest of us. He was a straight up kinda guy and so the girls liked him a bit. He was mean, moody and magnificent.'

John was, naturally, blunter. 'We were pretty sick of Pete Best, too, because he was a lousy drummer. He never improved. And, uh, there was always this myth being built up over the years that he was great, and Paul was jealous of him because he was pretty, and all that crap. They didn't get on that much together, but it was partly because Pete was a bit slow, you know. He was a harmless guy but he was not quick. All of us had quick minds but he never picked that up. We were always going to dump him when we could find a decent drummer.' Three days after Best's dismissal, The Beatles made their first TV appearance, and the world wobbled a little more on its axis.

When Hunter Davies tracked him down six years later, he was working in a bakery slicing bread for £18 a week. He was philosophical if clearly still haunted by that August morning in 1962: 'Twice I was really at the bottom, really low and didn't know what to do with life ... I know my mother thinks they were jealous of me but I don't think it was that ... I might accept help from them if I sort of met them again and we got on and they said, off the cuff, "here you are" but if they offered me X amount just out of charity then I'd say no.'

Thirty-three years later, in 1995, when the *Anthology* project was about to be released, Best was contacted and told that ten of his tracks would be included. Paul is rumoured to have insisted on using the early songs, knowing it would represent a substantial payday for Best. 'It came completely out of the blue. I knew *Anthology* was coming out but I didn't pay too much attention to it because I never figured that they would include me on it. But then I got the offer from Apple and lo and behold, I ended up on ten tracks which was great ... The bulk of the royalties came through when it was released and it was the icing on the cake after so many years. They keep drib drabbing in but you move on.'

It's been estimated that Best received several million pounds payment for his twenty-four-month tenure as a Beatle and perhaps as recompense for his much longer time as the man who once was a Beatle and can now forever never be anything else.

23. Astrid Kirchherr

'All I wanted was to be with them and to know them.'

They called it Operation Gomorrah; the terrible RAF bombing raids on Hamburg starting in July 1943 named after one of the cities God destroyed by fire and brimstone in the Old Testament. This too was a biblical immolation, unmatched by any other single Allied air attack in Europe during World War II. A thousand-foot-high tornado of twisting flame that sucked the air from the lungs, that swept people up like leaves and litter, or trapped them in the melting asphalt of the streets. Over forty thousand people perished. Yet while memories were still raw and rubble still strewn in the streets, in 1960 Hamburg welcomed five young Englishmen with open arms and hearts, and no Hamburger more warmly than a girl called Astrid Kirchherr.

Astrid and her friends Klaus Voormann and Jurgen Vollmer were not the first anglophile youth from their city. A generation before, a bunch of brave, jazz-loving, long-haired kids who called themselves the Swingjugend had sported Union Jack badges, smoked pipes, carried umbrellas and danced to British dance bands and US swing in defiance of and opposition to the Nazi's sinister, banal Hitler Youth. Metaphorically, perhaps even literally, these were the parents of the 'Exis' as Astrid and her friends were called, impossibly cool art students in love with foreign philosophy, literature and movies. Against stiff competition, Astrid was the most glamorous 'Exi'.

One night, drifting aimlessly around St Pauli after an argument with Astrid, Kirchherr's then boyfriend, Voormann, had chanced upon some English beat groups playing in the Kaiserkeller and been electrified by The Beatles, who he'd struck up a friendship with. But when he suggested that Kirchherr join him on a trip to the seedier side of Hamburg, she was initially reluctant. A good middle-class

Ford executive's daughter from the bourgeois Altona suburb, even an 'Exi' did not hang out in the shady, sleazy environs of the Reeperbahn. Voormann though was adamant, and eventually his excitement won her over. She went along to hear and meet his new English pals – perfectly, it was on a dodgy street with a glorious and symbolic name; Gross Freiheit. The Great Freedom – and Astrid was immediately smitten in every way. 'It was like a merry-go-round in my head. They looked absolutely astonishing … my whole life changed in a couple of minutes. All I wanted was to be with them and to know them' she recalled, which is a great testament to their personal magnetism since, for the entirety of his first two seasons in Hamburg, George never bathed or showered.

But one Beatle in particular entranced her. 'I fell in love with Stuart that very first night. He was so tiny but perfect in every feature. So pale but very, very beautiful.' They soon became lovers, something Voormann cordially accepted. 'At that time, Klaus was my boyfriend, but he sensed what was happening. He saw it and, in a way, forced it, which is strange to understand now, but Klaus always wanted me to be happy. He knew I wasn't happy in our relationship. He and I were great friends, we shared the same tastes, the same sense of humour, but we just could not live together as lovers, that was impossible. So he encouraged Stuart and me a little bit.'

Kirchherr remade their style and aesthetic, starting with Sutcliffe, feminising and softening the macho Brando-esque biker look into what would become their early defining image. Sutcliffe was the first Beatle to modify his hairstyle having seen and been impressed by Voormann's longer tresses, shaped by Kirchherr to conceal his prominent ears. Lennon and McCartney stuck to their rocker quiffs the longest till they were restyled in Paris by Jurgen Vollmer, now working there as a photographic assistant. 'Astrid was the one who influenced our image more than anyone else,' said George Harrison.

One November afternoon in 1960, that aesthetic nexus between Kirchherr and The Beatles would be sealed forever in celluloid. The band had been impressed and flattered when the art student had asked to take 'proper' pictures of them and so she took them to the deserted daytime fairground, the Hamburg Dom, draping and positioning them on the various trucks used by the riggers.* The results are justly famous, capturing The Beatles in creative transit and in embryo. They are pioneering, visionary even. Nearly all photos of pop groups of the era were cheesily goofy, the band mugging for the camera or throwing some crazy shapes. In Astrid's monochrome portraits at the fairground, The Beatles are unsmiling, pensive, bored even. Her pictures that afternoon established what would become the dominant 'cool' iconography of rock and prefigure the way alternative bands like Joy Division or The Smiths would be captured decades later.

In the years to come Voormann would have the most regular personal contact with The Beatles, going on to play bass on tracks by Lennon, Harrison and Starr, appear at the Concert for Bangladesh and design sleeves for (among many) *Revolver* and the *Anthology* series. But Astrid's part in The Beatles' story is in its own way just as intimate, crucial and, for her, complex. 'I became The Beatles' photographer, not a photographer in my own right. That was very hard. So that's why I gave up photography ... people didn't bother unless it was a Beatle, so that made me very, very sad. I just said to myself, you're not good enough, give it up, and do something else.' She never exploited her Beatle connections. Until the Nineties, she did not even collect the payments on the usage of her – and for once the word is justified – iconic pictures in countless publications around the world. When she passed away in 2020, the tributes reflected a real and heartfelt love within The Beatle family. 'God bless Astrid, a beautiful human being,' said Ringo. Olivia Harrison tweeted that Kirchherr was 'so thoughtful and kind and talented,

---

* This picture is nearly always cropped understandably tight to the band. The full original with the roller coaster in the background is even better.

with an eye to capture the soul'. Mark Lewisohn spoke of her 'immeasurable' contribution to the group; 'intelligent, inspirational, innovative, daring, artistic, awake, aware, beautiful, smart, loving and uplifting'.

Astrid's penumbral, luminous, black and white pictures are the abiding images of Stuart Sutcliffe, whose tragic early death from a brain haemorrhage is told elsewhere. Late in life Astrid would still say of her lover of sixty years ago, 'I have never got over his death. He is still the love of my life, even though I have been married twice since. I still wear Stuart's ring. I never found a love comparable to Stuart's. John used to say "Either you live or you die", and I have always remembered that and so I decided to live and be happy with my memories. When I am in trouble, I talk to Stuart, so my life is not unhappy because he's not with me in flesh and blood; he's with me in spirit.'

There is something very beautiful and very sad here. Something profound and mysterious about youth and time and fate, of lives changed and shaped forever by the energy and love that The Beatles generated. 'The Beatles were brave. They had to be to go through what they did in Hamburg, living in the most horrible places, with no parents there to support them, with very little food, only one pair of shoes each, and earning so little. If they hadn't endured all that, rock music would not have evolved in the way that it did. They changed my life, and there's not one day that I don't think about them ... I am proud to have been part of a process that changed a whole generation ... they are wonderful people who deserve everything they got because they gave so much joy to the world.'

24. Horst Fascher

'Mack Schau!'

Both Hamburg and Liverpool have city centre streets called the Ropewalk, and both are lively places of nocturnal revelry. But Hamburg's, the Reeperbahn, is the more salacious and more storied. I spent an evening here once with Depeche Mode and even they were, I think, a little taken aback at the relentless bracing sleaziness and vibrancy of a street that, while these days a tourist destination of a kind, nevertheless retains a disreputable ambience. But back in the late 1950s it was positively dangerous if wildly seductive, 'die sündigste Meile', or 'the most sinful mile' as locals knew it. One hot night on the Reeperbahn in 1959, Horst Fascher, Germany's young flyweight boxing champion and a gold medal hope for his country at the forthcoming Rome Olympics, got into a street brawl with a sailor over a girl. Fascher threw his not inconsiderable punch, the sailor went down striking his head and a few hours later was dead. Fascher spent nine months in jail for manslaughter and his boxing career was over. 'I thought my life was over ... all my dreams were gone.' What he didn't know was that new dreams and a new life were coming in the shape of five teenage Scousers in a cramped minibus on the ferry from Harwich.

Banned from the ring forever, he recruited some fellow pugilists and hard men from the Hamburg Boxing Academy and put together a formidable security crew called Hoddel's Gang (Hoddel was Fascher's nickname), who began working as bouncers at Bruno Koschmider's Kaiserkeller club in the St Pauli district. Koschmider, in Philip Norman's memorable description, was 'a small barrel-chested West German gentleman with a quiff of sandy hair, a turned-up nose and a disabled leg', the latter gained during his time in a Panzer division in the war. On a scouting trip to the famous 2i's coffee bar in

London, he'd begun to recruit from promoter Allan Williams various English rock and roll bands like Tony Sheridan and Derry and The Seniors. Derry Wilkie later implored Williams not to screw up a good deal by sending 'a bum group like The Beatles'. But when Rory Storm and The Hurricanes were unavailable thanks to a summer season at Butlin's and Gerry and The Pacemakers didn't fancy a couple of months in a chilly German North Sea port, he did just that. Despite Derry's fears, Hamburg and Horst Fascher loved them.

It was perhaps just as well. Fascher and his pals were allegedly feared. But hard man Fascher grew to love The Beatles, taking them under his wing and warning anyone who gave them trouble that he would 'find them'. He became their informal bodyguard during their Indra and Kaiserkeller days when they slept four to a room next to the toilets in the Bambi Kino cinema and even took them home to Neustadt to meet his mum, who would cook them pea soup in the same cauldron she boiled their underpants in.

At the end of their second Hamburg stint at the slightly more salubrious Top Ten Club, according to Pete Best, Fascher 'was in tears. Here was this outgoing man who had the reputation of being hard and could handle himself, openly shedding tears over the fact that his boys were leaving Hamburg, and he didn't know when he'd be seeing them again.' In fact, he would see them very soon. Within months, he travelled to Liverpool to seal a deal with the band's new manager Brian Epstein for a residency at a new Hamburg venue. The Star Club which Fascher co-founded and managed.

In the small hours at the Star Club, Fascher would often take the microphone for a rendition of Eddie Cochrane's 'Hallelujah, I Love Her So'. He sings, uncredited, on the album *The Beatles Live! At the Star Club in Hamburg, Germany, 1962*. (His brother Freddie also got up to sing 'Be-Bop-A-Lula', but he is credited as Herr Obber, 'Mr Waiter' in German). The night this was recorded, New Year's Eve 1962, was the last Hamburg show the unknown Beatles would play. 'Love Me Do' had nudged into the UK charts and 'Please Please Me' was about to be released on an unsuspecting world to become their first Number 1. Horst toasted Lennon and said he'd see him again soon. Lennon replied 'Horst, we'll never come back … I'm telling you now – this is it. If we ever come back here, you'll have to roll out a fucking red carpet.'

Fascher never saw John Lennon again. He did though have further contact with Paul. In 1994, Fascher called McCartney's office in desperation. Having already lost one child in a tragic accident, he and his new partner had been told that their baby daughter, Marie-Sophie, would not live long because of a heart defect. 'So in my angst that I lose a second child I called Paul. I thought Paul has better doctors in England.' Fascher wept on the phone to an assistant. 'Then after twenty minutes he called me back. And he said, "What's happened?" I said, "Paul, can you help me?" He was saying, "Horst, whatever I can do for you, I do for you."'

And he did, arranging flights and accommodation for the Faschers in London in January 1995 while 11-month Marie-Sophie was admitted to Great Ormond Street Hospital. McCartney also flew in a team of American surgeons to operate on the child, but to no avail. She died thirteen days later. 'When it came to the payment, Paul said, "I take care of everything. You don't have to [worry],"' says Fascher. 'And he flew us back and all of that. I said, "Paul, how can I pay you back?" He said, "Horst, forget it. Only don't tell anybody."'

In the many YouTube videos of Fascher at various reunions and anniversaries, this once fearsome man who sported knuckledusters, night sticks and gas guns, who once turned up at the club with someone's tooth embedded in his fist, seems a genial old soul. But he must have been very different then, when he was an integral part of that darkly, electrically formative booze-and-Preludin frenzy of The Beatles' days in St Pauli, playing six sets a night, six hours in total, thirty-one sets per week, 'the equivalent of 800 hours in the rehearsal room' as Paul later described it, all the while being implored by Koschmider to 'mack schau', to put on an act that might involve

Beatle goose stepping, playing in his underpants or with a toilet seat around his neck. That was John Lennon of course, who said of those days, 'I grew up in Hamburg, not Liverpool.'

25. Billy Preston

'It's Billy!'

On 11 September 1964, The Beatles were scheduled to play one of the biggest stadiums in America, the Jacksonville Gator Bowl, Florida, when they were told by a young reporter Larry Kane that the show would be racially segregated. 'To a man, they argued against it' he remembered. 'They said they weren't going to do it. There were nineteen days of negotiations. Eventually the Jacksonville Gator Bowl was desegregated for the first time.' To The Beatles, raised in a multi-ethnic city on the black music of Tamla Motown, segregation and its implicit rationale, racism, was 'just stupid'.

When he was asked around this time who his idols were, Paul McCartney replied 'coloured girl groups'. The phraseology comes across as wincingly anachronistic today, but the sentiment is heart-felt, and it resonated powerfully. When Smokey Robinson states in the Martin Scorcese produced *Beatles 64* documentary that The Beatles were the first white performers he had ever heard respect and praise black artists, the passion in his eyes is striking. And when the *Get Back* sessions are mired in torpor and confusion, it's a black artist who comes to save the day and save The Beatles. For a while at least.

The Beatles had first met Billy Preston in Hamburg in the early 1960s when the keyboardist was playing with Little Richard. Eighteen-year-old George Harrison bonded with the 15-year-old American but, in a twist unexpected by everyone, in mid-January 1969, Preston flew to London to do Lulu's TV show and ended up joining The Beatles. This is how.

George had gone along with his friend Eric Clapton to see Ray Charles at the Festival Hall. 'Before Ray came on there was a guy on stage playing the organ, dancing about and singing "Double-O

Soul". I thought, "that guy looks familiar" but he seemed bigger than I remembered. After a while Ray came on and the band played for a few songs and then he reintroduced … Billy Preston! … It's Billy! Since we had last seen him in Hamburg in 1962, when he was just a little lad, he had grown to be six foot tall.'

Messaged privately later by Harrison, Preston came along to the Apple HQ where The Beatles had relocated after their chilly, unprofitable sessions at Twickenham. Billy recalled, 'It was a struggle for The Beatles. They were kind of despondent. They had lost the joy of doing it.'

'He got on the electric piano' recalled George 'and straight away there was 100 per cent improvement in the vibe in the room. Having this fifth person was just enough to cut the ice that we'd created among ourselves … Billy didn't know all the politics and the games that had been going on, so in his innocence he got stuck in and gave an extra little kick to the band … It's interesting to see how nicely people behave when you bring a guest in, because they don't want everybody to know they're so bitchy. Suddenly everybody's on their best behaviour.'

It's a joyous moment, immortalised now in the *Get Back* documentary. When Preston enters on day eleven, Wednesday, 22 January, the change of mood is palpable. The room becomes illuminated by smiles not least Preston's own megawatt beam. The musical atmosphere improves immediately too. Billy contributes Fender Rhodes and Hammond organ to eight tracks and joins them for the rooftop performance.

Preston released two albums on The Beatles' Apple label, and sold three million singles in the early 1970s. He toured and recorded with The Rolling Stones and appeared on solo albums by George Harrison, John Lennon, and Ringo Starr. Conflicted by his homosexuality and devout Christianity, he battled cocaine addiction and served time in prison on assault and drugs charges in the 1990s. He died of kidney failure in 2006 at the age of 59. But he lives on, thanks to *Get Back*, beaming, grooving, taking a childlike joy in a Stylophone and immeasurably improving 'Don't Let Me Down', 'Let It Be', 'Get Back' and the rest. He is the only non-Beatle to receive a credit on one of their records.

26. Chas Newby

'They'd done their 10,000 hours ... mind-blowing.'

The young couple I asked directions from must have assumed that I had a doctor's appointment that chilly February morning as I walked up Hatton Hill Road. Because Litherland Town Hall is an NHS drop-in centre now. Or maybe they'd been asked before by some earnest YouTuber in search of prime Fab Four Beatle archeology. Ask a Beatle fan which show they'd wish they could have attended and they might pick the Apple rooftop gig or Shay Stadium or the fare-well in Candlestick Park. Ask a Beatlemaniac though, and the answer may well be a performance that lasted some twenty-five minutes in a building in north Liverpool that is now a drop-in health centre. The Litherland Town Hall show of December 1960 is regarded as a galvanising, pivotal moment in The Beatles' story. And memorable certainly for Chas Newby, one of the four occasions he played with them, the man who was a Beatle for two weeks.

Newby was a school pal of Pete Best who played alongside him in The Black Jacks and hung out at Mona Best's club. It was here that he met the fledgling band in the summer of 1959. When they returned from Hamburg in December 1960, they were missing Stuart Sutcliffe who had stayed behind to spend Christmas with Astrid Kirchherr and her family. With a borrowed leather jacket and bass guitar (played left-handed, like an illustrious successor), he was drafted for four gigs that Christmas and New Year; two at The Casbah, one at The Grosvenor Ballroom, Wallasey and, the day after Boxing Day, at the Town Hall, Litherland.

British pop in late 1960 was liminal, transitional, shadowy. The first incendiary fires of US rock and roll had guttered and died; Elvis was in the army, Jerry Lee Lewis disgraced, Little Richard returned to the church. Britain's teen music scene, like America's, was now the preserve of zestless, uninspiring young men exemplified by the Larry Parnes stable, all dressy outfits and prim choreography. The patrons at the regular Litherland Town Hall 'post-Boxing Day' dance would have come expecting saccharine records alongside the toe-tapping pop of The Searchers and The Deltones. What they got, a last-minute addition 'direct from Hamburg', was The Beatles in all their raging, amphetamine glory bolstered by a steely professionalism honed by long nights on the Reeperbahn.

It was immediately apparent to fill-in Newby that Hamburg had changed them. 'They'd done their 10,000 hours … mind-blowing … Paul started screaming "Long Tall Sally" and all the dancing stopped. People went to dance not to listen to the band. But they were assaulted. Instead of having these neatly attired suits mincing about … they got five guys dressed in black leather and cowboy boots jumping all over the place and screaming.'

John Lennon remembered, 'It was that evening that we really came out of our shell and let go. We stood there being cheered for the first time. This was when we began to think that we were good. Up to Hamburg we'd thought we were OK, but not good enough. It was only back in Liverpool that we realised the difference and saw what had happened to us while everyone else was playing Cliff Richard shit.'

Such was the response from the thousand and a half crowd that promoter Brian Kelly initially thought there was a brawl. When he saw that it was, in fact, unhinged enthusiasm, he immediately signed up The Beatles for more gigs. But by then Chas would be gone. While Lennon reportedly wanted Newby to continue with the band, Newby went to Uni. 'Music was never going to be a living for me … I wanted to do chemistry.'

In 2016 though, now living in the Midlands and retired from teaching, he began performing again with the reformed Quarrymen. 'People sometimes don't believe me when I say I've no regrets,' he reflected 'but I really haven't. I have enjoyed my life immensely.' He died on 22 May 2023 aged 81. Opinions differ as to where we can pinpoint the beginnings of Beatlemania, that madness that would soon grip the world, but there's a strong argument that what's now an NHS practice in Litherland ushered its birth, and Chas Newby was there.

1961

27. Neil Aspinall

'It's got nothing to do with you, you're only the driver.'

There are, by my estimation, at least nine people who have been dubbed the fifth Beatle. Seven of them have strong claims to the title either musical (George Martin, Billy Preston, Stu Sutcliffe, Pete Best), promotional (Derek Taylor, Murray 'The K') or managerial (Brian Epstein). But in the last category falls the one whose case is strongest, one whose link was more than professional but, literally and emotionally, familial.

Neil Aspinall shared a Woodbine with George Harrison on their first day at Liverpool Institute and through him met the other three. He first drove the band to a gig in Knotty Ash in his grey and maroon Commer van and then fell into a routine, taking the gear to the venue, coming home to work on his accountancy correspondence course ('I hated taking abuse from some fellow 300 miles away. It was like sending it off to the moon just to get shit on.') then going back to pick his new charges up. In July 1961, he abandoned accountancy to become The Beatles' full-time road manager for five shillings a gig. He also, aged 19, moved first into his pal Pete Best's West Derby home and then into a clandestine relationship with Best's mum Mona, fathering a child born the following year. Aspinall's name was not on Roag Best's birth certificate but later in life he maintained a relationship with him. Three weeks after Roag Best was born, his half-brother Pete was ejected from the nascent Beatles. As Pete's good chum, Aspinall was upset but was rebuked by Lennon, 'It's got nothing to do with you. You're only the driver.' Any awkwardness was offset by Aspinall's pragmatic, unsentimental streak. He remained with The Beatles for the next fifty years.

He was soon promoted, though to what was unclear. 'We went on the Helen Shapiro tour and the first theatre we got to the tour manager was a guy called Johnny Clapton. I remember just standing to the side of the stage about 3 or 4 in the afternoon when we got there, and Johnny Clapton was saying, "Who's The Beatles' road manager?" I'd never heard the term before, so I didn't answer. So he ended up saying, "Is there anybody with The Beatles?" So I said, "Yeah, I am!" "OK, you're their road manager." Oh, OK! I still don't know what a road manager is, quite frankly.'

Neil Aspinall, Nell, as Paul dubbed him, stayed with them for life. He was, effectively, their longest serving manager, taking over their affairs and Apple's in 1970 and handling both till his death in 2007. During the final years of the band, it was suggested he take steps to plan for posterity. 'In '69, in all the chaos, the traumas – things were falling apart but they were still making *Abbey Road* – Paul called me saying "You should collect as much of the material that's out there, get it together before it disappears."' So Aspinall began compiling and sourcing warehouses full of Beatle material. From this archival footage Aspinall assembled a ninety-minute feature film provisionally entitled *The Long and Winding Road* which he completed in 1971 without much Beatle input. 'I sent it to everybody and it just got put on the shelf and that was it for the next twenty years.'

Eventually though, and with the addition of much more and rarer footage and the involvement of the 'Threetles', this became *Anthology*.

He knew everything but said little, at least publicly. Along with Jane Asher, he is the only Beatle insider not to write a book. Philip Norman called him 'brusque and hollow cheeked with hair already thinning ... both friend and servant, their equal yet their errand boy'. Peter Brown claimed 'his opinions weighed with equal respect with any of them. He was an outspoken guy with a northern trait. He spoke the plain truth. He saw everything and knew everything.' Hunter Davies found him to have a 'dry, austere rather resigned cynical view of most people'. Certainly, this is how he appears via Norman Rossington's version of him as 'Norm' in *A Hard Day's Night*, uttering an irascible, exasperated 'Come ed!' in almost every scene. The dour foil to the genial Mal Evans, he was utterly devoted to The Beatles but also could be wry and sardonic. An eye roll never seemed far away. He once said of an early tour with Roy Orbison 'in five weeks ... I lost three stones. No one will believe it, but it was true. I went down from eleven stone to eight stone. I just didn't eat or sleep for five weeks. There was no time.' Many years later McCartney would admit to Paul Du Noyer 'Poor old Neil ... He's been a real solid guy for us. But I don't think we've always been good for him.'

As Du Noyer noted, 'In the unhappy years when The Beatles had ceased to trust anybody, including one another, they still trusted Neil.'

28. Bob Wooler

'Remember all you Cave Dwellers ...
The Cavern is the best of cellars.'

There is a history of violence lurking in the shadows of The Beatles' story. It would be unusual if it were other, given the tenor of the times and the places their story was forged; two tough seaports ravaged by war, an era of knuckledusters and coshes, of Horst Fascher's gang roughing up drunken sailors at the Kaiserkeller and Teddy Boys kicking Stu Sutcliffe's head in outside Lathom dance-hall. Both John and Ringo admitted to acts of violence against women and, as we all know, the former's story ends in savagery and darkness. But perhaps the most 'celebrated' incident of this kind was ultimately not hugely injurious to any party; in fact, one came out of the whole affair two hundred quid better off. But it offers an insight into some of John's anxieties and insecurities, and also gave them their first piece of national press.

A YouTube search for Bob Wooler will turn up, for those so minded to look, several, nearly identical newsreel-style features all called things like Liverpool a Go Go or The Sound of Liverpool or Rockin' and Reelin'. In these, various bands of whey-faced, pimply youths play fairly formulaic R&B on the Birkenhead ferry or the top deck of a bus while 'the Merseybeat' is eulogised (in that creamy commercial radio tone still employed by figures as diverse as Nigel Farage and Paul McKenna) by an older man standing to one side, swaying awkwardly beneath Peter Ustinov's Caesar haircut. Philip Norman in *Shout!* seems to have picked up on the voice and the look, too. 'Somehow, in the shabby jive halls, he maintained the gravitas of a Roman senator ... yet his voice, through the microphone, was as rich and relaxed as the best to be heard on Radio Luxembourg.'

Wooler, then, was an unusual casting as a key player of Liverpool's febrile early 1960s beat scene. But it was a role he threw himself into with gusto. Having flirted with songwriting under the name Dave Woolander – he was convinced all the most successful songwriters were Jewish – he became a DJ at The Cavern and a generally benign, enthusiastic, more senior champion of Liverpool music. It was he who convinced promoter Brian Kelly to give The Beatles, recently returned and battle-hardened from Hamburg, that pivotal December 1960 gig at Litherland Town Hall when they electrified the crowd.

Wooler, then, should be remembered for his tireless championing of The Beatles and their peers, and to a degree he is. But what happened to him on the evening of 18 June 1963 at Paul McCartney's 21st birthday party in his Aunt Jin's back garden is the most indelibly inscribed entry for Wooler in Beatle lore. Lennon and Brian Epstein were not long returned from a holiday they had taken to Spain. Tongues had wagged over this, and Wooler, in John's earshot, speculated on a gay tryst of some kind. 'Bob had insinuated that me and Brian had an affair in Spain' remembered Lennon later. 'I was out of my mind with drink ... you know when you're twenty-one,* you want to be a man ... I was beating the shit out of him, hitting him with a big stick and for the first time I thought "I can kill this guy ... if I hit him once more, that's going to be it." He sued me afterwards. I paid him £200 to settle it that's probably the last real fight I've ever had from then on apart from occasional hitting my dear wife ...'

The incident gave The Beatles their first national press, a back-page splash in the *Daily Mirror* headlined 'BEATLE IN BRAWL SAYS "SORRY I SOCKED YOU"' and opening 'Guitarist John Lennon, 22-year-old leader of The Beatles "pop" group, said last night: "Why did I have to go and punch my best friend?"'

---

* Lennon was actually 22. Wooler was 37.

In his book *One Two Three Four*, Craig Brown is assiduously hilarious on the competing accounts of the assault in various Beatle books, which range from mild horseplay to GBH to near-murder. Hunter Davies and Philip Norman dismiss it as a 'fight'. Peter Brown calls it a 'pummelling'. Ray Connolly adds a stick (also the remembrance of one John Lennon) while Bob Spitz, Pete Shotton and Albert Goldman (of course) arm John with a shovel. It's a wonder of course that Goldman didn't make it a Howitzer.

Bob liked his slick wordplay. His stage patter would begin 'Remember all you cave dwellers. The Cavern is the best of cellars.' Brian Epstein was christened 'The Nemperor' while *Mersey Beat* editor Bill Harry was 'the Boswell Of Beat'. In 1967, it was Harry who arranged for Wooler to be given an audition as a DJ for the new Radio 1 network but he never turned up and never explained why. In 1973, Wooler was divorced from his wife Beryl Adams, Brian Epstein's secretary, who he had married in 1967. He became a bingo caller but was always in demand at anniversaries and conferences to recount all the old tales with the usual polish.

Almost all the old tales that is. Jude Kessler, author of the epic, ongoing, multi-volume John Lennon Series biographies, asked Wooler what exactly he had said that night in 1963 that prompted Lennon's vicious attack. He replied, 'I absolutely will never repeat that again this side of heaven. All I can tell you is I deserved it.'

Five years later, when The Beatles were being filmed for *Let It Be*, a moment captured in Peter Jackson's *Get Back*, there's a jokey altercation during which John laughingly threatens, 'Hey … I've had some wine … remember Bob Wooler?' Whether with shame or pride, John clearly did.

29. Raymond Jones

'I couldn't believe what I was hearing and watching.'

One day in 1797, Samuel Taylor Coleridge awoke from a (possibly opium-induced) dream in his lonely Exmoor farmhouse with a whole, fantastical poem swimming around in his head. He was trying to write it all down when 'he was unfortunately called out by a person on business from Porlock and detained by him above an hour, and on his return to his room, found, to his no small surprise and mortification, that though he still retained some vague and dim recollection of the general purport of the vision, yet, with the exception of some eight or ten scattered lines and images, all the rest had passed away like the images on the surface of a stream into which a stone has been cast ...'

If the hapless 'person from Porlock' has become emblematic of the petty 'civilian' distraction that stymies true creativity, Raymond Jones is the polar opposite, the anti-person from Porlock, if you will, without whom the whole Beatles story as we know it might never have happened.

Jones was a 20-year-old printer's apprentice from Knotty Ash when he walked into a shop in Liverpool and changed the history of the world.* KB Printers was based in Dale Street, a five-minute walk from The Cavern Club and Jones was a lunchtime regular there. 'The first time I saw The Beatles I was totally blown away. I couldn't believe what I was hearing and watching. It was a sound I had never heard before.' After being given some free tickets by Bob Wooler, a customer at KB, he became one of the excitable, devoted tribe that followed them around Merseyside. 'It is impossible to even attempt to guess how many times I saw The Beatles ... Aintree Institute,

---

* Bill Harry has a different version of events. See his entry.

Blair Hall, The Casbah, Litherland Town Hall, Civil Service Club, Hambleton Hall, Knotty Ash Village Hall and The Tower Ballroom …'

His brother-in-law Kenny, a local musician, passed on the gossip that The Beatles had recorded a single in Hamburg with singer Tony Sheridan and so, on Saturday, 28 October 1961, Raymond Jones walked into the NEMS shop in Whitechapel and asked for this disc, 'My Bonnie', from manager Brian Epstein. While it's hard to believe that Epstein was unaware of The Beatles, he also prided himself on knowing every record on current release and with his interest piqued, he paid a visit to The Cavern Club just over a week later to see the local group in question. 'The rest is history' is a hackneyed, almost meaningless, old saw. In this case, it's indisputably correct.

Here's some of the 'rest' and the 'history' that isn't so hackneyed though. When The Beatles broke and this part of the origin story began to be told and retold in newspapers and magazines, Jones became, in one quote from Epstein in a national newspaper piece an '18-year-old leather-jacketed youth'. Livid, Jones wrote to NEMS saying, 'not everyone wore suits and that some people had to work for a living'. Typically conciliatory, Epstein apologised in person over drinks at Rigby's pub off Dale Street. 'He was asking me all sorts of questions and taking notes at the same time. He didn't say so, but I think he must have been planning the book', the book being Epstein's *Cellarful Of Noise* memoir.

Even more annoyingly for Jones, in later years Epstein's assistant Alistair Taylor began to claim that Raymond Jones didn't even exist, saying that he'd invented the name to place an order for 'My Bonnie' at the main NEMS shop, claiming that customers had been asking for it but Epstein wouldn't stock discs without a firm order. 'I wrote an order in the book under the name Raymond Jones and, from that moment, the legend grew.' Quite why Taylor claimed this is impossible to say now, but the Liverpool music historian Spencer Leigh, acting on a tip from Bob Wooler, tracked down the real Raymond

Jones in the 1990s and set the record straight. Even so, Paul McCartney finds it hard to believe that Epstein did not know of the band till Jones entered the store. 'Brian knew perfectly well who The Beatles were; they were on the front page of the second issue of *Mersey Beat.*'

As for 'that' record, Raymond lost his copy and the signed edition of *Cellarful of Noise* Epstein later sent him. A pity, not least for his pension and his kids' mortgages. But, retired to Spain after a lifetime in printing, Raymond Jones of Knotty Ash seemed genuinely content to be a fascinating footnote in an amazing story. 'People have told me that my name will go down in Beatles history. That may be true, but all I did was buy a record by a group that gave me so much pleasure and enjoyment.'

30. Brian Epstein

'He was just a beautiful fella.'

Hyde Park Corner throbs at five o'clock on a mid-week evening, that time of day when the workers head home for tea and 'Meet the Wife' according to Lennon's *Sgt. Pepper* track 'Good Morning, Good Morning'. But a private road leads you away from the bustle and into a handsome, sweeping curve of Belgravia, a different world of billionaires, oligarchs and embassies. I walk on past the ones of Argentina, Turkey and the United Arab Emirates, under the fluttering flags of the Romanian Cultural Institute and the Malaysian High Commission, and to the corner of Chapel Street, where the Italian embassy, poignantly for some of us, still flies the standard of the European Union alongside its tricolore. A young Deliveroo driver looks incongruous here, but then even the fabulously wealthy must eat. Across the road, at number 24, when at home here, Brian Epstein would have been served food by his butler Lonnie Trimble, or his Spanish housekeeper Maria. And it was they who, unable to get in to take him breakfast on the morning of 27 August 1967, alerted his assistant and doctor who came and broke down the bedroom door …

'I was expelled from Liverpool College at the age of 10 and, though my parents found this most unamusing at that age, I was not greatly worried, for Liverpool College was not the last school in the world nor certainly was it one of the best.' So reads the almost Dickensian opening to the chapter 'Beginnings' in Brian Epstein's 1964 memoir *A Cellarful Of Noise*.* The young Epstein, born into a well-to-do Liverpool Jewish family, the owners of the NEMS furni-

---

* The terrific title refers, of course, to The Cavern but the line comes from Tony Hatch's 'I Know A Place', a hit for Petula Clark.

ture store in Whitechapel, was educated at nine schools and happy at none, filling his exercise books with drawings of dress designs ('suggestive' according to the Liverpool College housemaster who expelled him) and dreaming of a career on the stage. After this latest expulsion, exasperated father Harry wailed 'I just don't know what on earth we're going to do with you.' The fates did though.

Epstein's favourite book as a child, one which he read and re-read, was *The Swish of the Curtain*, Pamela Brown's madcap soufflé about children's amateur dramatics, which perhaps gives an idea of why his National Service was such a farce (he was discharged as a 'compulsive civilian') and hinted at what the future might hold for him; curtain calls rather than curtain rails. Initially, he hoped it would be him taking those calls and bows. He became friendly with many theatrical types at the Liverpool Playhouse and via their encouragement successfully auditioned for RADA. Like his National Service though, this didn't go well. On a visit to Stratford, where he mixed with players from the Royal Shakespeare Company, he found 'They were really frightful and I believe that nowhere could one discover such phoney relationships nor witness hypocrisy practised on so grand a scale.'

Returning to Liverpool, the prodigal worked in his father's furniture store, setting up a record department that soon became one of the most successful in the north. Two hundred yards away was a club called The Cavern where he would first see and be captivated by the young men that would change his life and the life of millions. 'I never thought that they would be anything less than the greatest stars in the world,' he later said. 'I sensed something big, if it could be at once harnessed and at the same time left untamed.'

What follows is folklore. How, despite having no previous impresario experience, he became their manager, persuaded them out of leathers and into Pierre Cardin suits, helped reshape them post Pete Best. As Ian Penman has written, Epstein's 'quiet overhaul after he became their manager kept their abrasive life force intact inside a subtly codified front of charm'. He hawked their demo around every music biz office in London, each time returning to be met at Lime Street station's Punch and Judy coffee bar to tell John and Paul the inevitable bad news. Until the day he announced that he had arranged a meeting with George Martin, a comedy producer on EMI's smallest label, Parlophone. So does Epstein become the manager of the biggest pop group there has ever been, as well as a roster of other Scouse acts from Cilla Black to Gerry and The Pacemakers. In 1963, while he was still living at home with his parents Harry and beloved mother Queenie, Epstein acts were Number 1 in the UK singles charts for thirty-seven out of fifty-two weeks.

Brian Epstein was, of course, both Jewish and gay. John Lennon suggested that he call his memoir Queer Jew, which amused him, we assume, but hurt Epstein deeply. Even though Liverpool had the oldest Jewish community outside London, Epstein still encountered antisemitism. But being Jewish was not illegal. Epstein's homosexuality was well known to The Beatles, and of course there is the famous Spanish holiday he and John took during which time they may or may not have been sexual (accounts vary, even Lennon's is nowhere consistent). But it did mean that he had to 'hide his love away' in darkness and secrecy. This, combined with a taste for what Oscar Wilde called 'feasting with panthers', meant that he was often robbed and beaten by the men he had picked up. Perhaps to keep up with his adored charges, he also developed a serious drug habit, initially just amphetamines but soon the whole panoply of recreational drugs they indulged in. Despite this, for most of his time on the road with them, and in his dealings with others, he was the model of elegance, suavity and charm, far removed from the caricature of the loud, aggressive showbiz huckster. That kind of manager was waiting in The Beatles' future.

Maureen Cleave suggested in a 1960s TV interview that The Beatles rather liked the fact that Epstein 'had a Bentley and Jaguar and a coloured manservant ... they like the riches and the glamour that his life seems to have'. But this glamour seems to have masked a trenchant, gnawing loneliness, one that drugs and boys could not assuage. The stresses of the final tours in 1966 made him ill; he became so anxious and unwell on the flight to Delhi that the pilot radioed ahead for an ambulance. With touring over, Paul felt that 'I think Brian felt his role was decreasing and that was a sadness to him. I think that actually was what was happening. I think the problem was, we were starting to feel we didn't really need much management. We were now in the studio making *Sgt. Pepper*, and Brian kept out. To again give him his credit, he kept out of our face in the studio. In fact, we actually wanted him to visit a little more, because we liked him, and it was always nice when he showed up. But he was very 'No, no, I won't interrupt. I'm just ... two seconds, da da da da. Gotta go.'"

Bouts of depression followed and increasingly desperate profligate self-medication with speed, acid and hashish. In a Murray 'The K' radio interview, he arrived slurring and semi-conscious having taken a fistful of Nembutals in his Waldorf Astoria hotel room. 'Eppy seems to be in a terrible state,' Lennon told his friend Pete Shotton one night before playing him a tape Brian had sent him. Shotton described it as 'one of the most harrowing performances I've ever heard ... barely recognisable as that of a human voice, alternately groaning, grunting and shrieking words which, even when decipherable, made no apparent sense whatsoever. The man on the tape was obviously suffering from great emotional stress, and very likely under the influence of some extremely potent drugs.'

On Friday, 28 August with The Beatles in Bangor with the Maharishi and his bank holiday plans for a weekend in his country house with friends old and new in partial disarray, Brian decided to drive back to London in his Bentley convertible. The next day, after the door was broken down, he was found dead in his bed with his system full of barbiturates and alcohol. The news was broken to The

Beatles in Bangor and they were almost immediately expected to comment for the TV cameras. Lennon in particular looks stunned. 'He was just a beautiful fella. It's terrible.' Later, privately, he was blunter: 'I thought "we've fucking had it".'

Almost everyone concerned with Brian and his adored boys thought his death was an accident and the coroner agreed. He had been in good spirits according to Hunter Davies who went for tea the week before when his recently widowed mum, Queenie, whom he doted on, was spending time with him in his London flat. Would Brian have put his mum through the loss of a husband and a son within weeks? It seems unthinkable. Paul has speculated, 'He had a few bevvies, then to console himself had a sleeping pill or two before bed. Brian always did that, he was quite into the pills. And then I think he woke up in the middle of the night and thought: "My God, I can't sleep. I haven't had a pill." Then he had a few more pills, and I think that could have killed him.' George truthfully – if somewhat brusquely – concluded, 'In those days everybody was topping themselves accidentally by taking uppers and or amphetamine and alcohol … loads of whiskey or brandy and uppers and then they'd choke on sandwiches. That was the favourite thing and that's the kind of thing that Brian did. He threw up and choked on the barf.'

An Epstein cinema biopic was released in late 2024 called *Midas Man*, whose title implies that everything Epstein touched turned to gold. To believe this, you must conveniently forget the terrible deal he did for the *Hard Day's Night* movie, the effective 'giving away' of their merchandising rights or the fact that he thought a new signing of 1964, a Bolton leather worker called Michael Tanner, was surely destined to be as big as The Beatles. He talks of Tanner and Cilla Black and Billy J. Kramer, not The Beatles, in the last pages of *A Cellarful of Noise*. He is brisk and optimistic, and then becomes suddenly lyrical for the sweet closing line 'I think the sun is going to shine tomorrow.'

Thirty-six months later, he was dead. His life had been short but astonishingly eventful, even by the standards of The Beatles' story, a phenomenon that would not have happened without him. Simon Napier Bell, later manager of Wham!, remembered a concert in 1966 when 'He told me that just once he allowed himself to go and stand at the back with all the girls in a concert in America. I think it was one of the stadiums where there were probably 25,000, 30,000 people, and he went into the crowd of girls and he just screamed like one of the girls, which he said is what he'd always wanted to do from the first minute he'd ever seen them. He had spent his whole life being restrained and wearing suits and suddenly he just screamed and became the mad fan he wanted to be.'

1962

31. George Martin

'Congratulations gentlemen,
you've just made your first Number 1 record.'

At the party after the 2024 premiere of the re-issued, re-mastered *Let It Be* film, I told record producer Giles Martin that the sharpest dressed, best-looking man in the whole movie was his dad. I was a couple of Negronis in at that point, but I meant it. In case you are thinking that this is a shallow, trivial way to begin, let me quickly add, he is also one of the greatest musical minds the world has ever seen and his influence on The Beatles is incalculable. All the more shocking and unforgiveable then that at the outset of the *Let It Be* project, Lennon told Martin he did not want 'any of your production shit'.

The result was one of their worst albums, chiefly because 'that production shit' was a crucial, indispensable factor in turning the native, instinctual genius of the Beatles into the most creative and accomplished exponents of popular music the world has ever produced. Martin's suggestions, interventions and contributions to The Beatles' musical canon are legion; all Beatles fans have their favourites. Mine include his crisp and lovely baroque piano solo on 'In My Life', the eerie, whirling, kaleidoscopic magicians final flourish of 'Being for The Benefit of Mr Kite' (all and solely Martin) and of course the double string quartet on 'Eleanor Rigby' inspired by the work of Bernard Herrmann, especially *Psycho*'s staccato motifs.*

The Beatles don't appear until Chapter 7 of Martin's memoir *All You Need Is Ears* and the original cover gives almost as much prominence to Cleo Laine, Spike Milligan and Rolf Harris as the Fab Four. This seems a little odd but then Martin did have a rich and fascinating 'backstory' before The Beatles. Self-taught, he wrote his first piano piece, the 'Spider Dance', at the age of six but his sonic horizons were capaciously broadened on hearing Debussy's 'L'Après Midi D'un Faun' on the Third Programme as a teenager. Later, he would study at the Guildhall where Jane Asher's mum was his oboe tutor. After a stint at the BBC, he became head of a funny little EMI label called Parlophone which he rapidly made an offbeat success. His sound design and experimentations on comedy records with The Goons and Bernard Cribbins are rightly cited as prefiguring The Beatles' audio adventures. He was also something of an electronic pioneer. In 1962, with Maddalena Fagandini, using the pseudonym Ray Cathode, Martin released an electronic dance single called 'Time Beat' the first commercial release of the BBC Radiophonic Workshop. And then, a few weeks later, he was introduced to a group from Liverpool called The Beatles.

Their early interactions are the stuff of legend: on asking them to point out anything they didn't like about the first session, George Harrison replies 'Well, I don't like your tie for a start'; Martin getting on the studio intercom when they had finished recording 'Please

---

* Martin actually marks it 'marcato' on the score, which requires a heavier, thicker treatment.

Please Me' and announcing 'Congratulations gentlemen, you've just made your first Number 1 record'.* What is less discussed is that Martin too was also keenly ambitious at that first meeting. While his comedy records were well received, he craved pop success being 'frankly jealous of the seemingly easy success that people were having with such acts, in particular Norrie Paramor, my opposite number on Columbia whose artist Cliff Richard was on an apparently automatic ride to stardom'.

Like many men of his generation (Alf Ramsey and Edward Heath spring to mind), Martin's patrician urbanity was, to a degree, self-created. He grew up in a working-class north London home with no electricity and a communal stove serving several flats. Later, he would serve with distinction in the Fleet Air Arm and he retained something of that suave military aviator mien all his life. John indeed referred to him as 'Biggles'. Brian Epstein compared him to 'a stern but fair-minded schoolmaster' while Martin himself said that being sixteen years their senior made him less a father figure than an older brother to 'the boys' and, despite Lennon's ungrateful remark about his production embellishments, they seem to have held him in deep affection and respect. His rare genius lay in his utterly democratic and catholic view of music, his gentle but firm hand on their creative tiller and his generous willingness to learn from them. 'They did flower, they blossomed, and they astonished me with their ideas. Each song they brought to me was a gem, and I said to myself, "It can't last." I'd say to them, "That's great, now give me a better one." And they did. I was so thrilled with what they gave me.'

The Beatles, however, did not make George Martin the wealthy man that he should have been, at least not initially. As Hunter

---

* Some of these tales have become so polished in Martin's retelling that the comedian and Beatles nut Kevin Eldon (whose impression is uncanny) has an affectionate, very funny routine about George Martin being kidnapped by urban guerrillas who eventually release him after being driven mad by the relentless Beatle anecdotes.

Davies puts it 'during that first phenomenal year of Beatlemania, 1963, he was probably the only person at all connected with The Beatles who did not make a lot of money because of them'. That year, Martin had a UK Number 1 single for thirty-seven weeks out of fifty-two with not just The Beatles but Gerry and The Pacemakers, Cilla Black, Billy J. Kramer, Matt Monro and others, the most successful producer in the history of British pop, yet was still just an EMI salaryman on £3,000 a year. 'I never made any money out of The Beatles' successes … I never participated at all in their huge profits … everyone at EMI thought I must be in on the profits somehow through one of their many companies, and The Beatles thought I must be OK because EMI must be looking after me.'

On his passing in 2016, Paul McCartney said 'From the day that he gave The Beatles our first recording contract, to the last time I saw him, he was the most generous, intelligent and musical person I've ever had the pleasure to know.' And, as discussed, he looked terrific.* When George enters No. 3 Savile Row on the day of the Apple roof-top gig in his superbly cut suit, white woollen polo neck and lustrous sweep of matinee idol hair, glancing wryly as Roger Moore's James Bond at the hidden camera, it is clear George Martin was more than just supremely talented. He was one cool guy. Contrary to George's opinion, I imagine that tie was great.

---

* In the 1970s and 1980s, the hair got out of hand and the medieval tabard jumper thing he is wearing on the cover of his memoir *All You Need Is Ears* is as ill-judged as its title. But frankly he can be forgiven anything.

32. Norman Smith

'They didn't impress me at all.'

As a small boy, one of my favourite albums was K Tel's garishly sleeved *20 Dynamic Hits*. While I very much enjoyed the singles by Deep Purple, Colin Blunstone and Santana, I would routinely lift the needle to skip 'Oh Babe What Would You Say' by Hurricane Smith, a slice of vaudevillian whimsy which lacked 'Purple's' denim-clad heft to say the least, though he did share their shaggy, fulsome coiffure, unusual on a man of his years. Others obviously disagreed since it reached Number 4 here and, astonishingly, Number 1 in the States. Pop stardom in middle-age was just another twist in the life and times of Norman Smith, RAF glider pilot, jazz wannabe, discoverer of Pink Floyd and the man who engineered 180 tracks, nine UK Number 1 singles and six best-selling albums for The Beatles.

After his war time service in the RAF and a failed attempt to launch a career as a jazz multi-instrumentalist and writer, Smith lied about his age – he was 35 and the job ad stipulated the position was for under 28s only – to become a staff engineer at EMI Studios. Working his way up to balance engineer, one of his jobs was to record the tests that every new act on the label had to undergo, which is where he first saw a new band from Liverpool that George Martin was interested in. 'I couldn't believe what louts they looked with their funny haircuts. They didn't impress me at all.' Neither was he taken with their tiny, tinny Vox amps. Nonetheless, their wit and vitality won him over; it was Smith who had the inspired notion of abandoning the usual screens and partitions and having them play all together as if they were on stage. It was his idea to 'fade in' the start of 'Eight Days A Week' and his calm, genial presence led to him being nicknamed 'Normal' by John. Smith was not averse to taking a hands-on approach in the studio. When a tape wobble removed the hi hat from 'Can't Buy Me Love' and Ringo wasn't around, he obliged again. Most notable of all, it's Norman's lightning bongos you can hear propelling 'A Hard Day's Night' along.

By 1966, he was keen to move into production but also wanted to remain The Beatles' engineer. George Martin told him he could not do both so he quit his engineer job to work with a new band he'd spotted in the underground UFO club in London; Pink Floyd. Smith was not hugely taken with their sound or material, but he was savvy enough to see they were both different and popular. 'With The Beatles we're talking about something really melodic, whereas with Pink Floyd, bless them, I can't really say the same thing for the majority of their material. "A mood creation through sound" is the best way that I could describe them ... In fact, I could barely call it music, given my background as a jazz musician and the musical experience that I'd had with The Beatles.' Nonetheless Smith took the production helm for the timeless hit single, 'See Emily Play' and Floyd's first four albums – *The Piper at the Gates of Dawn*, *Saucerful of Secrets*, *Umma Gumma* and *Atom Heart Mother*. He also produced what is generally reckoned to be the first concept album, The Pretty Things' *S. F. Sorrow*.

Norman was clearly an engaging character. Pink Floyd's Roger Waters, not renowned for his easy-going ways, 'liked him enormously'. Geoff Emerick's memoir has almost as much about Smith as The Beatles, including such choice details as how he taught the teenage Emerick how to twirl his spaghetti fork at the Black Tulip Italian restaurant by Abbey Road. But few could have foreseen that career turn awaiting in his early fifties. Norman had written a song that he thought would suit John Lennon's voice while they were short of material for *Help!** Years later, he played it to his chum, the producer Mickie Most, who insisted he release it under his own

---

* They nearly used it too, but plumped instead for Ringo's cover of Buck Owen's 'Act Naturally'.

name, or almost his own name anyway. 'Don't Let It Die', an early eco-ballad, became a Number 2 hit for the newly rechristened Hurricane Smith. He followed this up with that piece of sentimental big band nostalgia written by his wife Eileen called 'Oh Babe What Would You Say'. Remarkably, as stated, this reached Number 1 in America, knocking Elton John's 'Crocodile Rock' off the top and occasioning a celebratory telegram from Lennon. Norman later incorporated John's affectionate nickname into the title of his auto-biography, *John Lennon Called Me Normal*, which came out in 2007, the year before his death aged 85.

33. Ivor Arbiter

'Ringo, Schmingo, whatever his name was.'

If you have ever found yourself in the Millstone pub in Manchester's Northern Quarter at 2 a.m. listening to a gravel-voiced brickie singing 'My Way' or sung a Roxy Music track with Scarlett Johansson in a Tokyo bar or drunkenly duetted 'Islands in the Stream' with a co-worker,* then you have Ivor Arbiter to thank. More importantly here though, when we think of the words The Beatles, the way they look in our mind's eye is all down to him.

One night in the late 1980s, Ivor Arbiter, former saxophone repairman turned musical instrument retail mogul, was visiting Tokyo on a business trip with his daughter when he heard some 'refreshed' salarymen singing along emotionally to a pre-recorded pop song coming from a small machine. Instantly seeing the potential of this activity with fun-loving Brits, he began to import these machines into the UK and made himself a second fortune. As the man who brought karaoke to the UK, Arbiter would have assured himself a crucial if eccentric place in popular culture. But in truth he had ensured himself of that over a quarter of a century earlier when, as he recounted, 'I had a phone call from the shop [his store, Drum City] to say that someone called Brian Epstein was there with a drummer. Here was this drummer, Ringo, Schmingo, whatever his name was. At that time I certainly hadn't heard of The Beatles. Every band was going to be big in those days!'

Epstein wanted a bespoke logo for the Black Pearl Oyster kit he was buying for Ringo. (He wanted the kit for free initially, but the business savvy Arbiter was having none of it.) On a scrap of paper Arbiter sketched the famous logo with capital B and dropped T to

---

* I have done two of the above.

emphasise the word 'beat'. It was painted on to the drum head by Eddie Stokes, a local sign writer and went on to be seen by millions around the world. It is still The Beatles' official logo to this day. Twenty-five years before he introduced the mixed blessing of karaoke to Britain, Ivor Arbiter came up with one of the most famous and widely reproduced visual icons ever, thus winning himself immortality, and the sum of five pounds.

34. Freda Kelly

'Good old Freda.'

She wasn't old enough to vote. She wasn't old enough to drink in a pub. She couldn't get married without her father's consent. Freda Kelly was just 17 when she took over the fan correspondence, their most direct link with their people, of the biggest entertainment phenomenon the world had ever known. On their Christmas message of 1963 when The Beatles chorus, 'Good old Freda!' their gratitude and affection is obvious. But 'old'? Even baby George was three years older than her. Her brilliance at her job, at coping with the storm she was part of, is a testament not just to her but to young working-class women the world over.

She was there at the beginning, and she was there at the end. The beginning was a lunchtime visit to The Cavern with two guys who took a fancy to the teenage girl in the typing pool at Princes Food. Epstein had yet to gloss and finesse The Beatles' Hamburg roughness, but she was immediately captivated: 'I loved everything about them … the leather gear, the mucking about, and the music.' She became a regular Cavernite, sitting in the same archway seat to see them a couple of hundred times, give or take a sweaty, smoky lunchtime.

She worked first as a secretary at NEMS and then, at Epstein's request, The Beatles' fan club secretary. On her first day in the job, the mailbag consisted of two letters. A couple of weeks later it was forty. Soon there were eight hundred a day, which made Freda regret giving her home address as the fan club contact. 'Dad was losing his phone bills and gas bills and he made them stop coming here.'

She saw The Beatles daily and was close to all their families, especially the Starkeys. Ringo's mum became a surrogate mother to her, Freda's having died when she was a baby. She was also close to all

The Beatles, though she is coy about just how close. When one interviewer asked if the friendship ever became more intimate, she answered 'Pass ... We were all teenagers – use your imagination.' To another, she rebuffed, 'That's personal ... once I joined The Beatles' organisation, I grew up overnight ... in lots of ways.'

When The Beatles moved to London, her father forbade her moving to the 'city of vice', but so valued was she that she continued to run the fan club, now a Herculean workload, from Brian Epstein's old office at NEMS. She wrote for *Beatles Monthly* and was on the *Magical Mystery Tour* charabanc trip when Ivor Cutler told her 'You've got a nice-shaped head.' She stayed loyal and hardworking right through the Apple years all the way to the final messy implosion. 'George finally spoke up and said, "well, you were there in the beginning and you're there at the end. Let's call it a day ... let's end the fan club."'

Freda's final message to Beatles fans around the globe ran 'Well, this is it. John Paul George and Ringo have each gone their separate ways and they are no longer collectively an item. There it is ... eleven years ... in which we have become a very strong happy and close circle of friends. There will not be another official fan club for The Beatles as individual artists. Please do not write again.' She had always understood the fans, especially the girls because she was one of them. She knew when writing that last message that 'this is going to break a lot of girls' hearts ... the lights went out didn't they?'

She has always resisted the temptation to write a book or profit from her memorabilia which she has largely given away. Eventually, now working as a legal secretary in Birkenhead, she was persuaded to allow the crowdfunded 2013 documentary *Good Old Freda*. At its close, she says poignantly, 'I don't know why Eppy picked me. Maybe it was just fate. I was taken along for this ten-year exciting ride and then dropped off on the corner where I started it ... I don't ever have to tell this tale again ... it's down now on record ... this is it ... end of.'

35. Rory Storm

'Forget it. The best of luck to the lot of you.'

A few years back I hosted a TV documentary in which various luminaries from contemporary music – Graham Coxon, Ian Broudie, Joss Stone, etc. – recreated that famed single day recording of The Beatles' debut album, *Please Please Me*. During it, at Abbey Road, I interviewed collectively several members of The Beatles' Merseybeat contemporaries from groups like The Fourmost, The Seniors and such. At one point, one of them, who shall be nameless, suggested that back in 1960 there had been 'hundreds' of bands as good as The Beatles, comparable talents who merely never got their lucky break. After an embarrassed silence, his protestations were drowned by a welter of 'come 'eds' and 'soft lads' from the rest until he was forced to retract and admit that, yes, The Beatles were something special.

One band though were nearly as highly regarded for a brief period around 1960. They had a compelling, vivacious front man, a raucous sound, an outrageous look and ardent fans. They also, for four years, had Ringo Starr. Rory Storm and The Hurricanes, like The Fourmost, The Big Three, Howie Casey, Derry and The Seniors and scores of others, are one of those groups chiefly known today for not being The Beatles; bands whose diehard fans kid themselves that but for a lucky break here or an Epstein there, it would have been Rory Storm's *Sgt. Pepper* whose anniversaries we celebrate, whose unreleased demos we hunger to hear, whose eight-hour fly on the wall documentaries we watch and re-watch.

As Alan Caldwell, milkman's son and cotton salesman with a pronounced stammer, he might not have attracted a second glance. But as Rory Storm, six foot of high-kicking, blond-haired, rock and roll athleticism, he was Liverpool's Golden Boy for a while. A powerful swimmer and runner, a charismatic self-promoter whose stammer disappeared when he took to the stage, he and his band The Hurricanes were Merseybeat faves as the 1950s became the 1960s. They were the most flamboyant and dynamic of all the local bands, a proto-glam rock troupe a decade before their time. The Hurricanes wore shades, Hawaiian shirts and pink suits while Rory, in turquoise and gold lame, would high-kick and clamber from the stage to the ballroom balcony or across the domed ceilings, occasionally bringing a pet monkey on stage with him. Unsurprisingly then, they were promoter Allan Williams' first choice as his Liverpudlian export to the clubs of Hamburg. But loathe to give up a lucrative Butlin's summer season at Pwllheli, during which their drummer Ritchie Starkey began calling himself Ringo, Williams was forced to send, with some reluctance, a band called The Beatles.

Rory's pretty sister, Iris, was an early girlfriend of Paul and gave George his first kiss too ('I ran into his arms and he gave me the best kiss ever. I can still feel it right in my tummy, even now. He was lovely …'). When The Hurricanes eventually went to Hamburg after their summer season was over, on their first night there, Storm and guitarist Johnny 'Guitar' Byrne heard amazing music coming from a club; 'It was raw and exciting. There was something about the way they looked too, rough and intense and a little bit rebellious … Rory and I turned to each other with a shocked look on our faces and we both kind of blurted out "It's The Beatles!"'

At the Kaiserkeller, they and The Beatles would play alternate sets. George wrote home that Rory 'does a bit of dancing around but it still doesn't make up for his phoney group … the only person who's any good in the group was the drummer'. On their return to Liverpool, on the very morning that Brian Epstein was sacking Pete Best in the NEMS office, John and Paul drove the 160 miles in Paul's green Ford Consul Classic to Butlin's Skegness far out on the Lincolnshire coast (where The Hurricanes had another summer season) in an attempt to lure Ringo into the fab fold. Accounts differ about this strange episode but, whether they broadcast an announcement over the camp's PA, Ruth Madoc in *Hi-De-Hi* style, or hammered on Johnny and Ringo's caravan door, they were successful. Ringo joined The Beatles and Rory, according to Brian Epstein's autobiography, was philosophical. 'I apologised, and Rory, with immense good humour, said, "Okay. Forget it. The best of luck to the lot of you."'

Epstein tried to repay the debt by producing a Hurricanes single, 'America', in late 1964 on Parlophone* with Ringo on percussion and backing vocals, but it flopped, and the band remained a purely local phenomenon for the rest of the decade. As sister, Iris, put it: 'He was happy to be the King of Liverpool; he was never keen on touring, he didn't want to give up running for the Pembroke Harriers … and he'd never miss a Liverpool football match!' Bill Harry agrees, 'They were Liverpool icons affectionately remembered on Merseyside but virtually unknown outside the area. They were the classic group who didn't make it. The favourite local group with the Golden Boy singer who were left behind.'

On 28 September 1972, Storm and his mother were found dead at their home 'Hurricaneville'. A post-mortem revealed both had alcohol and sleeping pills in their systems. Ringo Starr pays tribute to him on the song 'Liverpool 8'. 'Played Butlin's camp with my friend Rory, It was good for him, it was great for me' goes the lyric, but the feeling that it was rather better for Ringo is sadly inescapable.

---

* Oddly, the press release read 'Another Brian Epstein production'. In fact, it was the only record he ever produced.

36. Geoff Emerick

'Three months in the army would have done you good.'

As rock music grows older, so its history becomes more canonical, more revered, more sacred. Any modern producer or engineer will attest that today's bands continually seek from them the touchstone sounds of this venerated past; the mellotron sound from The Zombies' *Odessey and Oracle*, Johnny Marr's jangling twelve string, Led Zeppelin's percussive punch, the *Dusty in Memphis* Muscle Shoals horn sound. To The Beatles, such retrograde thinking was anathema. They wanted sounds no one had used before, and Geoff Emerick helped find them.

As always there's a crowd around the zebra crossing, even on a freezing January dusk. The motorists merely trying to negotiate their North London commute eye roll and horn blast as first a German family, then three Japanese girls, then an intense African man and then four middle-aged South American ladies slowly selfie their way across the world's most famous pedestrian crossing. The graffiti on the wall is testament to this site's international appeal as a place of pilgrimage; Croatia, Pakistan, Argentina, Bulgaria, Sweden ... the names of Penarol and Nacional have been written over each other, the two great rival football teams of Montevideo confirming a Uruguayan contingent have been here to this unremarkable, but for one building, corner of St John's Wood. Along the famous wall, covered in daubings, a blood-red exhortation to 'Bring all the Hostages Home' stands out among the 'Give Peace A Chance's' and 'Love Is All You Needs'.

None of this would have been here when the 16-year-old Geoff Emerick walked over that famed crossing for his first day at work at what was then still EMI Studios. The very next day, he met George Martin who had brought a new band called The Beatles to the studio. The first thing that struck Emerick was their skinny ties, a style he soon adopted. He was assistant to engineer Norman Smith for much of the band's early studio work but then moved off through EMI's formal training ladder – lacquer cutter, mastering engineer, balance engineer – which meant he missed *Help!* and *Rubber Soul.* During the recording of the latter, Smith seems to have lobbied to become a producer, annoying George Martin who responded by offering Emerick the job as Beatles' engineer. He was 20 and on his very first day in the new post, he helped create 'Tomorrow Never Knows', at that point probably the most sonically revolutionary production ever included on a mainstream pop record.

John wanted his vocal to sound like 'the Dalai Lama chanting from a mountaintop a thousand miles away' so Geoff came up with the idea to put Lennon's voice through a 'Leslie' cabinet. The result doesn't really sound like holy chanting from a distant peak, but it did sound like nothing else heard before in the world of pop; disconnected, alien, remote. Another innovation of Emerick's was to muffle the bass drum with an eight-armed promotional sweater hanging around the studio, an unused promo item from the period when the movie *Help!* was to be called Eight Arms To Hold You. For 'Yellow Submarine' John now wanted to sound as if he were singing underwater. Emerick put the microphone in a condom found in Mal Evans' bag (which seems to have rivalled Mary Poppins' in its capacity and the variety of its contents) and put the mike in a milk bottle filled with water. George Martin recalled that 'Geoff used to do things for The Beatles and be scared that the people above would find out. Engineers then weren't supposed to play about with microphones and things like that, but he used to do really weird things that were slightly illegitimate with our support and approval.'

The sessions for *Sgt. Pepper*, begun in the depths of winter and conducted often late at night, were intense if productive. 'All our social lives were going for a Burton. We were just living for the record. Towards the end we were getting a bit overwhelmed ... so whenever things were slowing up, we'd play "A Day In The Life" to cheer us up.' Despite being an integral part of these sessions, Emerick didn't even get a credit. Worse, when he won a Grammy for his work on this landmark of the summer of love, the award was delivered to Abbey Road studios where the venerable EMI studio manager E. H. Fowler took delivery and put it in his office without telling Geoff.

These details are taken from Emerick's memoir, *Here There and Everywhere* (co-written with Howard Massey) and should thus perhaps be viewed with some scepticism. Fellow Engineer, Ken Scott, has pointed out the many factual errors and *The Beatles Naked* podcast describes it as 'largely a work of fiction'. The tone can often veer between the peevish and the self-aggrandising, and there are many odd if amusing digressions into such tangential matters as childhood UFO sightings and the complexities of the London Underground system. The exchanges are stilted and test the credulity. For instance, this chat with Paul before the recording of 'Paperback Writer' seems unlikely. 'Geoff,' he began 'I need you to put your thinking cap on. This song is really calling out for that deep Motown bass we've been talking about so I want you to pull out all the stops this time …' Harrison emerges as sour and underwhelming as a musician and there are swipes at many colleagues though never at George Martin. On the other hand, there are fascinating insights. One of the reasons McCartney's bass lines are so 'creamily' sublime on *Sgt. Pepper* is that they were usually added last, with Paul working alone into the small hours, honing and embellishing.

The *White Album* sessions were fraught. While Geoff was struggling to get the required overheated guitar sound on 'Revolution', Lennon muttered snarkily, 'You know, three months in the army would have done you good.' Emerick took this to mean that Lennon viewed him 'as some kind of upper-class twit who had never been exposed to the real world'. Emerick quite rightly thought this was somewhat rich coming from a man whose nearest experience of soldiery was dressing up as one for an art house movie. 'I kept my cool and I thought, "I'm not going to take this anymore."' Emerick walked out, but was persuaded to return later and for the next studio album.

Emerick chain-smoked Everest cigarettes during these recordings and this became the working title for the developing album after weeks of kicking around throwaway silliness like 'Billy's Left Boot'. Eventually, though, the album became *Abbey Road*, which in turn became the new name for EMI Studios. If 'Revolver' had found Emerick tasked with finding sounds that did not exist, *Abbey Road* is simply a superbly engineered pop record played by seasoned and skilled musicians augmented by beautiful and appropriate instrumentation. In this, it's a template for Emerick's 1980s production masterpiece, Elvis Costello's *Imperial Bedroom*.

Emerick was part of a generation that essentially invented modern pop production. Before him and his kind, producers were white-coated boffins, more lab technicians than artist. Emerick and his peers turned the increasingly ambitious sonic dreams of The Beatles into reality. Tape loops, reverb, multi-tracking, all the things now taken for granted as part of the arsenal and toolkit of music recording were invented by men (or even boys) like Geoff Emerick.

37. Tony Barrow

'John must have built himself a set of leather tonsils …!'

Of the two men* most famously tasked with liaising between The Beatles and the world's press, Derek Taylor was perhaps the more dashing. Witty and suave, he hung out in LA, was an early adopter of LSD and held court from his peacock throne in Savile Row. Tony Barrow was more stolid and conventional perhaps – he quit being a PR completely in the early 1980s revolted by the 'new wave' groups – but he was just as vital; ever present during the maelstrom of Beatlemania and contributing not one, but two treasured and enduring facets of their story.

He began his media life as teenage pop reviewer, 'Disker', at the *Liverpool Echo* before moving to London to work for Decca writing liner notes for their albums (the fact that this was even a full-time job then is an indication of how much the music 'biz' has changed). It was Barrow who arranged the unsuccessful Decca audition but out of this grew a warm relationship with The Beatles. For the fee of £20, Barrow created a press kit for 'Love Me Do' which impressed Epstein enough for him to offer him twice his Decca salary to become NEMS press officer handling the publicity affairs of Cilla Black, Gerry and The Pacemakers, Billy J. Kramer, The Fourmost and, of course, The Beatles. His excitable yet oddly formal style was beloved by early Beatles singles buyers; 'John must have built himself a set of leather tonsils in a throat of steel to turn out such a violently exciting track!' he declaimed on the rear of the *Twist and Shout* EP in 1963. In one of the early press releases he also invented the phrase

---

* Huddersfield's Brian Summerville, their first, tends to get written out of history. It's said that unable to get along with John, he told Epstein 'Either he goes or I do.' And so, in short order, Brian was gone.

'the Fab Four' which instantly stuck and continues to endure over half a century later.

Barrow's other lasting contribution to Beatle lore also came in 1963. Unable to countenance the amount of unopened fan mail piling up at the NEMS office, Barrow suggested the band record a flexi-disc Christmas message sent out to all 'loyal Beatle people' in lieu of individual replies. The band sang 'Good King Wenceslas' and 'Rudolf The Red Nosed Ringo' and riffed individually and collectively on a script written by Barrow.*

'I was relying on them to mess around with my words and make them funnier. They didn't let me, or themselves, down. Although part of their Christmas message was a genuine "thank you" to fans, the rest of the material I gave them provided ample scope for plenty of clowning around. I took the finished recording to Paul Lynton's place just around the corner from my Monmouth Street office and we edited it to fit on one single side of a 7" flexi-disc. When I say edited, I mean we actually cut the tape recording with scissors, patched the pieces together and let the discarded bits drop to the floor. Lyntone's [sic] staff pulled out all the stops to produce some 31,000 copies of the edited disc and we got the eagerly awaited Christmas present in the post just in time to beat the seasonal rush. Epstein's grudgingly given budget for the venture left us with little cash to spend on a conventional EP-style cover or sleeve to house the disc. We had to make do with a cheap, vomit-yellow-coloured container, overprinted in black and made of an inexpensive cross between paper and board. It was put together with staples that came open too easily. This was the one part of the product of which I felt ashamed. Otherwise, the record did the damage limitation job for which it was intended, and much more.'

The Beatles' Christmas message became a beloved seasonal fixture

---

* In an early script, he invented the nonsensical word 'Chrimble' for Christmas, now a commonplace.

for thousands across the globe and ran from 1963 to 1969, their last Christmas together. As for 'damage limitation', Barrow also had to contend with the fall-out from Maureen Cleave's infamous 'more popular than Jesus' Lennon interview (which he accidentally facilitated by sending it to *Dateline* magazine's Art Unger), the supposed snub to the Marcos' family in the Philippines, the 'Paul Is Dead' rumours and, by his tally, at least ten sackings by the temperamental Epstein (always followed by a next day reinstatement). He seems to have borne it all with grace and good humour, a 'class act' as many recalled. When he passed away in 2016, Paul said on social media 'Tony Barrow was a lovely guy who helped us in the early years of The Beatles. He was super professional but always ready for a laugh. He will be missed but remembered by many of us.' Whenever someone mentions 'the Fab Four', the consummate PR man that he was would surely consider it a job well done.

38. Dick Rowe

'Groups of guitarists are on the way out, Mr Epstein.'

Has history been unfair to Dick Rowe? Was he really 'the man who turned down The Beatles'?, as the inevitable postscript to any mention of his name has it (and the title of his unpublished autobiography). Perhaps posterity has done him a disservice; did the decision to pass on The Beatles for Brian Poole and The Tremeloes have less to do with music than the British arterial road system of the early 1960s?

Rowe never claimed to have 'golden ears' or musical expertise. He was, by trade, like his father and grandfather before him, a stockbroker for Decca's chairman Sir Edward Lewis. So he was staggered when Lewis asked him to take over the running of Decca. But he ran it well, having a string of hits throughout the 1950s from the likes of Winifred Atwell, Lita Rosa, Anthony Newley, Billy Fury, Marty Wilde and Tommy Steele (who had been turned down by George Martin at Parlophone).

Encouraged by his A&R man, Mike Smith, who'd been impressed by The Beatles on a trip to The Cavern and badgered by Epstein, Rowe arranged for the band to come to London for an audition/test recording. A hungover Smith recorded fifteen songs by them (all covers, at Epstein's insistence) on 1 January 1962* and on the same day recorded a session by Brian Poole and The Tremeloes. After this, things get a little murky. Rowe apparently told Smith that they could only sign one of the two bands and Smith – not Rowe it's said – went with The Tremeloes. But was this because they were musically superior? Or was it because they lived around the corner from Smith in Barking, were pals of his who mixed with him socially and even

---

* New Year's Day only became a public holiday in the UK in 1973, incredibly.

celebrated their signing by going to Smith's mum's for Sunday tea? Add to this that, in the pre-motorway days, while Barking was just east of Decca's offices and studios in the capital, Liverpool was eight hours away by A-roads. (The night before their audition, having been driven all day by Neil Aspinall, The Beatles only arrived in London at 10 p.m.). As Rowe later put it 'Liverpool could have been Greenland to us then.'

Whatever the reason, at lunch in Decca's dining room, (though in the Epstein biopic *Midas Man*, this has become a boozy, braying, brandy and cigars affair at what appears to be The Savoy) Rowe infamously declared 'groups of guitarists are on the way out, Mr Epstein'.* Epstein apparently tried to convince Decca that with his retail connections he could guarantee sales of 3,000 copies of any Beatles single but Rowe maintained 'I was never told about that at the time ... if we'd been sure of selling 3,000 copies we'd have been forced to record them whatever sort of group they were.' As it is, it was a strange decision by Rowe, given that he could probably have taken a punt on The Beatles for less than he spent lunching Epstein. But it was not an entirely fruitless exercise for the band. It gave them a well-produced 'demo tape' which George Martin heard and liked, as long as they changed their drummer ...

For Rowe though, it was a decision he'd come to regret bitterly. A year and four months later, in the first week of May 1963 at the height of UK Beatlemania, Rowe was a judge at a talent show at the Philharmonic Hall, Liverpool alongside George Harrison, now one of Britain's most famous and feted stars. Rowe told Harrison he was still berating himself for his stupidity. George, graciously, replied that he had probably been right as their audition was awful, adding that Rowe should check out an interesting new band down south.

---

* Or 'guitar groups' or 'groups of guitars' or other variants. I have used the phrase Epstein quotes in *A Cellarful Of Noise*. Rowe always denied saying this or indeed that he was at the lunch.

Rowe immediately went to see them at their Richmond Hotel residency and was impressed by both them and their smart young manager Andrew Loog Oldham. He signed them as, naturally, he did not want to risk making the same mistake again and reject another potential rock phenomenon, which is of course just what those young bucks at the Richmond Hotel were to become. While no Beatles (obviously), the 'blues covers band' as Macca cheekily described them in 2021, The Rolling Stones have done pretty well it has to be said, if not perhaps well enough to rescue Dick Rowe from what E. P. Thompson termed, 'the enormous condescension of posterity' as 'the man who turned down The Beatles'.

39. Anello & Davide

'They were a cool thing before The Beatles,
but afterwards they were mandatory.'

It's a commonplace among actors, possibly originating with Stanislavski, that the key to inhabiting a character is getting the shoes right. And it's understood that while raw talent was the prime driver of The Beatles' success, something about their story and its mystique is alchemical, dependent also on chance, accident, meeting the right people, making the right decisions. Once The Beatles had begun to ensnare the world, what people (especially men) most wanted to emulate about them was not just their tightknit bond, their blazing charisma or their musical prowess – it was the hair and the clobber. Like all good actors, they had found the right shoes and found them at Anello & Davide on the Charing Cross Road.

Anello & Davide was founded in 1922 by Anello and Davide Gandolfi, supplying bespoke dance shoes and theatrical footwear to London theatres and ballet companies. Though The Beatles had been wearing 'Chelsea boots' since Hamburg, it was Brian Epstein who directed them towards Anello & Davide as part of his astute and sophisticated remodelling process, with them first visiting the store at 96 Charing Cross Road when they travelled to the West End on New Year's Eve 1962 for the Decca audition. That, of course, was unsuccessful, but within not much more than a year, The Beatles were wearing handmade Anello & Davide 'Beatle' boots to their own specification, a streamlined silhouette with Cuban heel, pointed toe and centre-seam stitch with an elastic gusset or a zipper.

Before long, every hip young man in town and beyond (who could afford it) was headed to 96 Charing Cross Road. 'As a band, like a thousand others' remembered Mick Fleetwood 'We all went to a shoe shop called Anello & Davide and bought ourselves Beatle boots, which were basically Spanish dancing boots. They were a cool thing before The Beatles, but afterwards they were mandatory.' More recently, fictional wearers include Austin Powers and Ned Flanders, a huge Beatle fan who sports a pair in 'Treehouse of Horror X'.

Aside from The Beatles, Anello & Davide's most celebrated customer was the late Queen Elizabeth II who wore Size 4 A&D leather slip-ons (a grand a pair) all her working life, with ten pairs in circulation at any one time. These would be 'worn in' by a junior staff member, 'Cinders', at the company, whose feet were the same dimensions as the late monarch, and who wore beige cotton ankle socks when testing the Queen's shoes and was only allowed to walk on carpets but for a sole trial run outside to test traction.

Anello & Davide are still with us, now in Kensington but still offering handmade shoes and ballet pumps for a discerning bespoke clientele. But for a pair of authentic period Anello & Davide Beatle boots you will need to scour the auction houses. A rare pair of men's Anello & Davide 'Beatle' boots of 1962 vintage handmade of black leather with elasticated sides, pointed blunt-tipped toes and shaped heels went to auction in 2013. The vendor had seen The Beatles perform at the Smethwick Baths in the West Midlands on 19 November 1962 and met the group after the show. Admiring their boots, he asked where they were from and Paul McCartney told him 'a theatrical shoemaker in Charing Cross, London called Anello & Davide'. The unnamed vendor commissioned an identical pair which sixty-two years later went to auction at Kerry Taylor auctioneers, estimate four hundred pounds, but they did not sell. A pair actually owned by George Harrison sold at Bonhams the year before for £61,250.

40. Maureen Starkey

'Thanks Mo!'

Of the nine Beatle wives, just two were Liverpool girls, and their entrees into Beatledom were quite different. While Cynthia Powell was a studious, middle-class art student somewhat derailed by John's rebellious nature and Bardot fixation, Mary Cox, Maureen as she was known, quit school at 14 to work at Ashley Dupree's beauty salon. At 15, she was a devoted Cavernite and by 16 was dating Ringo Starr to the envy and resentment of many another Cavern regular. 'The other girls are not friendly at all,' she told Hunter Davies in his official biography of 1968. 'They were playing at the Locarno once. Just before they finished Ritchie told me to go outside and sit in the car and wait for him so no one would see me. I was sitting in the car when this girl came up ... I'd forgotten to wind the window up. Before I could do anything, she had her hand through the window and scratched me down my face but I just got the window up in time. If I hadn't, she'd have opened the door and killed me.'

However, their relationship was in abeyance when, in June 1964, on the eve of their first world tour, Ringo collapsed with tonsillitis and pharyngitis and was confined to hospital. Maureen nursed him with daily visits and care packages of ice cream and they grew close again. They married when she was 18. After three days of their honeymoon in Brian Epstein's lawyer's holiday home in Hove, they were doorstepped and Maureen gave one of her first and last broadcast interviews, telling the press pack tartly: 'I don't like reporters.'

Children followed and she settled into the role of little seen but supportive wife. Like the other Beatle partners, she rarely visited the studio. When she once did, she recalled, 'It was like watching a couple of actors rehearsing a scene in a movie. I would sit there with a cup of coffee in my hand and watch them for a while or maybe gossip with Linda or Mal. When I did watch them, I always thought to myself, "So this is what he's been doing for the last six years!" I sometimes felt like a fly on the wall, but I knew that I had to be the luckiest fly in the world.'

Cynthia Lennon said of her: 'Maureen was one of the most down to earth, honest people I ever knew', which makes it seem all the harder to believe, but true, that after The Beatles split, in 1973, Maureen and George had an affair, one they seem to have done little to hide. When wife Pattie eventually caught them in flagrante at Friar Park, in a very British act of retaliation, she squirted them with water pistols. In what must have been an excruciating moment, Harrison told Ringo, in front of Pattie and Maureen, 'I'm in love with your wife.' When Lennon found out about the affair, he famously declared it was 'virtual incest'.

Neither marriage survived the decade. In July 1975, her and Ringo's divorce was finalised on the grounds of his affair with an American fashion model. She received a lump sum of £125,000 plus £2,500 a year for each of their three children. Maureen was distraught and rode a motorcycle into a brick wall in an apparent suicide attempt. She later married Isaac Tigrett, the founder of the Hard Rock Cafe chain who is said to have described her as 'the ultimate collectable'. In 1994, at the age of just 48, she succumbed to leukaemia, despite bone marrow donation from her son Zak. He, her other children, Tigrett and Ringo were all at her bedside when she died.

For those of us who never knew her though, 'Mo' comes alive in the latter stages of Get Back, dark-eyed, vivacious, delighted. At the rooftop gig, she is the most excitable of all, especially when seen alongside Yoko's basilisk gaze. Ringo has borrowed her shiny red plastic coat and as they finish, the 'Thanks Mo!' that Paul yells is heartfelt and loving. After her death, he wrote a beautiful song about her, 'Little Willow', on the Flaming Pie album.

41. Peter Pilbeam

'John Lennon – yes, Paul McCartney – no'

Manchester's Hulme is not as 'edgy' a place as it once was in the late 1960s and 1970s when the cramped terraces were replaced by the infamous curving brutalist Crescents, described in the Manchester University archive as 'perhaps the most dysfunctional housing estate in Britain'. Even so, an outsider with a notebook and a man-bag can feel vaguely uncomfortable wandering around looking for a vanished landmark as dusk comes on and, in the words of local laureate Guy Garvey of Elbow, lippy kids begin to settle on the corners like crows.

On one such corner the Niamos Centre sits on an unprepossessing corner of Manchester's inner-city district of Hulme. Now a community hub, it's been a Caribbean arts centre and the headquarters of an evangelical church as well as languishing through periods of neglect and disrepair. But from 1955 to 1986, it was the BBC Playhouse, a jewel in the 'Beeb's' northern crown, host to Ken Dodd, Les Dawson, Jimmy Clitheroe and that radio stalwart The Organist Entertains. In the early 1960s, it was home to a show called *Teenager's Turn – Here We Go* where The Beatles made their first ever radio performance, largely due to the slightly grudging enthusiasm of a BBC producer called Peter Pilbeam.

The BBC at the time had a policy of offering free auditions for radio slots to any number of variety acts; ventriloquists, comics, skiffle and trad jazz acts and, increasingly, pop groups. Pilbeam remembered, 'With some of the groups, where noise could replace musical values, it did … there was masses of rubbish … then out of the blue this group turned up at one of our audition sessions called The Beatles – a weird name and everybody said, "Whoa, yuck!"'

It was not quite 'out of the blue'. Pilbeam had caught The Beatles at The Cavern and been impressed by their verve and brio as well as

142

Epstein's crisply formal letter of application. After their audition, a mix of covers and Lennon and McCartney originals, he gave his lukewarm verdict on their vocal abilities ('John Lennon – yes, Paul McCartney – no') but was more generally positive. 'An unusual group ... not as "rocky" as most, more country and western, with a tendency to play music. Yes.' The contract was signed; The Beatles would perform on *Teenager's Turn* for a fee just shy of twenty-seven quid plus the cost of four return rail tickets to Liverpool at eight shillings and sixpence each.

It was a pivotal moment. Coming just a few weeks after their failed Decca audition, this was a major fillip; a vote of confidence from the national broadcaster. A month later, at the Playhouse, Hulme, on 7 March 1962 (broadcast the next day), the band, still with Pete Best, rehearsed from 3.45 p.m. then changed for the first time into the new suits Epstein insisted they adopt and at 8.45 p.m. played three covers, 'Dream Baby (How Long Must I Dream?)', 'Memphis, Tennessee' and 'Please Mister Postman'. Host Ray Peters became the first person to announce The Beatles on the radio; in the audience was Stuart Sutcliffe, visiting from his new home in Hamburg.

Over the next three years, The Beatles would make at least fifty-two musical performances for the BBC in addition to hundreds more cameos, interviews and unscheduled appearances, together or individually. But none feels more important to this story than that night in Hulme, thanks to Peter Pilbeam.

1963

42. Helen Shapiro

'I looked up to him not in a fatherlike way,
but as a teenage girl with a wild crush.'

Susie and The Hula Hoops were not really a band, more a bunch of East End schoolkids with ukuleles and plastic guitars. Nevertheless, two of them, nine-year-old guitarist Marc Feld (later Bolan) and 12-year-old singer Helen Shapiro would later go on to have Number 1 hits and to become bona fide pop stars. Shapiro was Britain's biggest female artist of the early Sixties, with 'Walking Back to Happiness', recorded when she was just 14, reaching Number 1 in the UK, Ireland, New Zealand, Israel and South Africa. But for Beatle people, her main claim to fame is that way down the bill on her 1963 UK tour was a support act setting out on their first national tour at a moment of volcanic change for them and us.

Helen met The Beatles in Bradford on a freezing 2 February 1963, for the first show at The Gaumont. They hit it off instantly as she told Gary James for the Classic Bands Blog. 'They'd call me Helly. I

WITH A LITTLE HELP FROM THEIR FRIENDS

used to smoke cigarettes at that time, secretly. So they used to make fun of me when I would dive into the ladies restroom somewhere for a cigarette. I couldn't be seen having one in public … It was just gentle, good-natured fun, really. That's all.' Though Shapiro's husky contralto belied it, she was still just 16, much younger than The Beatles and she seems to have brought out the big brother in John. With her recent chart positions flagging, a *Melody Maker* article headlined 'Is Helen Shapiro a has-been at 16?' upset her and he was consoling. 'He would always look after me. I looked up to him not in a fatherlike way, but as a teenage girl with a wild crush. He never took advantage of me.'

Also on the tour were Kenny Lynch, The Red Price Band, The Kestrels,* The Honeys and the compere was Irish comedian and later TV star, Dave Allen. Paul and John would play and write compulsively on the tour bus; Shapiro remembers them composing 'From Me To You' and offering her 'Misery' which her manager Norrie Paramor (George Martin's rival and chart nemesis at the time) turned down. 'They introduced us to all that Motown stuff that they loved that none of us had heard before.' Together the contingent criss-crossed England in the worst winter in living memory. In Carlisle, at the Crown and Mitre hotel they gate-crashed a golf club dinner dance. 'I think I was twisting with Ringo. There were these ladies with their long gowns who made a beeline for The Beatles in their leather gear. Then suddenly this guy came over, a much older man, and he was huffing and puffing, getting red in the face. He ordered us to leave. "Who invited you?" he asked. It was a shame really because nobody seemed to have a problem with us, apart from the one bloke.'†

---

* Bristolian outfit featuring the later hugely successful song-writing duo of Roger Cook and Roger Greenaway.

† The 'bloke' was Dr George Jolly, a Carlisle GP who died in 2006 at the age of 91. Speaking to the city's *News & Star* he recalled 'I was having a meal with Bill and his wife and my wife. Somebody had introduced four rather scruffy

The reception for The Beatles was growing more fervid every night, boosted by a mid-tour TV appearance on *Thank Your Lucky Stars*. Soon they were promoted up the bill. By the time they got to Southport 'Everyone was screaming for The Beatles,' recalled audience member Plum Connolly, wife of later Lennon biographer Ray, 'it must have been so difficult for Helen,' though Shapiro says she never minded. In Sheffield, one reviewer was particularly percipient. 'Halfway down the bill in small letters are a group called The Beatles but don't let the fact that they are not top of the bill mislead you. The Beatles are NEWS.'

The next night, Hanley was The Beatles' final performance. They parted with hugs and laughs bound for a future that was becoming increasingly electrifying. Two days after Hanley, they recorded that bus composition, 'From Me To You'. It became their second Number 1. Ironically, Helen Shapiro's perky, pizzicato pop was about to be consigned to history by her new friends from Liverpool.

young men into the dance. They were leather-jacketed and all the rest. We saw them across the room and Bill said to me "I think we should ask them to leave. What do you think?" I said "Yes, I think maybe we should." I didn't recognise them and neither did Bill. They were just coming into their fame. Bill went across to have a word with them. They left without any ill-feeling. I suppose it is something to say you were involved in asking The Beatles to leave.'

43. Sean O'Mahoney

'What on earth are you going to put
in it after the first three issues?'

Millions of Beatles fans around the world knew and devoured the work of Sean O'Mahoney without ever knowing his name. They knew his alter ego though, the more racily monikered Johnny Dean, the man behind the journal of record, the *Pravda* of Beatledom, *The Beatles Book* (or *Beatles Monthly* as it was also known), and the man who gave the first byline and published the first pieces by the leading Beatle authority of our time.

Sean O'Mahoney had worked in music publishing since the mid-Fifties but the release of each of The Beatles' first three singles fired him with increasing entrepreneurial vigour and new ventures. On hearing 'Love Me Do', while working for Robert Stigwood's *Pop Weekly*, he rang Brian Epstein to ask if they might run a piece on his charges, The Beatles; he readily agreed and even took out a paid ad. With the release of 'Please Please Me', O'Mahoney, a shrewd judge of promise, left to start his own magazine, *Beat Monthly*, which featured The Beatles on the cover of the first issue. When 'From Me To You' was released, Sean pitched the notion of an all-Beatles magazine, sent to all Beatles fan club members around the world and sold on newsstands. While the band and Epstein were keen, Paul did wonder 'What on earth are you going to put in it after the first three issues?'

That was not to prove a problem. *The Beatles Book* was an instant hit, built upon unparalleled access for O'Mahoney (now writing as Johnny Dean) and photographer Leslie Bryce. It featured regular columns by Neil Aspinall and Mal Evans as well as lyrics, candid photos and Bob Gibson's distinctive graphics and caricatures. It ran for the rest of the decade, but the 1969 editions make for particularly fascinating reading; the uncritical, almost hagiographic tone of the magazine becoming increasingly censorious regarding the band's lifestyles. Eventually, seventy-seven editions after Paul's sceptical remark, *The Beatles Book* ended with the dissolution of The Beatles at the end of 1969.

Seven years later though, with passions rekindled by EMI's singles re-issues programme in 1976, the magazine was re-launched. Enter the young Mark Lewisohn, an accounts clerk at the BBC and Beatle obsessive who persuaded O'Mahoney to give him a column (written as Johnny Dean) answering readers' Beatle queries. 'He paid me one pound a letter, so I was actually being paid for my Beatles knowledge for the first time,' he told Joe Wisbey on *The Beatles Book*'s podcast and soon became an integral part of the magazine working under O'Mahoney's strict regime. 'He was a very upright individual, quite conservative both with a small and a large C. Quite a stickler. He had to be called Mr O'Mahoney by his employees and he had quite a temper. I often wonder what The Beatles thought of him … the more way out The Beatles became from '66 onwards, say, the less he understood them and then obviously with the drugs era and then the nudity era of 1968 onwards he really couldn't understand them at all anymore. They began to distance themselves from his magazine. It was right that it came to an end in 1969.'*

As a print entity, *The Beatles Book* ended with issue 321 in January 2003. It now continues as a social media repost of classic articles. But more importantly, back in those now unimaginable days before the internet, *The Beatles Book* was an invaluable resource and more, a way for Beatles obsessives from Accra to Zagreb, Accrington to Zaragoza to share their passion and feel connected and nurtured by it. The 'Personal Ads' section put Beatle fans around the world in

---

* In February 1979, three years into the revived magazine, Lewisohn thrust a copy into George Harrison's hand in the foyer of Broadcasting House when he arrived for Kid Jensen's *Round Table*. Harrison was irate that this was being republished and had Neil Aspinall serve O'Mahoney with a writ.

touch with one another so, who knows, there may even be someone reading this who owes their very existence to the business savvy of Sean O'Mahoney.

44. Maureen Cleave

'They look beat up and depraved
in the nicest possible way.'

Dr Johnson had Boswell. Delius had Fenby. Lou Reed had Lester Bangs. For much of their pomp, The Beatles had Maureen Cleave, a writer so close to them – intimate even – that she was their trusted scribe for many years, part of their inner circle. Ironically then, it was Maureen Cleave who nearly ruined their career, if not worse.

These days, the once august and rarefied pages of the broadsheets overflow with the chatter of pop. Most have a resident 'music critic', usually a graduate of the now defunct weekly rock press. But in the early 1960s, 'Fleet Street' (as was) regarded popular music as trite schlock, vacuous fodder for addled teens, to be mocked in a tone of amused hauteur. A young woman called Maureen Cleave changed all that. Born in India in 1934 and raised in her mother's native Ireland, after Oxford she was hired as a secretary at London's *Evening Standard* but persuaded the newspaper's editor to give her a column on pop music, a full page called Disc Date and the first of its kind in the national press. A friend of Cleaves and later doyenne of radio critics, the Liverpudlian Gillian Reynolds, persuaded her to take the train to Lime Street in 1963 to report on the burgeoning phenomenon that was Beatlemania. Her subsequent piece, 'Why The Beatles Create All That Frenzy' is a lemon-sharp, highly personal, very much 'of its time' profile:

'John Lennon has an upper lip which is brutal in a devastating way. George Harrison is handsome, whimsical and untidy. Paul McCartney has a round baby face while Ringo Starr is ugly but cute. "Their physical appearance," said my friend, who is a Liverpool housewife, "inspires frenzy". They look beat-up and depraved in the nicest possible way.'

She was clearly charmed; 'They just made me laugh, immoderately … more fun than anyone else and terrible teases. The interviewer was outnumbered four to one: they might put your coat in the wastepaper basket, offer to marry you, seize your notebook and pencil, pick you up and put you somewhere else, demand you cut their hair … On the other hand, they were often kind, offering you cigarettes or a swig from their bottles of Coke, making sure you never got left behind.' They in turn were hugely taken with her, as indeed were most. Her smart Sixties bob and fringe, prim but cute delivery and individual fashion sense secured her a berth on the panel of *Juke Box Jury*. She quickly became The Beatles' most favoured journo, one of the chosen few who, at a secret signal, would be allowed to remain in dressing rooms and hotel suites when Neil Aspinall would dismiss the rest. She travelled first-class with them on Pan Am flight 101 on that first American trip and in the Maysles brothers' documentary, we hear her calling up The Beatles' suite from her own. Ringo answers and the exchange reveals their easy familiarity, 'We're waiting for a very important phone call from London and you're blocking the line' he laughs, signing off 'Alright love, see you later.'

Over the next few years, she would write many pieces, trivial and serious, about the group. Sometimes this might be an entire article centred around George's first experience with an avocado but the conversations could also be frank and revealing. As part of a series of profiles of them all entitled 'How Does a Beatle Live?', she interviewed John Lennon at home in Weybridge, Surrey. The conversation touched upon spiritual and philosophical matters with Lennon mentioning his readings on religion and offering the insight 'Christianity will go. It will vanish and shrink. I needn't argue about that; I'm right and I'll be proved right. We're more popular than Jesus now; I don't know which will go first – rock 'n' roll or Christianity. Jesus was all right but his disciples were thick and ordinary.'

The comments attracted little attention in Britain. But Beatle PR Tony Barrow offered the four profiles to a US magazine called *Datebook* as evidence of the moptops' growing maturity and intellectual curiosity. This didn't work out quite as planned. *Datebook* editor Art Unger ran a line from Lennon's interview on the cover: 'I don't know which will go first – rock 'n' roll or Christianity!'* In contrast to the more measured and, let's face it, grown-up response in The Beatles' home country, America, to use its own vernacular, 'lost their shit'. First, two Alabama DJs destroyed Beatle records on air and invited listeners to bring theirs in to be crushed in a piece of agricultural machinery. Bonfires of Beatles records were organised across the Bible Belt South.

Brian Epstein was initially sanguine, remarking 'If they burn Beatles records, they've got to buy them first.' But when the stock of their publishing company Northern Songs began to plummet and stations in Mexico and South Africa boycotted the band and, most worrying of all, the violent white supremacists of the Ku Klux Klan became involved, Epstein grew so concerned for the band's safety on the forthcoming US tour that he considered calling it off. As it was, the tour passed off without incident, apart for some firecrackers thrown during the show in Birmingham, Alabama and a famous TV cameo involving a Klansman before that show in which, while looking about as laughably idiotic as a dangerous far-right nutjob can, he explains that the Klan are a 'terror organisation' and would use 'ways and means' to stop the show. They didn't.

Lennon issued a grudging, anguished apology and Cleave herself made several radio appearances (until Epstein told her to stop) offering explanations and justifications for Lennon's remarks. But the damage was done. Loathing the tour as much as they did surely

---

* The cover star though was Paul, and Unger expected greater controversy for a more prominent frontpage quote from McCartney about America, shocking to modern ears, viz 'It's a lousy country where anyone black is a dirty nigger.'

contributed to their decision soon afterwards to stop touring alto-gether. A quote from Lennon was later used in a book in 1986: 'If I hadn't upset the very Christian Ku Klux Klan, well, Lord, I might still be up there with all the other performing fleas.'

Exactly how close Lennon and Cleave were has long been a subject for conjecture. She knew that he was instantly attracted to her 'because I had a fringe and a pair of red boots, considered rather daring'. Lennon himself claimed they had had a sexual relationship, possibly the one described in 'Norwegian Wood', but Cleave denied this, and Lennon later recanted. What is not in doubt is that Maureen Cleave, for the obvious reason of her sex, is never given the credit she deserves for her seminal role in the history of music jour-nalism. Without her column in the *Evening Standard*, the first to take pop musicians and their views seriously, there would never have been a rock press at all. I, of course, am glad there was, but opinions may differ.

45. Derek Taylor

'Spring is here and Leeds play Chelsea tomorrow and Ringo and John and George and Paul are alive and well.'

The Q Awards, given by the now defunct monthly magazine I used to write for, were a bibulous highlight of the music biz calendar. In 1996, it was typically glittering (I was at a table between Brian Eno and Jarvis Cocker if memory serves) and when The Beatles *Anthology* won Best Compilation, Peter Blake, famed designer of the *Sgt. Pepper* sleeve, took to the stage to accept it. His speech, however, soon diverted down a rather well-trodden path concerning the paltry two hundred pounds he had been paid for this 'iconic' cover. After some minutes of this, from an adjoining table, a clear, well-modulated voice rang out, 'Shut up, you pompous c**t!' Perhaps not Derek Taylor's most elegant sentence, but typically effective.

When I was a music journalist, I used to tell young bands 'Don't read your press, weigh it'; an old PR saw meaning that, by and large, getting your name out there is often more important than the nature of the write-ups. The 'heft' of course, will depend on how good your press 'person' is. I have known a lot. Some may even be reading this so I should say that (nearly) all have been helpful, friendly and efficient. Theirs is often a thankless task, chaperoning idiotic, penniless music journalists around the world and acting as thankless intermediaries between these and their illustrious charges. Their role though has changed this century from Pandarus to Praetorian Guard, from eager solicitor of any publicity to stern denier of access. Derek Taylor, the world's only famous press officer (Alastair Campbell may disagree) was all these things and more during his close association with The Beatles, a game of two halves, with a glittering Californian half-time interval.

The music writer Jon Savage, who wrote an excellent foreword for the re-issue of Taylor's memoir *As Time Goes By*, has stated that, in early 1963, Taylor 'was the only person at the time who recognised the full significance of what was happening'. He realised it immediately as well, one Manchester night that year when he was dispatched by the *Daily Express*, then a hugely successful mass market newspaper, to review a pop group called The Beatles. One suspects that this commission was issued in the hope and expectation of a sardonic, haughty dismissal of this latest teen fad. But Taylor and wife Joan were instantly smitten in the kind of joyous epiphany Epstein had experienced that lunchtime at The Cavern. After the show, he dictated his copy down the phone extempore.

'The Liverpool Sound came to Manchester last night, and I thought it was magnificent … Indecipherable, meaningless nonsense, of course, but as beneficial and invigorating as a week on a beach at the pierhead overlooking the Mersey. The spectacle of these fresh, cheeky, sharp, young entertainers … is as good as a rejuvenating drug for the jaded adult.'

Soon after, he profiled Brian Epstein for the *Express* though he was not hugely impressed. 'He was awfully remote. He had this kind of sniffy front, but that didn't fool me, because I was from Liverpool. I didn't ask him anything very cheeky anyway. I just wanted to be nice about him and about The Beatles, because I was truly stunned by how marvellous they'd been at that concert.'

Like Epstein, he was Scouse, born and raised in Hoylake. Like Epstein, he was elegant, urbane, well spoken and, like Epstein again, this proved an attractive novelty to The Beatles. He soon became part of their inner circle, ghost-writing both George Harrison's newspaper column and Epstein's memoir. For this, the pair decamped to a Torquay hotel for the weekend, during which time Epstein told Taylor he was 'queer'. Taylor effectively shrugged and told him he didn't care and, more importantly, 'I won't ever let you down.'

He was soon on the payroll as The Beatles' press liaison and Epstein's personal assistant. He was embedded with them on their 1964 World Tour, five insane and intense months that were both exhilarating and wearying thanks to what Taylor saw as Epstein's constant peevishness and control-freakery. 'I joined in April and by May he was treating me with massive cruelty.' This culminated in Epstein throwing a tantrum when Taylor commandeered Epstein's limo to ferry some journalists (including Gloria Steinem) around. On the last night of the tour, Taylor slipped a resignation letter under Epstein's hotel room door. The pair spent an icy flight back to the UK together until, over champagne and tears, Brian begged him to reconsider. Derek gently declined saying 'We can be friends, but I can't work with you.'

Taylor relocated his family to LA where he became the most gilded publicist of the West Coast rock scene. He made stars of The Mamas & The Papas and garage pop acts Paul Revere and The Raiders and The Beau Brummels, moulded The Byrds as the American Beatles and was largely responsible via his skilful promotion for *Pet Sounds* becoming hailed as a masterpiece. His Californian sojourn was golden, but his heart was elsewhere. Brian Wilson, of his charges The Beach Boys, once turned to him and said 'The Beatles are always going to be number one for you, aren't they Derek?' Taylor replied, 'Sorry, but yes.'

This much becomes obvious when you consider that, at two days' notice and despite being in the middle of organising the Monterey Pop Festival, he and wife Joan flew 6,000 miles just to be at Brian Epstein's *Sgt. Pepper* party at his country house in Sussex where a loving welcome and tea spiked with acid awaited. Soon he was back permanently in The Beatles' employ, at George's urging. When Alistair Taylor asked what Taylor might do in the sclerotic Apple organisation, Harrison (to whom Derek was always the closest) replied 'we'll think of something'. He oversaw the launch of Apple Records (which included sending a box set of singles to The Queen and PM Harold Wilson) and was its press officer till the bitter end.

'I was as free as a bird and if this thing was going to be weird then it was going to be weird.' In his office, two projectors beamed psychedelic light shows and on the desk was a tray of water into which several plastic birds dip their heads hypnotically. Taylor, by now 'an inebriated, psychedelic visionary' as Peter Brown called him, would hold court from his vast peacock-feathered wicker chair at the centre of what became a famed bacchanal where scotch and coke and stronger fare was available to anyone who cared to drop by, from Fleet Street hacks to visiting Hell's Angels. At one point, Taylor even put out a fey press release announcing, 'Lebanese export companies, we learn, are pleased by the amount of business we're putting their way.' *Beatles Monthly* publisher Sean O'Mahoney said 'the entire room was a haze of cannabis. It was ridiculous. You could hardly breathe. I asked Derek for some new photos of The Beatles and he wandered around the room in a daze and eventually gave me some which turned out to be the same ones I had given them. But that was what Apple was like.'

Or at least, until Allen Klein arrived. Taylor survived the first cull and stayed on, seeing himself as 'the keeper of the mood'. Philip Norman reported that Taylor wrote a great deal in that final tumultuous, bleak year; remarkable, revelatory musings, memos and notes to self like this; 'Whatever the motivation, the effect is slavery. Whatever The Beatles ask is done. I mean, whatever The Beatles ask is tried. A poached egg on The Underground on the Bakerloo line between Trafalgar Square and Charing Cross? Yes, Paul. A sock full of elephant shit on Otterspool promenade? Give me ten minutes, Ringo. Two Turkish dwarves dancing the Charleston on the sideboard? Male or female, John? Pubic hair from Sonny Liston? It's early closing, George but give me until noon tomorrow. They make Lord Beaverbrook look like Jesus.'

In response to speculation about their demise, Taylor drafted the last ever Beatles' press release typed by his secretary Mavis Smith on 10 April 1970. It read 'Spring is here and Leeds play Chelsea tomorrow and Ringo and John and George and Paul are alive and well and full of hope. The world is still spinning and so are we and so are you and when the spinning stops, that'll be the time to worry not before then. Until then The Beatles are alive and well and the beat goes on, the beat goes on.' Peter Doggett calls it 'the weakest pronouncement that this strikingly articulate man ever made'. But I disagree; I think its tenor of wearily vague optimism speaks to the sadness and confusion that surrounded the final days of the band.

Taylor left to become director of special projects at Warner Brothers records where he was involved in the release of The Rutles movie and album. In it, he becomes PR man Eric Manchester, an oblique, geeky gag on the fact that The Beatles had initially teased him for being an exiled 'fake' Scouser living in their great rival northern city. He was back though to do the PR for *Anthology* and is one of only three non-Beatles involved or interviewed. During the project, he died of cancer.

Almost every reference to Taylor mentions his (usually described as 'Italianate') good looks. Stevie Nicks, with whom he had a brief affair, wrote the song 'Beautiful Child' about him on the *Tusk* album. Reflecting on Epstein asking him to become his personal assistant, Taylor mused 'I suppose it was because he fancied me that I got the job even though in all the time I knew him he never as much as laid a finger on my knee.' Add to this that he was charming, kind and droll, and Taylor seems to have been loved by all who knew him, except perhaps Paul McCartney for a few fractious months in 1968, and by Derek's death, Paul could say from the heart, 'He was a beautiful man. It's a time for tears. Words may come later.'

Hunter Davies said, 'Derek was the most amusing, most likeable, most urbane and possibly the most talented of all The Beatles' insiders.' That last adjective is debatable, but I take Hunter's point. In his turn, through all the sturm und drang of their lives together, Derek

Taylor never fell out of love with 'the boys' ... 'They were much more than a pop group ... They were like the weather only much more constant ... Life was going to be good now because we have The Beatles. They were alive for all our sins. They could absorb it all and make life seem enormous fun ... In The Beatles the world had found the truest folk heroes of the century or, indeed, of any other time. From that day, 30 May 1963, I have never wavered in my certainty that they painted a new rainbow right across the world, with crocks of gold at each end and then some ...'

46. Brian Matthew

'She likes Saturday Club.
She always listens when she's digging in the yard.'

I was fortunate right at the start of my radio career to work alongside some real legends of the medium coming towards 'the mature phase', as we might say, of theirs: Terry Wogan, Jimmy Young, David Jacobs, Johnny Walker and, thrillingly for any Beatlemaniac, Brian Matthew. He was as urbane and avuncular in the flesh as he was in the countless interviews with the band that we know him for. Matthew spoke to The Beatles, most usually on the *Saturday Club* show, more than any other radio broadcaster. He may well have been the best. But we should point out that he was not the first.

On 27 October 1962, Monty Lister (along with assistants Peter Smethurst and teenager Malcolm Threadgill) spoke to the rising local band from across the Mersey for Radio Clatterbridge, a hospital radio station in the Wirral. Though the band claim during the chat that the experience is 'nerve wracking', they are already exhibiting the insouciant wit and playfulness that would soon charm the world, cracking gags about war wounds, knowing 'a man in Chester' and reciting the catalogue number of 'Love Me Do' ('Parlophone R4949.') They sign off with a request for Maddy and Eileen in Robert Carr Ward and Monty quips 'And I'm sure for them, the answer is P.S. I love you!'

Seven months later, they first spoke to Brian Matthew at their debut performance on *Saturday Club*. Matthew, a former Coventry milkman who studied at RADA was perhaps unique among the presenters of that time in that, while clearly of a different generation, one of National Service and Brylcreem, he never patronised his young listeners or treated them like idiots. His signature greeting, 'Hello, it's your old mate, Brian Matthew,' always seems more sincere and meaningful than most of the DJ prattle that was to come in the Sixties and Seventies and The Beatles seemed genuinely fond of him. George speaks warmly to him on the phone from their hotel suite during their first US visit, captured on film by the Maysles brothers; John affectionately dubbed him 'Brian Bath-Tube'. He interviewed them in their suite at the Warwick Hotel before the Shay Stadium show and was generally there or thereabouts through their touring years. He became a good friend of Brian Epstein's and was on close enough terms with 'the boys' to be cheekily candid with them, asking Ringo in 1966, 'On the whole, would you say you've had a fairly easy life?'

Matthew hosted the first major BBC Radio documentary series on the band, *The Beatles Story* on Radio 1 in the summer of 1972. It's his distinctive voice you hear often during *Anthology* and on *The Beatles at the BBC* set. All in all, they appeared on *Saturday Club* ten times, joyous occasions all, with a highlight being the 1964 edition when George mentions his mum – 'She likes *Saturday Club*. She always listens when she's digging in the yard.'

But I particularly like to think of him presenting the show on 6 July 1957, John and Paul listening, as they surely did, to his warm, husky tones introducing songs by skiffle outfit The Black Diamonds before these two music-mad teenagers head separately down to the Woolton fête, about to meet, and about to change the world.

47. Mal Evans

'You're big and ugly enough.'

The 'Auteur' theory of film making holds that the director (classically a white man) is the creative engine and guiding solo visionary of a movie. I've never really bought into this theory to be honest. Without writers, actors, producers, gaffers, runners, best boys, make-up artists and catering trucks dispensing bacon butties, Welles, Hitchcock, Spielberg and the rest would never have finished a reel. In the same way, though the incendiary talent of Lennon, McCartney, Harrison and Starr burned at the group's core, The Beatles (as this book seeks to point out) had many significant others around them to facilitate their particular genius, and no one more than Mal Evans. Roadie was too small a word for this gentle giant.

Like many people, a chance encounter with The Beatles in The Cavern changed Post Office engineer Malcolm Evans' life. He was firstly a fan, then at George Harrison's instigation ('You're big and ugly enough') became Liverpool's most benign bouncer, useful extra money for a man with a wife, Lily ('Lil'), and new baby son, Gary. Sick with jaundice one night, Neil Aspinall needed fresh air and bumped into Mal on The Cavern's Mathew Street doorstep. The band had a London engagement the next day that Aspinall was clearly not fit for and so he asked Mal to step in. It was to prove a fateful, folkloric trip. On the way back, a stray pebble shattered the windscreen of their van.* As Paul recalled, Mal came into his own in a defining moment. 'He just put his hat backwards on his hand, punched the windscreen out completely and drove on. This was winter in Britain and there was freezing fog and Mal was having to

---

* Probably the White Commer, reg 208UFM, they used before upgrading to a Ford Thames 800 Express in cream, van fans.

look out for the kerb all the way up to Liverpool … two hundred miles.'

Impressed by this, and the fact that Mal returned the van with a new windscreen, Neil and The Beatles insisted that Epstein offer him a permanent job as road manager. On 4 July 1963, in Epstein's office, Evans negotiated a salary of £25 a week, handsome compared to his current £15 with the GPO and considerably higher than the average Briton's weekly wage at the time. He still agonised over the situation though, especially because of the pressures it would put on his family life. Lil was blunt: 'I didn't want him to. I told him "You're a person in your own right, you don't need to follow others." But he was starstruck.' She told him, 'It's right for you but it isn't right for me. I am going to be left alone a lot.'

She was right. For the next six years, Mal would travel the world with The Beatles, occasionally accompanied by Lil and Gary, as in their stay at the George V hotel Paris, but more often than not, as in the 'Jimmie Nicol' visit to Australia and the infamous Philippines trip, of which more elsewhere. He contributed the much-loved Mal's Diary to *Beatles Monthly* and kept an archive which qualifies him really as the first Beatle historian. He leased the bus for *Magical Mystery Tour* and scoured the libraries of London for the celebrity images that appear on the cover of *Sgt. Pepper*. Sweet-tempered, genial and genuinely adoring of his family, he nevertheless found himself seduced by the hedonism of The Beatle lifestyle as the Sixties progressed. He wove himself into The Beatle tapestry in countless ways, part Jeeves, part Passepartout, part Tonto, part Little John, reliable, self-effacing, kind, engaging. Lennon's later assistant, Dan Richter (who, incidentally, played the lead ape in the opening section of *2001: A Space Odyssey*), called Mal 'the sweetest human being that ever lived'. He holidayed with Paul, was the Channel Swimmer in one of the many silly moments in the *Help!* movie and carried a bag that Mary Poppins would have been proud of; a legendary, capacious receptacle from which he would produce everything from screwdrivers to condoms, plectra to band-aids. His size and physique – six foot three in an age when that height was highly uncommon among working-class males and superbly fit from swimming and cycling – made him imposing but never aggressive, a calm and supportive presence and a first rate photobomber, as so many pictures attest.

He's on the records too. He plays Hammond Organ on 'You Won't See Me', bass harmonica on 'Being for The Benefit of Mr Kite', tambourine on 'Dear Prudence', trumpet on 'Helter Skelter' and backing vocals on 'Yellow Submarine'. His is one of the hands slamming the E chord at the close of 'A Day In The Life' and, most famous of all since *Get Back*, he plays the anvil he personally sourced on 'Maxwell's Silver Hammer'. But there may be an even more significant musical contribution. According to his extensive diaries, while living with Paul in Cavendish Avenue, Mal co-wrote 'Fixing A Hole' with him but was persuaded out of a credit as it would complicate the Lennon/McCartney brand: 'I didn't mind because I was so in love with the group that it didn't matter to me.'

With the dissolution of the band and separated from Mal moved into an apartment in LA with a new girlfriend Fran Hughes and was busy for a while producing Badfinger and collecting and organising his diaries and archive for a book deal with Grosset & Dunlap. (Somewhat cruelly, when John Lennon heard of this, he responded '"Tuesday 1965 … got up … loaded van" … should be a laugh.') But Badfinger and other production projects stalled and, without the band he loved and an estranged family on the other side of the world, Mal became vaguely and fatally unmoored, developing a then very Californian appetite for booze and cocaine. In a David Frost TV interview in 1974 he now sports blond highlights and the specs have gone. His colourful shirt is open to just north of his navel and jewellery glitters at his throat and wrists. He looks chubbier though not unwell. In fact, he looks fine in a very 1970s LA way. He just doesn't look like Mal.

John Lennon once said that Mal knew every police chief in every city in the world. This didn't help him when he needed it most. In the *Living The Beatle Legend* biography, his son Gary writes 'On January 4th, 1976, when he simply couldn't stomach the act of living another day, my father orchestrated his own demise in a Los Angeles duplex.' Mal had a long-standing, unsettling obsession with guns, sometimes replicas like the ones mounted on the wall behind the breakfast table in Sunbury On Thames. But also the real and lethal kind. After taking Valium on that early New Year evening and getting maudlin looking over pictures of his children, he began to fool around with a Winchester rifle. Concerned, Fran told him if he didn't put the gun down, she'd call the cops. Mal replied 'Frannie, call the police.' When they arrived and asked him to drop the gun, he told them 'No. Blow my head off' and began to raise the rifle. Officers Krempa and Brennan shot him six times. Mal, 40 years old, died instantly, surrounded by pictures, clippings and diary entries, the ephemera, the flotsam and jetsam, the mosaic of a life.

Let's remember him a different way though. In his green fringed suede jacket and jam-jar bottom glasses, banging gleefully on that anvil on 'Maxwell's Silver Hammer', the unlikely star in many ways of *Get Back*, with the light of childlike joy and undying love on his sweet, good-natured face.

48. Dougie Millings

*'We'd get into our jackets and suddenly
we're the four-headed monster'*

Did Brian Epstein force The Beatles out of leather and into suits?
Hardly. No one could ever tell The Beatles what to do. But even the
ever-dissentient Lennon was smart enough to know that their
manager was right that if they ever wanted to graduate from back
street cellars, they would need to lose the biker jackets and greasy
quiffs and smarten up. Hence 'We all went quite happily over the
water to Wirral,' remembered Paul in *Anthology* 'to Beno Dorn, a
little tailor who made mohair suits. That started to change the image.'

Much later, they would sport psychedelic shirts by Mr Fish and
Tommy Nutter took great pride in dressing three of the four men on
the Abbey Road crossing (George preferring denim). But the tailor
most associated with The Beatles was Dougie Millings, who from
1963 until their split made their signature suits, at a time when The
Beatles were transforming the nature of masculinity and male fashion almost hourly.

Millings had already established a celebrity clientele* – Sammy
Davis Jnr, Tommy Steele, Cliff Richard's white snakeskin stage suit
– by the time Epstein visited his Old Compton Street shop in Soho,
handily just around the corner from that crucible of UK pop
pre-Beatles, the 2i's coffee bar. Dougie's son Gordon recalled that
'Epstein told dad he needed a look that made The Beatles look like
a modern group, rather than the rock 'n' roll leather jacket look
they'd had for their time in Hamburg … Dad had no idea who
Epstein was and, of course, at that point nobody had heard of The

---

* Later he would dress The Who: 'Keith Moon died in one of my suits,'
Dougie Millings said in 2000. 'In fact, he hadn't paid for it.'

Beatles. But Dad had cut these round-collared jackets for ship stewards and thought that idea could work. It was the kind of thing that the like of Pierre Cardin was doing at the time, too. So that's what he came up with, these jackets with half-inch braiding on the edges, flared cuffs and a three-pearl button-fastening, and tight, flat-fronted trousers with no pockets to keep the lines lean – and because Epstein said he didn't want the band members to have pockets to put their hands in.'

Millings also added two small vertical slits to the jacket for ease of movement during performances and when fleeing from mobbing fans. But the thinking behind the suits was psychological as well as practical: 'We'd get into our jackets and suddenly we're the four-headed monster,' as McCartney has put it. 'I was always keen that The Beatles had uniforms. We didn't look like any four guys; it was a unit.' Hanif Kureishi posted on his substack in 2024 'The suits ... made them look French or what we used to call Continental. They resembled Alain Delon or Jean-Paul Belmondo in moody thrillers about good-looking, stubbornly original people who weren't prepared to fit.'

In the years that followed, Millings designed over five hundred garments for them. He provided them each with half a dozen blue-grey lightweight wool and mohair suits with velvet collars for their first American tour and the 'Soldier Boy' suits they wear in *Help*. They wore his suits for all their TV appearances and he made the morning suits they wore to Buckingham Palace to receive their MBEs. He even dressed their Madame Tussauds Waxworks. They called him 'Dad' and insisted on him having a cameo in *A Hard Day's Night* as a tailor frustrated by their boisterousness at a fitting. Paul stayed close to Millings even after The Beatles. He designed the suits Wings wore on their 1972 debut tour and those worn on the cover of *Band on the Run*.

'When The Beatles came around everybody freaked. They just loved the look. It revolutionized how people dressed' said Tommy

Hilfiger, while fashion historian Fausta Urte Geigaite has commented, 'In essence, The Beatles taught us that fashion, much like music, is a platform for personal expression and cultural dialogue.' Former *GQ* editor Dylan Jones was more succinct; 'The Beatles were the best dressed group of all time.' Dougie Millings had a skilful, chalky hand in that.

49. Jane Asher

'We all fancied her.'

Two young women pass me as I stroll down Wimpole Street one February morning. They are northern though sadly not Scouse; that would be too perfect. One is jokingly moaning to her mate. 'I came to London thinking it would be quite exciting but then I look at my life and I think it's really quite boring. I don't drink. I don't party. I could be anywhere ...' Sixty years or so before, another young Northerner was having rather a better time in the heady crucible of swinging London, much of it right here at number 57, the 1960s home of the remarkable Asher family and their daughter Jane.

'I always feel very wary including Jane in The Beatles' history. She's never gone into print about our relationship, while everyone on Earth has sold their story ...' said Paul in *Anthology*. Discretion has sometimes been at a premium around The Beatles and their associates, their workmates, friends and hangers on. Some have kissed and told, traded and sold their time, however fleeting, 'with The Beatles'. But not Jane Asher. Her tactful silence concerning her five hectic years as Paul's girlfriend seems all the more gracious and attractive now in a new world of relentless over-sharing and hubristic self-regard. But her influence and that of her family on the enquiring mind of the young Macca cannot be overstated.

On 18 April 1963, at the BBC's *Swinging Sound* live broadcast Jane Asher was possibly the only girl in the Royal Albert Hall not screaming. Not because she didn't like the group who were performing; everyone loved The Beatles. But she had been sent to cover the show for the *Radio Times* and was a peer as much as a fan. Asher was an unusually sophisticated 17-year-old who'd been acting since she was six in films like *Mandy*, *The Quatermass Experiment* and *The Greengage Summer* and a regular panellist on 'appointment to view'

169

TV pop show, *Juke Box Jury*. After a photoshoot together for the magazine feature, she joined the group backstage in the green room. 'We all fancied her,' remembered Paul 'so we immediately tried to pull her, you know, that being the order of the day. We went back to the Royal Court Hotel where we were staying and then to Chris Hutchins the journalist's flat on the Kings Road and it was all very civilised* … But at the end of all that I ended up with Jane.'

It was to prove a life changing encounter for him, as mind expanding and consciousness broadening as any later drug experience. At this point, he and the other Beatles were sharing a tiny, bleak flat at 57 Green Street Mayfair, the only time all four Beatles lived together. 'We kept saying, we must get a table, we must get a kettle, but we were pretty hopeless about all that. It was a very cold place. There was no homeliness about it … there was nobody's touch … I hated it.' When his new girlfriend's mum suggested he might like to move into the sixth-storey spare room at the Ashers' home on Wimpole Street next to the bedroom of Jane's brother Peter, he was delighted. 'It was everything Green Street was missing. There were people there, and food in a homely atmosphere and Jane being my girlfriend … it was kind of perfect.'

Paul and the Ashers soon fell for each other. Jane's father, Dr Asher, was an eminent and evidently eccentric psychiatrist who would inject himself at the dinner table and, prescribing Paul a nasal inhaler, urge him to eat the Benzedrine pad inside later (the trick learned from poet Royston Ellis back in squalid Gambier Terrace but that Paul feigned ignorance of). Mum Margaret was an oboe teacher whose former students included George Martin. Sister Claire was on air every day in the popular daily radio soap, *Mrs Dale's Diary*. Jane was a film and TV star and brother Peter would soon become a pop

---

* Hmm. According to Hutchins himself, John, wired on amphetamines and Mateus Rose, was reliably smutty and unpleasant. Also present was Norman Jewry aka Shane Fenton, later the creepy gloved glam rocker Alvin Stardust.

star himself in the duo Peter and Gordon, thanks to a tranche of songs gifted from Paul like 'World Without Love' and 'Woman'. This extraordinary household was perfect for Paul's enquiring mind and ravenous appetite for culture. Whereas John would surely have bridled at being introduced to jazz, classical music and dinner table vocabulary games, for Paul, never shy of asking questions, confident but not arrogant, it was a kind of university; the best kind, in the heart of swinging London, living with a brilliant, beautiful girl and her absorbing, supportive family and with considerably more than a student grant to fund his adventures into this thrilling new world of theatres, galleries and concerts.

As The Beatles' star rose, 57 Wimpole Street was often besieged with fans to the extent that Dr Asher devised an ingenious escape route from the house for Paul. 'I used to go out of the window of my garret bedroom, on to a little parapet. You had to be pretty careful, it wasn't that wide, it was only like a foot or so wide, so you had to have something of a head for heights. You'd go along to the right … number 56, and there was a colonel living there, an old ex-army gentleman. He had this little top-floor flat, and he was very charming, it was quite amazing going through. "Uh! Coming through, Colonel!" "Oh, oh, okay, hush-hush and all that!" and he'd see me into the lift and I'd go right downstairs to the basement of that house. There was a young couple living down there and they'd see me out through their kitchen and into the garage. I remember I bought them a fridge later on to thank them.'

In 1966, Paul and Jane moved to Cavendish Avenue (just around the corner from both Abbey Road and Lord's cricket ground, price £40,000) while the other Beatles were now domiciled in suburbia and the stockbroker belt. But the couple were spending increasing amounts of time apart, Paul with his constant Beatles commitments and Jane with her acting career in movies like *Alfie* and *The Masque of The Red Death* and on stage and on tour with the Bristol Old Vic. Paul would make a point of seeing all Jane's opening nights but there were tensions over the demands of their creative lives which neither wanted to sacrifice. When she was touring America in *Romeo And Juliet*, Paul went out to celebrate her 21st together in Denver, walking barefoot in the snowy Rockies. Even so, Jane was moved to say, 'I'm in this country as a Shakespearean actress, not just as the friend of a Beatle' to a reporter whose story then ran headlined 'Shakespeare's The Topic, Paul Not To Be Mentioned!'

When Jane returned after the five-month tour, she later told Hunter Davies that Paul had 'changed so much. He was on LSD, which I hadn't shared. I was jealous of all the spiritual experiences he'd had with John. There were fifteen people dropping in all day long. The house had changed and was full of stuff I didn't know about.' After finding Paul in bed with Francie Schwartz, she moved out of Cavendish Avenue. Despite this, oddly, on Christmas Day 1967, at a McCartney family get together, they announced their engagement and the next year they travelled to the Maharishi's ashram together, an experience Jane seems to have found interesting. 'I think it [meditation] calms you down. It's hard to tell because it was so different, you know, the life out there. It'd be easy to tell now that I'm back, or when we're doing ordinary things, to see just what it does.'

But on 20 July 1968 when asked about their engagement by Simon Dee on his hit BBC chat show, Jane replied 'I haven't broken it off, but it is broken off, finished. I know it sounds corny, but we still see each other and love each other, but it hasn't worked out. Perhaps we'll be childhood sweethearts and meet again and get married when we're about 70.' Paul later said of the sundering of their relationship 'I got cold feet ... that and a few other personal things.' Soon afterwards, she appeared in a triumphant revival of John Osborne's *Look Back in Anger*, a play in part about the tension between a beautiful posh girl and a young working-class autodidact.

Neither of them, particularly Jane, have spoken much about their relationship since. But its legacy is both lovely and profound, not least in the songs written either about Jane ('Things We Said Today', 'Here There And Everywhere', 'I'm Looking Through You', 'You Won't See Me', 'And I Love Her', 'We Can Work It Out') or in Wimpole Street such as their first US hit 'I Want To Hold Your Hand' or the imperishable 'Yesterday'. Journalists still ask Jane about their time together but she is always elegantly firm. 'I know what you're interested in … but my connection to that is personal, so it opens up a whole thing. You have to make a blanket rule and that's the decision I made, many years ago.'

In 2025, as I stand across the street sheepishly making notes on my phone, number 57, like its neighbours, does not radiate luxury (though its asking price would be doubtless eye-watering). There is litter and scaffolding and the only plaque reads 'Bicycles parked or chained to these railings will be removed without further notice'. But its place in Beatle lore is radiant. In the *Lyrics* book of 2001, Paul recounted that, many years after their parting, he was walking down Wimpole Street on his way to a doctor's appointment and passing no 57 thought '"Wow, so many great memories there" and I was just pressing the bell when I sensed someone behind me. I turned around and it was Jane … I said "Oh my god, I was just thinking about you and the house."'

'That was the last time I saw her, but the memories don't fade.'

50. Dick James

'Robin Hood, Robin Hood … riding through the glen.'

On 10 January 1969, music publisher Dick James dropped by on the *Get Back* sessions, chatted a little about how Peter Cook had been rude to Zsa Zsa Gabor on the previous night's TV and then showed Paul and Ringo the huge collection of old standards they have just acquired via the Northern Songs publishing company.* Ringo is amused by some of the more comic titles ('Nobody Loves A Fairy When She's Forty') while Paul is impressed at some of the familiar material they now own such as 'Aint Misbehavin'' and 'my uncle Ron's favourite!' 'Carolina Moon'. 'Oh yes' says James 'there's some real golden oldies in there.' James suggests Paul include some on the album he's producing for a new young artist fresh from success on the *Opportunity Knocks* TV talent show. Perhaps, she could perform 'Burlington Bertie from Bow' or the Welsh standard 'We'll Keep A Welcome in The Hillside', a hit for stentorian Goon, Harry Secombe in 1956. Paul deadpans that they 'would be just right for Mary Hopkin.'

Dubious musical judgements aside, it attests to James' close relationship with the band at this stage that, alongside George Martin and Brian Epstein, he was one of the very few non-Beatles who could turn up unannounced like this at sessions. It's also a testament to how strange and strained that relationship was that during his visit, out of his earshot, John Lennon can also be heard calling James a 'fascist bum' and a 'pig'.

Reginald Isaac Leon Vapnick was the son of a Polish emigree East End kosher butcher and was a sometime pop singer himself at the

---

* It was the collection of Lawrence Wright, the first man to set up a music store on Denmark Street, Britain's Tin Pan Alley and founder of *Melody Maker* magazine. Northern Songs beat Lew Grade to the collection, but all Grade had to do was wait of course.

Cricklewood Palais and beyond. Signing to Parlophone, he had hits with the ballad 'Tenderly' and the rousing theme tune to ITV's hit 1950s serial *The Adventures of Robin Hood* (both produced by George Martin), the latter parodied by Monty Python as *Dennis Moore*,* and wrote Max Bygraves' weird children's hit 'You're A Pink Toothbrush, I'm A Blue Toothbrush' before turning to music publishing.

He and Martin were both keen for The Beatles to record Mitch Murray's 'How Do You Do It' as the follow up to 'Love Me Do', which James had been underwhelmed by – 'just a riff – and which had been under-promoted by EMI's in-house publishing wing, Ardmore & Beechwood. James thought Murray's slight but catchy toe-tapper was 'going to make The Beatles a household name like Harpic'.† He was disappointed then to hear that they wanted to release a song of their own called 'Please Please Me'. But when Brian Epstein brought an acetate to James' tiny Charing Cross office, he was electrified. He immediately rang the producer of 'appointment to view' pop TV show *Thank Your Lucky Stars* and played it to him down the phone. He instantly gave The Beatles a slot the very next week.

It's often said in the music business that publishing issues are what splits bands up and sours their legacy. Few bands and performers even today have the inclination in those thrilling early days of fame and fun to forensically analyse the small print and legalese of their songwriting percentages. That certainly applied to the barely out of their teens Beatles of 1963 as Paul has recalled. 'John and I didn't know you could own songs. We thought they just existed in the air. We could not see how it was possible to own them. We could see owning a house, a guitar or a car, they were physical objects. But a

---

* 'Dennis Moore, Dennis Moore/Galloping through the sward/Dennis Moore, Dennis Moore? And his horse Concorde', etc.

† It did, of course, become a Number 1 for Gerry and The Pacemakers.

song, not being a physical object, we couldn't see how it was possible to have a copyright in it. And therefore, with great glee, publishers saw us coming.'

Rather than the usual one-off publishing deal, James suggested the creation of a company called Northern Songs which would handle all Lennon and McCartney songs henceforward. Financially, this was not appreciably worse than most deals of the time. But it was binding into perpetuity and the devil was lurking in the details.* No one is quite sure of the actual figures of the deal but it is usually thought that, after a 10 per cent 'cream off' for Epstein, the profits would be split with 25 per cent each to Dick James and his account-ant and financial partner Charles Silver, with Lennon and McCartney each receiving 20 per cent. Basic maths will tell you that this meant of course that Paul and John would always lack any power over their own creative handiwork. 'There was always this voting share that could beat us,' said Paul. 'We could only muster 49; they could muster 51.† They could always beat us. John and I were highly surprised to find that even though we'd been promised our own company, it actually was a company within Dick James's company that was to be our own company. And we thought that's not fair at all, but this was just the way they pulled the wool over our eyes.'

The arrangement that Dick James and The Beatles arrived at concerning their publishing is now the matter of some debate among Beatle historians. Did he show admirable confidence, foresight and canniness in backing them into the unknowable future? Or did he just screw them over? The Beatles certainly felt the latter. Paul called it a 'slave deal' while John seethed that he had created a 'fucking multimillion music industry company Northern Songs not owned by us … He actually said that he made us. I'd like to hear Dick

---

* This phrase is actually a misquotation of Dutch designer Mies van der Rohe's 'god is in the details', and I have just misquoted him again.

† The maths here is wonky I know but the point holds.

James music … please just play me some!!' It is not recorded whether at this point anyone played John 'You're A Pink Toothbrush, I'm A Blue Toothbrush' or the Robin Hood theme.

Even as he chatted with them at Twickenham about acquiring the rights to 'Ain't Misbehavin'', 'Lazy Bones' and the rest, James was considering selling his share of Northern Songs to ATV's Lew Grade who had long coveted them. James had been increasingly anxious about Lennon's attitude and behaviour, and Yoko Ono's hold over him, evidenced as he saw it in their joint heroin use, naked album sleeves and new habit of performatively sitting inside bags. Crucially, he was nervous about the effect it might have on the value of his shares. By March, James and Charles Silver decided to sell to ATV for roughly one and a half million pounds, without giving John and Paul advance warning and thus the chance to buy them out. ATV now owned over a third of the company. James told the *Daily Mirror* 'What I did, I did in their interests as well as mine, and the rest of the shareholders. I hope that one day, I can justify my decision to them. I was not acting behind their backs. I believed I was acting for them and for the whole future good of the company … I just hope that our friendship can go on. I have great faith in the boys, but I felt that, as magnificent songwriters as they are, I had to relieve them of the responsibility for the company's future affairs.' George Martin saw it differently. 'I told him he was a rat.'

A few months before he dropped into the Twickenham *Get Back* Sessions, James, at the encouragement of his son Steven, had signed a young pianist from Pinner called Reg Dwight and his Lincolnshire lyricist partner Bernie Taupin, a meeting cornily dramatised in the Elton John biopic, *Rocketman*. The film, sanctioned and developed by its subject, depicts Dick James (played by Stephen Graham) as a cigar-touting, foul-mouthed, philistine concerned solely with sales and money, who at one point calls John a 'fucking poofter'. James's son Steven, perhaps unsurprisingly, was not pleased with this portrayal. 'They basically depict my father in the film completely opposite to the way he was in real life. It's rather upset me because my father was a nice guy ... They have turned him into this stereotype with a big fat cigar, swearing every other word ... He just wasn't like that. He never got aggressive. He never lost his temper. He never swore. But that's how they have made him in the film.'

Did Dick James, like the Nottinghamshire bandit he once sang of, steal from the rich? Or merely take his share for helping them get that way? Like the tale of Robin Hood himself, it seems to depend on which folklore you prefer.

51. Marsha Albert

'Why can't we have music like that here in America?'

George Orwell thought that 'only by resurrecting our own memories can we realise how incredibly distorted is the child's vision of the world'. Many of my earliest memories are Beatles related and though indubitably distorted they are vivid; being stood on a seat back aged three to watch tiny figures being screamed at when they played Wigan ABC cinema, hearing 'Can't Buy Me Love' in my cousin Eileen's bedroom in Swinton. Strangest of all though was being told by Anne Rudd in the playground of St Jude's Primary School that Paul McCartney was dead.

The rumours that Paul had died in a car crash at some point in the mid-Sixties and been replaced by a lookalike, which had swirled pointlessly for years, reached an apogee on 12 October 1969 when a Detroit DJ called Russ Gibb devoted a phone in (and later a two-hour special) to 'confirming' the story. Gibb explained how The Beatles had done this to spare the world's anguish, but now, racked with guilt, offered clues to the grim truth such as various messages hidden in songs like 'Paul is dead man, miss him, miss him, miss him' on 'I'm So Tired' and 'I buried Paul' on 'Strawberry Fields Forever' (a bit 'on the nose'). Paul's bare feet (or rather those of the imposter replacement) on the *Abbey Road* sleeve were also a sign of mourning in Sicily apparently. As the critic Edmund Wilson declared haughtily of Tolkien's popularity 'some people have a lifelong appetite for juvenile trash'. (See also 'Jim Morrison is alive', 'Bill Gates is monitoring you through Covid vaccines' etc.)

Gibb may have been talking rubbish, but at least he was talking about them. For the first two years of their career, US DJs had little time for The Beatles; in fact, had probably never even heard of them thanks to Capitol Records, EMI's US subsidiary's, complete indifference to them, despite their success here and the urgings of George Martin and Brian Epstein. Thus, on 17 December 1963, as they rehearsed and recorded in London for a two-hour Christmas special on the BBC, they had as yet never been heard on American radio. That was about to change.

Marsha Albert, a ninth grader at Sligo Junior High, Silver Spring, Maryland, had been watching Walter Cronkite on the CBS Evening News on 10 December when she saw an item on a phenomenon sweeping the UK called Beatlemania and the mayhem they had caused at shows in Bournemouth. Most of Cronkite's adult viewers would have watched with amused bafflement. But 15-year-old Marsha was captivated by the boys and their music and immediately fired off a letter to DJ Caroll James at her local radio station WWDC in Washington DC asking 'Why can't we have music like that here in America?' Intrigued, James 'pulled strings and called in favours', wangled a copy of 'I Want To Hold Your Hand' from a BOAC flight attendant and invited Marsha Albert to the studio to introduce it, reading from a few scribbled lines on the back of a traffic bulletin.

'So, Marsha Albert of Dublin Drive, Silver Spring has the honour of introducing something brand new and exclusive here at WWDC. Marsha, the microphone here on the Caroll James show is yours ...'

'Ladies and gentlemen for the first time on the air in the United States, here are The Beatles singing "I Want To Hold Your Hand".'

Calls were coming in before the opening riff had ended, as DJ James recalled: 'The switchboard just totally went wild, every line lit up ... (I) played it again in the next hour which is something I'd never done before.' He went on to play it every night that week, often interjecting with a station 'ident' to prevent rival networks taping it and acquiring a bootleg copy of what had become the hottest record in America. Previously unenthusiastic Capitol record executives were stung into action, bringing forward a proposed New Year release (which they had only agreed to at the insistence of EMI's UK chairman, Joseph Lockwood) to 27 December. Within three days, it had sold a quarter of a million copies across the States. By 10 January it had topped one million. By 13 January it was selling ten thousand copies an hour in New York City alone and by 16 January it was Number 1 across America.

As Wille Dixon once sang 'the men don't know, but the little girls understand'.

52. Nicky Byrne

'Ten per cent is better than nothing.'

What was waiting beneath the tree for the kids at Christmas in 1963? A Matchbox car or Sindy doll? The new board game, Diplomacy, perhaps ('the game of political intrigue and military power in Imperial Europe')? Or maybe a wig or sweater or plastic guitar or jigsaw or belt bearing the image and name of The Beatles, flotsam and jetsam from a tide of tat that was flooding the British and American markets. There was no such thing as 'merch' then which is perhaps why Brian Epstein made the business mistake of his life, indeed one of the greatest commercial blunders of all time and one that would haunt him till he died.

The David Jacobs that was a household name in most British households in the early Sixties was the suave and debonair presenter of *Juke Box Jury*. But his solicitor namesake was just as famous within showbiz and media circles. This David Jacobs, six foot plus, flamboyantly coiffured and made-up, discretely if obviously 'homosexual', had a pink-and-maroon Rolls-Royce and kept a table on permanent reserve at Le Caprice in Piccadilly. His string of famous clients included Judy Garland, Diana Dors, Lionel Bart, theatre director Peter Hall, Laurence Olivier and Gene Vincent, and he was the man who helped celebrity pianist Liberace go 'crying all the way to the bank' after winning him damages in wake of the the *Daily Mirror*'s bizarre and clearly homophobic description of him as a 'luminous, quivering, giggling, fruit-flavoured, mincing, ice-covered heap of mother-love'.

In the winter of 1963, directly prior to the first momentous US visit, Epstein found himself overwhelmed and baffled by the mushrooming volume of merchandising requests. So he tasked his lawyer Jacobs, with whom he had much in common – monied, dandified, doting Jewish matriarch, gay – with the problem. Jacobs in turn recruited an old Etonian amateur racing river, former Guards officer and playboy member of the self-styled Kings Road Rats called Nicky Byrne, whose qualification for the job seems to have chiefly been that he and his ex-wife Kiki, a skiwear designer, threw fabulous parties. After some qualms, Byrne agreed, later saying, 'They couldn't wait to get somebody else to do this, because they were in a mess themselves.' He invited five friends in, all from his 'set', all in their twenties and none with experience in the field.

In December 1963, Byrne took over Stramsact in the UK and then set up Seltaeb (Beatles spelt backwards) in the United States to handle the merchandising. When he went to sign the contract in Jacobs' office, Jacobs asked Byrne what percentage rate he wanted and Byrne, as a crazy opening gambit one assumes, asked for 90 per cent. Astonishingly, Jacobs agreed, advising Epstein '10 per cent is better than nothing'. As far as Epstein was concerned these hats, badges, clocks, pens, plastic wigs and assorted ephemera represented merely good PR and exposure, although a cursory spot of research would have revealed that Elvis Presley grossed twenty million dollars in 'merch' in 1957 alone.

When Epstein met Byrne in New York in early 1964, he was impressed not just by his gorgeous astrakhan coat but also the cheque he was handed for $9,700, a handsome return it seemed, especially when you consider he'd agreed a fee of ten grand for all three *Ed Sullivan Show* appearances.* Epstein assumed Byrne had yet to take his cut and asked what Byrne was owed. 'Nothing, Brian,' Byrne replied. 'That's your 10 per cent.'

---

* Byrne has claimed that he was responsible for the welcome they received at JFK when arriving in the US for *The Ed Sullivan Show*, getting a local radio station to promise a free t-shirt for every kid who went to the airport. 'For all Capital and CBS cared, they were just going to walk off the plane and go to the hotel. Nobody would even have known they were in America.'

As the magnitude of the money Byrne was making became apparent, Epstein's mood began to sour. Suddenly the posh coat made sense, as did the permanent suites for the five Seltaeb partners at the Drake Hotel, Park Avenue, the offices on 5th Avenue, the two limos on 24-hour call and the private helicopter hired to ferry potential partners to and from the airport. Essentially, Seltaeb couldn't stop making money. They had already sold more than a million t-shirts made by the Reliant Shirt Co. Remco, one of America's largest toy manufacturers, had bought the licence for Beatle dolls, produced one hundred thousand and had orders for half a million more. The (frankly ludicrous) Beatles wig was so popular that even the thirty-five thousand leaving the Lowell company's factories a day were nowhere near enough. Then there were the eggcups, scarves, mugs, bath water, bubble gum, ten million sticks of liquorice, even empty cans of purported 'Beatle Breath'. Seltaeb licensed, and took a cut from, over one hundred and fifty Beatle 'products' during that first frenzy of US Beatlemania. It's believed that Epstein's rash decision subsequently cost The Beatles an estimated one hundred million dollars. No wonder that a horrified Epstein felt he couldn't tell John, Paul, George or Ringo. He was well on the way to losing them a billion dollars.

Epstein immediately forced re-negotiations, finally achieving by August 1964 a more realistic 49 per cent. An orgy of suing and counter suing and legal wrangling continued until Epstein's untimely death in 1967. Jacobs was later implicated in a Panamanian coup and, extraordinarily, a crucifixion on Hampstead Heath. He too was found dead in mysterious circumstances in his garage in December 1968. Conversely, Byrne retired to a yacht in the Bahamas and later a country pile in Wiltshire. Another of Byrne's chums in the venture, Peregrine Nicholas Eliot, 10th Earl of St Germans, later founded the chaotic Cornish festival Elephant Fayre which became the extremely chi chi Port Eliot Literature Fest.

For me, the really fascinating thing about this whole bizarre, chaotic, salutary story is the light it sheds on the relationship between The Beatles and the 'aristocracy'. The English upper class seemed to have courted them and craved their energy and glamour but clearly felt them to be little more than trophies to be exploited for profit and amusement. One obvious if perhaps glibly 'Spartist' reading then of the Seltaeb debacle is that it's all typically illustrative of how the monied class exploits the labour and skill of the proletariat. But the really dismaying 'takeaway' is that, when we look at the cronyism and corruption that still dominates British life, most obviously during the Covid pandemic, the rigid, classist society that The Beatles and their vibrant, gifted working-class peers seemed set fair to destroy, still persists; the old boys' network and that old school tie, which is not the one of Quarry Bank or the Liverpool Institute but of Eton.

53. Melanie Coe

'I can't listen to the song. It's just too sad for me.'

Fourth October 1963. Television House in London. While three of The Beatles are mugging their way through a cute/cheesy tableau with Helen Shapiro miming to her song 'Look Who It Is', Paul is in a different part of the studio where, ever amenable, he's been roped into judging which of four young women mimes and dances best to Brenda Lee's raucous 'Let's Jump The Broomstick' ('You're keen on budding Brenda Lees are you, Paul … I'll bet you are' leers host Keith Fordyce, creepily). After some frenzied frugging, Paul extends the prize of an LP and a brisk handshake to his winner, Contestant Number 4, Melanie Coe, after which she exits his life forever. Or so he, her and everyone thought.

Four years after her brush with Beatledom, Melanie's teenage life was less rosy. Seventeen, pregnant and fearing the wrath of her father, who 'gave me everything but never told me he loved me', she slipped away from her affluent parents' desirable house in Stamford Hill, North London with her croupier boyfriend. This detail though did not appear in the *Daily Mail* story about Melanie's disappearance that Paul McCartney read on 27 February 1967. Inspired, Paul set about writing 'She's Leaving Home', recorded the next month and one of the jewels in *Sgt. Pepper*'s crown.

In the *Lyrics* book, Paul says 'This one is based somewhat on a newspaper report of a missing girl. The headline was something like "A-Level Girl Dumps Car and Vanishes". So, I set out to imagine what might have happened, the sequence of events. The detail of leaving a note that she "hoped would say more" is one of the strongest moments in the song … in addition to the newspaper report, I'm pretty sure another influence was *The Wednesday Play*. It was a weekly television play that often addressed "big" social issues. It's the kind of thing people would be discussing at the bus stop on Thursday morning. It was a very important part of the week.'

Melanie was discovered in Bayswater a week later. Her father forcibly repatriated her and arranged a discrete abortion. She married at 18, later divorced, went to live in LA where she had a relationship with Burt Ward (Robin in the campy Sixties TV version of *Batman*), came home, re-married, had kids and became an antiques dealer. Paul did not know till decades later that his chosen Brenda Lee impersonator and the 'A-Level Girl' who dumped her car and vanished were one and the same.

By any reasonable reckoning, 'She's Leaving Home' is a masterpiece. Ian MacDonald called it 'imperishable popular art'. Composer Ned Rorem thought it 'equal to any song that Schubert ever wrote'. Paul played it on the piano to Brian Wilson in the hope of jolting him out of his post *Pet Sounds* torpor and made him cry, for several reasons one imagines. Lennon's ghostly parental Greek chorus is inspired and haunting, but the whole arrangement is superb. But for once, it was not by George Martin, busy with Cilla Black, but Mike Leander, later to write and produce the early, extraordinary and now utterly verboten Gary Glitter singles. Paul later commented regretfully, 'George Martin was offended that I used another arranger. He was busy and I was itching to get on with it; I was inspired. I think George had a lot of difficulty forgiving me for that. It hurt him; I didn't mean to.'

'I was surprised and hurt,' Martin admitted. Leander was paid eighteen pounds for the arrangement.

No Beatle plays an instrument on the record. The harp is played by Stella Bromberg, the first woman on a Beatles track. Rapturously beautiful as it is, Melanie Coe 'can't listen to the song. It's just too sad for me. My parents died a long time ago and we were never resolved. That line, "She's leaving home after living alone for so many years" is so weird to me because that's why I left. I was so alone. How did Paul know that those were the feelings that drove me towards … one-night stands with rock stars? I don't think he can have possibly realised that he'd met me when I was 13 on *Ready Steady Go!*'

One final thing. The Beatles had already told us in song that 'money can't buy me love'. Yet according to 'She's Leaving Home' 'fun is the one thing that money can't buy'. Both statements are untrue and, furthermore, contradictory. We'll let them off, shall we?

54. Peter Yolland

'Really unfunny!'

Readers of a certain vintage may remember a programme called *The Tomorrow People*, a teatime drama about a group of teen harbingers from a new race of 'homo superior' who could 'jaunt' through time and space and boasting one of the greatest opening TV sequences ever featuring paranoia inducing graphics and Dudley Simpson's amazing theme.

Earlier that day in 1974, younger siblings might have enjoyed Geoffrey, Bungle and the colossally irritating Zippy on pre-teen favourite *Rainbow*, or perhaps its musical spin-off *Rod, Jane and Freddy*. A few years later, as students perhaps, they may have relaxed with a recreational 'cigarette' and an episode of the dreamlike puppet show *Button Moon* about an ensemble of sentient spacefaring kitchen utensils led by benign dictator 'Mr Spoon'. The man who directed all of the above may have been helped by his previous experience working with talkative, combative, wacky, spaced out, adorable characters. In 1963 and 1964, Peter Yolland was the mastermind behind the very odd thing that was The Beatles' Christmas Shows.

Yolland had just completed a series of Schools' TV French Language programmes when his agent Joe Collins approached him with an offer to produce a Beatles Christmas show at The Astoria Finsbury Park. Though he had some pantomime experience, it would leave him just six weeks to write and rehearse the whole thing, so it's testament to The Beatles' ever-growing stardom and cachet that he agreed. Dialogue was written within days. Then, one Sunday night in mid-November, he travelled to The Hippodrome Birmingham, where the band were playing, to record The Beatles reading some linking dialogue. This would be played out over The Astoria's PA to the audience. Quite a large audience in fact. Tickets went on sale on 21 October 1963, and by 16 November all one hundred thousand tickets for the sixteen-night, two-shows-a-night run had sold out.

Clearly, the whole Christmas show idea was Epstein's, a man with thespian tendencies and theatrical aspirations; indeed, his name appears above The Beatles on the souvenir programme. Effectively, the show seems to have been something between a panto, a concert, a night at the music hall and a student revue. In between very brief appearances by the likes of The Barron Knights, Tommy Quickly and Billy J. Kramer and The Dakotas, The Beatles would appear in a series of what must have been fairly excruciating – they certainly thought so, see below – comedic skits. In one, the youthful and baby-faced George was cast as a helpless heroine in a cod Victorian melodrama sketch, tied to the railway tracks by John as wicked Sir Jasper only to be rescued by 'Fearless Paul the signalman'. Despite their stilted acting, the crowd went predictably and volubly nuts. 'Let's face it,' said McCartney, 'they would have laughed if we had just sat there and read the Liverpool telephone directory.' PR Tony Barrow recalled 'The Beatles were never much for rehearsing. That never really mattered as far as songs were concerned, but the fact that they were so bad at doing the sketches was an added extra for the show. It was organised chaos, but it was very funny chaos.'

One audience member recalled that at one point 'The four Beatles came on as doctors, in white coats and stethoscopes, and John was wearing glasses (the first time he'd worn them in public, I think). A sign came up "Three out of four doctors ..." (obviously referring to a current advert for medicines or such). Then Paul, Ringo and George left the stage, leaving John alone. Another sign came up saying "Leaves one doctor". Really unfunny!' Perhaps mercifully, The Beatles were each evening's final act, with an eleven-song set, performances lasting twenty-five minutes. After the Christmas Eve evening's performance, The Beatles and the largely northern cast and crew flew to Liverpool to spend Christmas Day with their families then straight back on Boxing Day morning in a private Viking aircraft chartered for £400 by Brian Epstein.

Funny or not, the Astoria shows were such a success that the format was repeated the following year at the Hammersmith Odeon. This time the supporting bill included new R&B sensation The Yardbirds with Eric Clapton. After them came a sketch featuring The Beatles as Antarctic explorers searching for the Abominable Snowman. Then Elkie Brooks, Freddy and The Dreamers and ubiquitous Epstein stablemates Sounds Incorporated before The Beatles closed the show again. Plans for a third festive season were hatched. The Beatles reportedly grew to hate the Abominable Snowman section so much that they refused to do it, or indeed anything like it, ever again.

I find these shows fascinating as a glimpse into an England and its entertainment culture that The Beatles themselves were in the process of dismantling; an end of the pier world of greasepaint and uneasy comedy, the milieu of Osborne's seedy Archie Rice. Certainly, each of the shows featured a then beloved if patently unsettling, now disgraced family 'entertainer' implicated in serious child sexual abuse. Jimmy Savile appeared in the second, while in the first it was Rolf Harris. His attempts to explain the role of the sun in Aboriginal spirituality, as an intro to his hit 'Sun Arise', were hampered by daft offstage interjections by Lennon over the PA. Later he confronted The Beatles in their dressing room: 'If you want to fuck up your own act, do it! But don't fuck up mine.' As it was, Rolf was going to do that himself fairly comprehensively several decades later.

By the way, 'Sun Arise', that droney anthem to Aboriginal sun worship of 1961 (later covered by Alice Cooper of all people), was produced by George Martin. He thought it was 'very boring'.

55. William Mann

'Aeolian cadences.'

By tradition, the British intellectual distrusts enthusiasm. Irony, sarcasm and languor have always been prized above joy, a pose that persists to this day. So when a classical music critic called William Mann wrote in the pages of 'journal of record' *The Times* at the end of that astonishing year that 'the outstanding English composers of 1963 must seem to have been John Lennon and Paul McCartney' and asserted 'one gets the impression that they think simultaneously of harmony and melody, so firmly are the major tonic sevenths and ninths built into their tunes, and the flat submediant key switches, so natural is the Aeolian cadence at the end of "Not A Second Time" (the chord progression which ends Mahler's "Song of the Earth")', the sniggers and guffaws were loud and immediate, largely from people who knew a lot less than Mann or The Beatles about how music works. As Clive James puts it in a brilliant essay, 'A Cavern in Arcadia', 'It was the joke of the decade, in a quiet way. People who had never listened to The Beatles quaked with silent laughter. People who had never listened to Schubert quaked along with them.'

If anything gives the lie to the notion that rock and pop music is innately more progressive than the 'reactionary' and 'conservative' classical world, it's how some of the various practitioners felt about The Beatles. While Sinatra sneered about 'kid singers wearing mops of hair thick enough to hide a crate of melons' and Noel Coward blustered that they were 'totally devoid of talent' and Lou Reed thought they were 'garbage', classical composers and critics, maybe smarter or perhaps just less bitter and envious, were often (and often very quickly) more embracing.

American composer Ned Rorem said in 1967 that The Beatles were 'colleagues' of his, 'speaking the same language with different accents'. Despite having never been on a *Now* album, Schubert was always getting dragged in as the sine qua non of songwriting excellence with Wilfred Mellors too claiming The Beatles were 'the greatest songwriters since Schubert'. Leonard Bernstein was an admirer and Peter Maxwell Davies was one of many modern musicians who chose a Beatles' track as a Desert Island Disc, saying of 'Yesterday', 'it's an inverted canon that works perfectly as a canon within itself ... there's so much more implied than is actually written. It's pregnant with further musical and literary meaning.' More recently, composer Howard Goodall has boldly asserted 'The Beatles almost single-handedly rescued the western musical system.'

It's William Mann who gets remembered, though, for those Aeolian cadences, whose mention provoked a very British cultural cringe at anything deemed 'pretentious' or hifalutin. Even Lennon felt he had to join in: 'I still don't know what it means at the end ... But it made us acceptable to the intellectuals. It worked and we were flattered.' Of those cadences he said 'to this day I don't have any idea what they are. They sound like exotic birds.'

William sounds a lot more fun than his detractors. He was a jaunty but informed regular on Radio 3 and even appeared on *Juke Box Jury*. He was still a Beatles fan five years later when he reviewed the *White Album*, wittily and perceptively, in *The Times* on its release in 1968. But look again how his 1963 eulogy to The Beatles ends:

'These are some of the qualities that make one wonder with interest what The Beatles, and particularly Lennon and McCartney, will do next, and if America will spoil them or hold on to them, and if their next record will wear as well as the others. They have brought a distinctive and exhilarating flavour into a genre of music that was in danger of ceasing to be music at all.'

William Mann was more than just an enthusiast. He was right.

1964

56. The Maysles brothers

'Who are The Beatles?
Are they any good?'

A small apartment in midtown Manhattan on the night of 9 February 1964. School books are scattered on the modest table, a tea service is neatly stacked on a dresser, dishes dry on the draining board. Centre stage are three young sisters variously between about 5 and 15. Like most of America on this late winter night, they are enraptured by something on the TV set in the corner of the room where The Beatles are appearing on *The Ed Sullivan Show*. But their response is not the full-throated tribal frenzy of the concert hall; it is, if anything, a sorcery even stranger and more powerful. They are transfixed, held by both a communal spell and secret inner epiphanies of delight and desire. Something is shifting inside them; the same stirrings that are being felt by millions of young people across the land at exactly this moment; a seismic wave that will shake America into a new way of being.

This scene is one of many quietly brilliant sequences in the movie *The Beatles: The First US Visit** by the Maysles brothers. Albert and David Maysles made over thirty ground-breaking films that helped revolutionise the documentary as we know it. Direct cinema, Kino Pravda, Cinéma Vérité, Fly on the Wall, however we style it, they were pioneers and masters of that new visual art. Two of their films, *Salesman* and *Grey Gardens*, are preserved in the Library of Congress. But nothing they did bettered their 1964 record of The Beatles' first visit to US shores. For devotees of pop culture, this short film has the same historical heft as if there had been a movie camera at the battle of Thermopylae or to film the Colossus of Rhodes or, a more appropriate analogy perhaps, when the Mayflower docked at Plymouth Rock with its eager, expectant cargo of English travellers, come to change the course of the New World.

While The Beatles were in the air over the Atlantic aboard Pan Am flight 101, the Maysles brothers received an urgent call from Granada TV in Manchester. 'They said The Beatles were arriving in two hours in New York at Idlewild Airport.† Would we like to make a film of them? I put my hand over the phone and asked my brother "Who are The Beatles? Are they any good?"' When David, the pop buff, assured Albert, the classical fan, that they were, the deal was sealed. They dashed to the recently rechristened JFK airport and watched the black speck of The Beatles' plane descend towards New York. 'We didn't know whether it was gonna be five people or 5,000 people showing up at the airport … it was of course much nearer the latter … It was like they were from another planet.'

They would spend the next five whirlwind days with them, unobtrusively recording almost their every move on the custom-built handheld cameras and sound gear that allowed them to be discreet,

---

* Originally *What's Happening! The Beatles In America*.

† It had actually been renamed John F Kennedy airport some five weeks earlier.

mobile and intimate in a cool 'underground' style The Beatles warmed to. Albert's dictum was always, 'As a documentarian, you are an observer, an author but not a director, a discoverer, not a controller.' The results are astonishingly intimate and revealing, from the early shots of them in the madness of their Plaza Hotel suite to the hysteria on their return to Heathrow. Packed into its initial eighty-one-minute cut are many incandescent moments; Ringo being endearing with the little girl on the train to Washington, the boys' genuine, gleeful interest in the Maysles' custom-built equipment, the feverish, thrilling ambience of the night at the Peppermint Lounge and the nasty, supercilious milieu of the ambassador's reception in which they are treated like animals by assembled chinless wonders. There is a beautiful, almost stately section where the boys faff about in their suite, erratically getting their stuff together before heading down to *The Ed Sullivan* studio. One by one they leave, then return, until finally Ringo looks back at the camera and heads off, unaware of his appointment with destiny and the era-changing event he is about to be part of.

Some of my favourite sections were excised from the original, such as the three sourpuss Freshman types sneering that they would 'rather see a good jazz show ... Mingus or Mulligan ... not The Beatles'. Or a clearly slightly drunk Paul being dropped back at the Plaza by Murray 'The K' (of whom there is slightly too much, it has to be said) after an incredible day and night. How did the Maysles get such access? By being relatively young, underground and groovy, and by being natural and warm. 'It's the empathy. It's the love if you will that you share that gets you the access and we liked these guys a lot.' Not even this though could circumvent the union rules that prevented them from getting into the Sullivan recording itself. So, in what turned out to be a genius move, they walked down the street a couple of blocks until they heard music coming from an apartment, knocked on the door and were allowed in to film the Gonzales family watching the show, as described above.

Forty years later, in 2004, the Maysles met two of the Gonzales sisters, Enid and Eva, again at a Beatles Gala at the Plaza Hotel to celebrate the DVD launch of the remastered documentary. 'I was such a Paul fanatic' said Enid who moved to Puerto Rico along with Eva over twenty years before. 'I would sit there for hours playing their songs over and over.' Eva was raising two teenagers while Enid was now a secretary with two grandsons. She was working on the fifth floor of the Roosevelt hospital on the night John Lennon was pronounced dead there. Half a century before, she had watched him and his friends on the night, as Albert Mayles put it, 'They'd taken another country in their hands … in the end, they were just kids. But there has to be some kind of magic quality to explain how they could take over a whole nation.'

57. Ed Sullivan

'The most repulsive group of men I have ever seen.'

Two things strike one forcibly watching The Beatles' first live US TV appearance that February.* The first is the sheer brio and energy of the performance, still astonishingly thrilling over half a century on. The second is how deeply odd Ed Sullivan is. Sweaty and Nixonian, awkward and curmudgeonly, he seems comprehensively ill-suited for his chosen career. *Time* magazine said of him 'What exactly is Ed Sullivan's talent? He doesn't sing. He doesn't dance. He doesn't tell jokes … His wincesome looks and quirky mannerisms – such as hunching his shoulders and reeling around like Quasimodo doing the lindy – still bring serious letters from shut-ins commending his courage for appearing despite such an obviously bad case of Bell's palsy. [He is] a stone-faced monument just off the boat from Easter Island. He moves like a sleepwalker; his smile is that of a man sucking a lemon; his speech is frequently lost in a thicket of syntax.'

Dip into almost any Sullivan televisual link and I guarantee you will be staggered by how unappealing and robotic he appears.† And yet he stayed on prime-time US TV for several geological epochs. Maybe regular guest comic Alan King was right when he said 'Ed does nothing, but he does it better than anyone else in television.'

Sullivan booked The Beatles for his show, he claimed, after he and

---

* It was not their very first US TV appearance. On 18 November 1963, NBC aired a four-minute report on Beatlemania. Days later, on 22 November, CBS Morning News ran a five-minute segment on the craze that was sweeping England.

† Exhibit A. The Supremes and The Temptations, 19 November 1967. Two of the greatest vocal groups in the history of pop music come together to sing each other's hits. Ed manages to introduce it with less verve than the voice that says you are fourteenth in the queue for car insurance.

his wife were amazed by the riotous scenes at London Airport in November 1963 involving 'hundreds and hundreds of youngsters. I asked which celebrity was arriving and they told us the teenagers were awaiting The Beatles … always on the lookout for talent I decided The Beatles would be a good TV attraction for our show, so I contacted Brian Epstein their manager.' This is partly true and partly Sullivan's classic penchant for self-aggrandisement. He may have witnessed the mayhem at Heathrow first hand, but it was the show's talent co-ordinator Jack Babb and PR man Peter Pritchard who persuaded him to book them after initial reluctance on his part. On 11 November 1963 in the Domenico Hotel, New York (where Ed and his family lived), the deal was sealed with a handshake between Sullivan and Epstein. The figures differ from account to account but as Sullivan recalled with his trademark wisecracking vivacity, 'We agreed on $10,000 for three shows plus five round-trip plane tickets plus their expenses for room and board.'

A few years back, I wrote and presented a documentary about The Beatles' *Ed Sullivan Show* appearance and its significance. Dennis Locorriere, singer with Dr Hook, told me how he sat in his class-room with a transistor radio under the desk and an earpiece listening to updates on the group's progress; 'And The Beatles are over Greenland!' Writer Roger Steffen remarked that a nation 'punch drunk' from the assassination of JFK just four months previously was desperate and ready for the joy and energy of 'these bright well-scrubbed, funny irreverent young men from England'.

On that first appearance, they opened with three numbers; 'All My Loving', 'Till There Was You' and 'She Loves You'. Later they close the show with 'I Saw Her Standing There' and 'I Want To Hold Your Hand'. As Blondie's Gary Valentine explained to me, 'It was very much a family type show supposedly with something for everyone; an unfunny comedian or a guy who could make a chicken talk.' So, in the gap between their sets, as America reeled with delight and the world changed for ever, viewers were treated to a Dutch magician, various comedic turns and larger than life Welsh musical stalwart Tessie O'Shea alongside ads for Aeroshave ('keeps drenching your beard right through the shave'), Anacin painkillers and Liquid Wax. During 'Till There Was You' the camera pans to each Beatle in turn. On reaching John, a caption appears that will become legendary (and a long-standing joke during my time at *Q* magazine whenever a less than pulchritudinous male pop person was pictured); 'Sorry Girls, He's Married'. Locorriere recalled 'Every time the camera would go close up on Ringo behind the drums bobbing his head back and forth from side to side, the whole place would erupt in laughter. But it wasn't mocking laughter. It was like, damn he looks like he's having a great time. Doesn't this music feel good? They came in like a freight train and left like a jet plane.'

After The Beatles have finished their set, Sullivan gesticulates stiffly, yelling charmlessly, 'Quiet! You promised!' Later he expresses his gratitude … to the New York Police Department. *Rolling Stone*'s verdict rings true. 'The most fun-obsessed civilization in human history comes face to face with The Beatles, and realizes they've been doing it all wrong until now. Everything else on *The Ed Sullivan Show* – puppets, acrobats, jugglers, magicians – will never cut it again. It's like a donkey race, and The Beatles showed up in a Maserati … They don't just make the rest of the show look corny and obsolete – they make it look cynical, phony, like nobody else has their hearts in it.'

That is not quite fair. Some of them were just unprepared and overwhelmed. The comedy duo and married couple Brill and McCall bombed with a sketch about theatrical agencies that Sullivan had unwisely tinkered with. They look stunned as they take their bows to a smattering of applause. 'We were in a daze,' says Brill. 'It was an out-of-body experience. I know we were onstage and I know we were doing something, but that's it.' 'It was a nightmare,' adds McCall. 'We just about wanted to kill ourselves.' Brill has still never watched the performance. 'If I watch it, I'm going to be right back on that stage.' Though the appearance didn't do much to advance their career, ultimately, McCall said, it was 'an honour' to be a part of it. 'We were there when the world changed,' she said.*

A troop of Swedish acrobats closed proceedings. For the whole sixty minutes of the show, it's said not a single crime was recorded in New York City, unless you count Frank Gorshin's impressions. But while the kids went nuts, the adult American media responded with massively wrongheaded hauteur. *Newsweek* sniffed, 'Visually, they are a nightmare: tight, dandified, Edwardian/Beatnik suits and great pudding bowls of hair. Musically, they are a near-disaster: guitars and drums slamming out a merciless beat that does away with secondary rhythms, harmony, and melody. Their lyrics (punctuated by nutty shouts of "yeah, yeah, yeah!") are a catastrophe, a preposterous farrago of Valentine-card romantic sentiments ... the odds are they will fade away.' The *New York Herald Tribune* pronounced the band '75 per cent publicity, 20 per cent haircut, and 5 per cent lilting lament'. They were 'not merely awful', sneered right-wing windbag William F. Buckley, but 'so unbelievably horrible, so appallingly unmusical ... that they qualify as the crowned heads of anti-music.' One reviewer bemoaned the fact that the girls in the audience were clearly smitten by these long-haired limeys rather than another Ed Sullivan regular, the singer Robert Goulet who they described as far more 'virile and mature' which is pretty weird. David Suskind, a popular talk show host, claimed they were 'the most repulsive group of men I have ever seen', which is even weirder.

Hipper America was captivated, however. Allen Ginsberg danced on a table in a nightclub. Bob Dylan was entranced and the seed of his electric future was sown. A teenage generation of emergent US rock performers sitting agog before their TVs were inspired to form

---

* It was six months before their agent called. Eventually they rebuilt their careers. Among other things, Brill played a Klingon on an episode of *Star Trek* and McCall was a voice-over artist, whose roles include *Ice Age*; 'I think I'm a turtle.'

bands and change America; Tom Petty, Bruce Springsteen, Alice Cooper, Mike Nesmith, Blondie, The Ramones. Seventy-three million people were watching: 40 per cent of the US population, the largest TV audience ever at that point. Britain had not been this influential on its former colony since 1775. It will probably never be as influential again. Sixteen years later, on 8 December 1980, America would exact a terrible price on The Beatles. Better to remember 7 February 1964, the night a nation fell in love.

58. Murray 'The K' Kaufman

'My station manager told me that The Beatles were coming.
I said, "Fine. Get an exterminator."'

'You asked for the Triple Ripple ... Well, here it is (blast of hunting horn) CHAAARRGE!

Triple Ripple! Triple Play! Three In A Row With No Commercial Interruptions! The Beatles have taken control ... CHAARRRRGGE! Here's what's happening baby ... THE BEATLES!!!'

This is how, with the muted understatement that was his stock in trade, Murray Kaufman AKA Murray 'The K' introduced The Beatles to his radio show on WINS, New York. A moment captured vividly in the Maysles brothers' movie of The Beatles' first US visit. Murray sports a jazzy sweater with a bold chevron and strange Homburg with strong Tony Hancock energy. 'Love Me Do' plays while behind him a tacky Beatles promotional item features the lads with idiotically wobbling heads. Seemingly inexhaustible, Murray continues to prattle energetically if incomprehensibly while various feline young women dance, pout, chew gum and generally radiate an air of sultry lassitude. It's a queer tableau, even by the standard of those times, when most entertainment, however goofy, came coated in a light perspiration sheen of showbiz creepiness, a world The Beatles had come to overhaul, or at least, put on hold.

As discussed elsewhere, putative 'fifth Beatles' range from the plausible to the ludicrous. But Murray 'The K' may have been the first to attract the epithet. Kaufman always claimed that he was given the tag unwillingly; 'I think it was Ringo who did it ... One reporter said, "Who's this fellow we see with you all the time?" They answered "Oh, don't you know him? My goodness man. That's the Fifth Beatle." That's where that was picked up. I was tagged with it after that ... I really didn't like it very much, but that was it.' However, in the Maysles movie, we see Murray, almost pleadingly, remark that he would be the fifth Beatle by the end of the week and 'would really like that'.

Kaufman was a former Borscht belt entertainer who is, on the evidence of the Maysles brothers' movie and from the perspective of our more cynical, analytical age, a loudmouth chancer straight from central casting. We see him clinging limpet-like to them at every stage of that first visit: thinning-haired, perspiring, comparatively ancient as he dances alongside Ringo and Ronnie Spector at the Peppermint Lounge, or bellowing inanities on air or gate-crashing their hotel suite for a radio show. His jabbering, nonsensical style is parodied in *The Rutles – All You Need Is Cash* with Bill Murray playing Bill Murray 'The K'.

Initially, he had been sceptical about the group's appeal; 'My station manager told me that The Beatles were coming. I said, "Fine. Get an exterminator."' But he soon embraced them with gusto, tirelessly promoting them, becoming their social secretary and staying in touch for the rest of his life (which ended aged just 60 from cancer). George wrote the foreword to his 1966 biography and he is part of the chorus of celebs (a thought-provoking roster that includes both Petula Clark and Timothy Leary) at John and Yoko's bedside during the recording of 'Give Peace A Chance'. He also conducted what was to be Brian Epstein's last proper interview, a melancholic affair on WOR FM with Epstein initially barely intelligible after necking a fistful of Nembutal and Seconal in his Waldorf Towers hotel suite.

Whether you think The Beatles regarded him as a champion and confidante or an annoying hanger on rather depends on who you believe. Apart from the 'fifth Beatle' stuff – which Epstein loathed to the point of threatening litigation – some say that George asked Kaufman to room with him on that first tour, others that he forced himself on to George. But McCartney has said 'Murray "The K" was the man most on to The Beatle case; he had seen it coming and grabbed hold of it.'

And but for Murray 'The K', they might have missed their first ever US concert. 'I did my radio show right from their hotel room. I wound up taking them out afterwards for dinner, and all that kind of stuff. We got kind of friendly. Then I found out that it was going to snow the next day. They were supposed to take off for their first concert in the U.S., which was in Washington, D.C., so told Brian Epstein he'd better hire a train. I told him to make arrangements to get a special train to get to Washington because they weren't going to be able to fly out of New York tomorrow.' Thanks to Murray, they made it. Twenty-three days later, they would be goofing and wise-cracking on a train once more (with Murray still hanging out just out of shot), but this time for Dick Lester's cameras on the shoot for *A Hard Day's Night*.

59. David Ormsby-Gore

*'I pulled out those little scissors from my purse
and I just went clip, clip, clip.'*

On the first day of the *Lady Chatterley's Lover* obscenity trial, prose-
cution barrister Mervyn Griffith-Jones, the British representative at
the Nuremberg war crimes hearings, turned and asked the jury, 'Is it
a book that you would even wish your wife or servants to read?'

Several jurors burst out laughing; the three women perhaps or the
docker or driver or teacher, none of whom we assume employed
domestic help. The book itself is of course about what happens when
the British aristocracy 'rub up' (literally, in the novel) against the
working classes. When something similar happened at the ambassador's reception for The Beatles' first US gig in Washington, the
coming together was much less fun.

In the silky, frictionless manner of these things, the future William
David Ormsby-Gore, 5th Baron Harlech, Knight Commander of
the Order of Saint Michael and Saint George, Privy Counsellor and
Deputy Lieutenant, left Eton and entered parliament as MP for
Oswestry, then joined Harold Macmillan's cabinet and in 1961 was
appointed ambassador to the US. His route then to the British
Embassy on the fateful night of 11 February 1964, was somewhat
different from Ringo Starr's. But their worlds were about to collide
with infamous results.

The Beatles had just played their first ever concert in America at
the Washington Coliseum, an unheated sports arena with a boxing
ring for a stage. The show was in the round and Ringo was continually, exhaustingly, forced to manhandle his drum kit around to face
each audience section in turn. Straight from the show, the band were
whisked to a gala reception at the British Embassy on Massachusetts
Avenue. They were met privately by Ambassador Ormsby-Gore and

his wife Sylvia and exchanged pleasantries, Ormsby-Gore even laughing good naturedly when Ringo gave him the once over and asked 'So, what do you do?' The cordial mood was not to last.

They were ushered into a black-tie party being staged that night for the National Association for the Prevention of Cruelty to Children and were immediately swamped by the British upper classes at their most superior, boozy and obnoxious. Autographs were gracelessly demanded; one embassy staff member thrust a piece of paper at them demanding 'You'll sign this and like it.' Various debutantes passed nasty, slighting remarks such as 'Look, he can actually write.' They were pressganged into doing the raffle with the injunction 'Come along now and do your stuff.' Matters came to a head (again, literally) when an 18-year-old called Beverly Markovitz snipped off some locks of Ringo's hair. For *Anthology*, he recalled, 'We attended a miserable event in the British Embassy in Washington. In the early Sixties there was still a huge disparity between people from the north of England and "people from embassies" ... But we went, God knows why. Maybe because we'd suddenly become ambassadors and they wanted to see us, and I think Brian liked the idea ... We were standing around saying, "Hi, that's very nice," and having a drink, and someone came up behind me and snipped a piece of my hair off ... I just swung round with a "What the hell do you think you are doing?"'

'People were sort of touching us as we walked past' remembered Lennon 'that kind of thing ... we were supposed to put up with all sorts of s**t from Lord Mayors and their wives and be touched and pawed like *A Hard Day's Night* only a million more times. At the American Embassy, the British Embassy in Washington, or wherever it was, some bloody animal cut Ringo's hair ... I walked out of that. Swearing at all of them and I just left in the middle of it.'

In Cynthia Lennon's book, *A Twist of Lennon*, she states, 'The true blue British high society abroad treated them like freaks as only the upper-class British at their worst could do.' Even George Martin, exemplar of patrician decorum, was moved to say in his autobiography that the event was 'full of the full quota of chinless wonders (who) behaved abominably'. Clearly to these stalwart members of the British ruling class The Beatles were the children of the lower orders. Worse, they were the runts of their kind who possessed the temerity to rise to fame and riches by virtue of talent rather than privilege, and breach the citadel that is 'high society'. Photographer Harry Benson, travelling with The Beatles, recalled, 'They were very sad. They looked as if they wanted to cry, John in particular. They weren't pugnacious. They were humiliated.'

The Ormsby-Gores, at least, seem to have had the good grace to be embarrassed by their peers, Mrs Ormsby-Gore telling them as they left: 'I really am terribly sorry about the scene in the ballroom.' Word of The Beatles' ill treatment travelled back to the UK to the concern of the Foreign Office. Conservative MP Joan Quennell asked Foreign Secretary Rab Butler to investigate but was told 'the suggestion they were manhandled by anyone is untrue'. Brian Epstein, meekly deferential, later wrote to thank the Ormsby-Gores 'for a lovely evening'.

The events in the Ormsby-Gore residence that night, so illustrative of how The Beatles were simultaneously courted and despised by the British upper classes, made The Beatles further mistrustful of their so-called betters and even less likely to dance attendance on their favours. It also has two fascinating postscripts.

The first reminds us that gilded lives may not be the happiest. David Ormsby-Gore became Lord Harlech on the death of his brother in a car crash. Then his wife too was killed in a car crash in 1967. Always close to the Kennedys, he was a pallbearer at Robert Kennedy's funeral in 1968 and the same year he proposed marriage, unsuccessfully, to Jackie Kennedy. Daughter Alice fell in love and lived with Eric Clapton although Ormsby-Gore hated their junkie lifestyle, threatening to turn Clapton over to the police if he didn't change his ways. In 1974, his son Julian shot himself in his apartment and Ormsby-Gore himself was killed in a car crash in 1985 attempting to avoid a stray dog on the road. Alice died of a drug overdose in a squalid 'shooting gallery' flat in Bournemouth aged just 43.

Then, fifty years after the rather more glittering scenes at that embassy ball, Beverly Markovitz, now Rubin, re-emerged to tell her local paper, the *Ottawa Sun*, that she'd actually gate-crashed the party and, at some late stage, 'pulled out these little scissors from my purse and I just went clip, clip, clip ...' Far from being chastened or remorseful, she added that if she'd had the time 'I'd do worse ... I mean I'd get a matching set of locks from John, Paul and George, if I was quick enough.'

She still has the locks pasted in a scrapbook. For The Beatles the takeaway was that, as Paul recollected in 2001, 'There's always the guy in the bowler hat who hates what you're doing. He's never going to like it, and he thinks you're offending his sensibilities. But you've got to remember, as we always did, there's the people who work for that guy. There's the young secretaries, the young guys in the office, or the tradesmen or the cleaners ... We always knew that there's the establishment and then there's the working people. And we were the working people.'

60. Buddy Dresner

'The Beatles are in my living room.'

There was definitely something funny going on at Northeast 160th Street, Miami on Saturday, 14 February 1964. Andi and Jeri, the Dresner girls, knew it. Their parents had told them that Uncle Harold from California was coming to dinner, but when the tables were being set for a more formal affair than normal, they became suspicious. Odd things were happening. Mom said Dad had forgotten that it was Valentine's Day, and where had he been all week? Eventually, Dad came clean. He had been assigned by the Miami Police Department as the security detail for The Beatles for their time in Florida for the second *Ed Sullivan Show*. And guess who was coming to dinner?

There's a picture Paul took of Sgt Louis 'Buddy' Dresner included in the *Eyes of The Storm* book and exhibition. He looks every inch the US TV cop with his blue-grey ensemble, badge and, presumably somewhere, gun. 'It was still slightly shocking for us to see a gun in real life, as we didn't have armed police officers back home,' remembered Paul. When The Beatles arrived, little Barry Dresner thought cousin Jess was here. Then a limousine pulled up and his Dad in full uniform and some strangers got out. 'Wait a minute,' I thought. 'This isn't a Jewish holiday. And The Beatles are in my living room.'

Buddy did much to make their brief stay in Miami a happy one. He took them fishing which they proved too squeamish for. According to *Life* magazine, 'he introduced them to gefilte fish, water skiing, Lucille Ball, Jackie Gleason and The Outer Limits'. He invited them back to his home at 160th Street for some suburban home cooking at its best; roast beef, peas, green beans and baked potatoes with side salad rustled up by Mrs Dresner. 'She wasn't fazed,' said Buddy proudly. 'It was a dynamite dinner.' Jeri drops a hot potato on George's lap while serving. He laughs. Neighbour Debbie Nelson (11) who has been allowed over under oath of secrecy stares mutely and adoringly at Paul all night. Dessert is strawberry shortcake oozing with whipped cream. Paul reads the Dresner children a story. Google the pic. It's adorable. At 11 p.m., they go back to their hotel to watch the floor show and be gently ribbed by waspish MC Don Rickles.

Buddy also arranged with some local high rollers to loan The Beatles a crewed yacht which took them on a tour of Miami Bay and a mansion. 'We borrowed a millionaire's swimming pool,' John gasped when back home, by then probably not far from being a millionaire himself. From Paul's pictures and the ones that *Life* magazine grabbed, we can see that in the eye of that storm, Miami was a paradise of blue skies, sun, sand, sea, pretty girls and good food. The Beatles look as relaxed and happy as they ever would. I hope Buddy Dresner knew that.*

---

* The line 'And so I quit the police department' on 'She Came In Through the Bathroom Window' was inspired by the police certificate for Eugene Quits that Paul and Linda saw in a New York cab. But on one of the takes of the song, you can hear John shout 'Buddy!' at this point. They never forgot him.

61. Diane Levine

'Who is this Paul McCartney calling you?'

Strolling through the National Portrait Gallery 'Eyes of The Storm' exhibition of Paul McCartney's 'lost' photographs from 1964, a cute girl in a smart blue outfit caught my eye. I know she's in blue because, suddenly, with The Beatles' first trip to the States, their monochrome world blooms into technicolour, especially in sun-soaked Miami where, like mine, Paul McCartney's eye was caught by Diane Levine.

From the very beginning, from the adoring fans at The Cavern and John's devoted barmaid Bettina of Hamburg to the screaming aisles of Beatlemania to the Apple Scruffs, 'girls'/women and The Beatles always enjoyed a powerful, almost alchemical mutual bond. Christine Feldman-Barrett's *A Woman's History of the Beatles* brilliantly and exhaustively analyses how this relationship was always more complex and layered than merely the dopamine hit of sexual attraction, as potent as that was. Women were crucial to the way that The Beatles interrogated and redefined masculinity amidst a burgeoning mood of female agency. Feminist scholars such as Barbara Ehrenreich cite Beatlemania as 'a dramatic uprising of women's sexual revolution'.

As true and thought provoking as this is, I'm not sure it was at the forefront of either of their minds when Diane Levine and Paul McCartney's eyes met in Florida in 1964. 'It started at a private beach' she remembered two decades later. 'Three of my friends and I were relaxing after taking the college boards. I was 17. We were Seniors at Miami Beach High School … We heard sirens. We thought it was an ambulance or something. There they were. They popped out of a car. They were white – blue-white, skinny. They looked white because everyone in Miami Beach is tanned. We couldn't believe our eyes for a minute. I backed up. I was totally blown away.'

The feeling seems to have been mutual. 'Some girls were chasing Paul. I was standing by myself. He was coming in my direction. At that point I was really thrilled. I held out my hand. I said, "I don't want an autograph. I don't want to rape you. I just want to shake your hand and welcome you to the United States ..." It's not like I was a spectacular beauty. I was really quite shy. He had sand and water on his hand. He sort of wiped his hand on his bathing suit and shook my hand. Then he said, "Come with me." We ran toward a house where the entourage was. He sat me down and just started to joke immediately. I felt so at home with Paul. We had this Gemini thing in common, I suppose. We really clicked. It was very nice.'

After about forty-five minutes of chat, Paul was whisked away to his car but shouted from the window that she should come to that night's concert. 'When the show was over, I was taken up to the room. The Beatles were just as excited about the show as everyone else. After they left, the hotel guard told me I had to leave. I gave the guard a note thanking The Beatles and wishing them luck. I said I was sorry I didn't get a chance to say goodbye. I left my father's number and my home number ... Then, next day, when I dropped by my father's office after school, he said, "Who is this Paul McCartney calling you?"'

They double dated at a drive-in movie with Ringo and Diane's friend Barbara Turchin, driving convertibles that a local dealership had loaned them. Here we dolly back and fade to black ... what we know for sure is that Diane got married, moved to Hawaii and had three kids. Twenty years on, she confided to *Rolling Stone*, 'Well, I've always kept it a secret. But for the 20th anniversary, it's okay. I hope Paul doesn't mind.' His lovely portrait of her, looking coyly bemused, captioned 'Diane Levine. My Miami Date' and featured prominently in the *Eyes of The Storm* book and exhibition, would suggest that he absolutely doesn't.

62. Bob Dylan

'But what about your song? The one about getting high?'

Like all the best relationships, each brought to the other something new. The Beatles injected Bob Dylan's spartan troubadour balladry with the excitement and dynamism of rock and pop. He in turn gave them, as he did to the entire lexicon of pop, the cryptic strangeness and complexity of the modernist poets. Even those of us mildly and heretically immune to the charms of Robert Zimmerman's music (especially his harmonica playing) would have to concede that his impact on popular music has been colossal and profound. His effect on John Lennon was just as transformative, extending not just to his songwriting and voice, but also to his headgear and general 'vibe'.

Dylan had initially dismissed The Beatles as 'bubblegum' before hearing 'I Want To Hold Your Hand' while driving through Colorado. Witnesses attest that he stopped the car and ran around it, banging on the bonnet, yelling his approval. 'They were doing things nobody was doing. The chords were outrageous ... just outrageous and their harmonies made it all valid. I knew they were pointing the direction of where music had to go.' As soon as he got back to New York, he acquired an electric guitar. Over in France, where they were performing a week of shows at the Olympia in Paris, The Beatles were reciprocating the love: 'Paul got the record (*The Freewheelin' Bob Dylan*) from a French DJ' remembered John. 'For three weeks in Paris we didn't stop playing it. We all went potty about Dylan.' 'We just played and played it ... just wore it out' added George. 'The content of the song lyrics and just the attitude.'

On 28 August 1964, as the Dylan biographer Clinton Heylin put it 'two cultures fumbled for a common creed via a bag of weed'. In a meeting for pop culture historians as charged with import as Stanley discovering Livingston or Cortez meeting Montezuma, Dylan visited

The Beatles in their suite at the Delmonico Hotel, New York. Searching for his usual tipple of 'cheap wine', he was informed by Brian Epstein that they only had champagne. When offered some pills, Bob suggested pot which The Beatles admitted sheepishly they had never tried.* 'But what about your song?' he asked. 'The one about getting high? You know ... and when I touch you I get high, I get high ...' Even more sheepishly John admitted 'Those aren't the words. The words are, "I can't hide, I can't hide, I can't hide ..."'

Dylan or not, one assumes that, ever on the hunt for new experiences, The Beatles would have found their own way to the new sensations of the counterculture in time. But the introduction arriving via someone they were so besotted with was epochal. In his diaries, their driver Alf Bicknell says Lennon viewed Dylan 'almost like a God' and there is something almost slavishly devotional about 'You've Got To Hide Your Love' on *Help*. 'Norwegian Wood' on *Rubber Soul* (their 'pot album' according to Lennon) had Dylan spluttering 'What is this? It's me, Bob. [John's] doing me! Even Sonny & Cher are doing me, but, fucking hell, I invented it.' Dylan, for his part, injected the whiny grain of his early Woody Guthrie homages with 'that wild, thin mercury sound', the shivery crackle and vigour that came out of a car radio in Colorado and electrified (literally) his magpie imagination and begat *Blonde On Blonde* and *Highway 61 Revisited*.

Like most relationships, they had their ups and downs. Car bonnet banging notwithstanding, Dylan could be snide, superior and frankly tin-eared about The Beatles' charm and appeal, as with all his competitors. He apparently dismissed 'Yesterday' as a Tin Pan Alley 'cop-out' and when Paul played him an acetate of 'Tomorrow Never Knows' in his Mayfair hotel room, he sneered 'Oh, I get it.

---

* In *Anthology*, however, George says 'We first got marijuana from an older drummer with another group in Liverpool. We didn't actually try it until after we'd been to Hamburg. I remember we smoked it in the band room in a gig in Southport and we all learned to do the Twist that night.'

You don't want to be cute anymore' before leaving the room. Years later, John was to find his old idol had feet of clay, dismissing Dylan's religious conversion album song 'You Gotta Serve Somebody' as 'pathetic'. But the echoes of that smoky, bibulous night in the Delmonico Hotel can still be heard and felt across the culture, and in the oddest places. Above the bed in room 211 of the Hard Day's Night hotel in Liverpool, artwork of Lennon and Dylan gaze down inscrutably at the bed's occupant. Also in the picture is an ashtray, in which something suspicious is smouldering.

63. Richard Lester

'The Citizen Kane *of Jukebox Musicals.'*

In the early Noughties, I interviewed the film director Richard Lester in the office at Twickenham Film Studios he had kept since the early 1960s. We talked beneath the posters for his big directorial film hits *The Three Musketeers, Superman II* and two films for a certain British pop group. In his biography of that band, Bob Spitz described Lester as 'irascible'. I wouldn't go that far. But I did find him wry, laconic, perhaps slightly superior. Certainly, I felt that the day he had chosen for the interview, Easter Monday, when the suburbs were silent and the trains irregular, and we were the only people in the building, was some kind of test of my seriousness. I liked him, but I could sense why George Martin didn't.*

Dick Lester was a prodigy. He finished high school at 15 and graduated from the University of Pennsylvania with a degree in clinical psychology aged 19. He played in bands and worked in TV directing in the States before setting off to satisfy his wanderlust in Europe. In London, he found work in the nascent commercial UK TV industry directing a jazz series before getting his own series, *The Dick Lester Show*, heavily indebted to the humour of The Goons. The show was short lived, but it did bring him to the attention of Peter Sellers with whom he made short comedy films such as *Idiot's Weekly, A Show Called Fred* and its sequel, *Son of Fred.* Then, for fun over a weekend, he made a movie with a bunch of friends like Sellers, Milligan and Bruce Lacey of pioneering absurdists, The Alberts, called *The Running, Jumping and Standing Still Film* which earned a surprise Oscar nomination and, perhaps more

---

* According to Mark Lewisohn, at the mention of the other's name, each would begin 'sniping' immediately.

importantly, was regular viewing for The Beatles in Liverpool news cinemas.*

It was this movie, a period piece of Goonish silliness that pre-dates Python, as well as his first two hits *It's Trad, Dad'* and *'The Mouse That Roared* that put him very much in the frame (by the astute Walter Shenson) for The Beatles' debut movie. Whole books and hours of documentary footage have been lavished on *A Hard Day's Night*. For our part we should simply re-state that it is a miniature masterpiece. Lester's genius was to celebrate the band's chaotic, breakneck, intoxicating life at this point by utilising handheld cameras and unusual angles (with the help of brilliant cameraman and editor Gilbert Taylor and John Jympson) imbuing the movie with the same surrealist verve – witness the scene where The Beatles are both inside the carriage and running along the trackside simultaneously – and sly wit that he had brought to those comic shorts. He and Shenson insisted the movie should be filmed in black and white; a nod to newsreel, the French New Wave and the fact that this was how the world largely saw The Beatles in newspapers and TV. He was also sympathetic to his young stars' raw talent but lack of film experience (they were proposed and seconded into the Equity union on the platform of Paddington station just before cameras rolled), shooting the whole movie largely chronologically (not usual practice) in order not to bamboozle them. Also, he was conscious of the fact that being on set for 6 a.m. meant 5 a.m. alarm calls, an hour when The Beatles might usually be just getting to bed.

Critics swooned for the finished film. *The Village Voice* dubbed it 'the *Citizen Kane* of jukebox musicals'. Roger Ebert has described it as 'one of the great life affirming landmarks of the movies'. More importantly, audiences loved it. It took eight million dollars in its

---

* These were small theatres often by railway stations that showed newsreel and short films continuously. They were dying out by The Beatles' era, though the last at Victoria only closed and was demolished in 1981.

first week, making it one of the most profitable movies of all time. At its London premiere, attended by Princess Margaret and Lord Snowdon, Piccadilly Circus had to be closed because huge crowds blocked the street. Four days later, one hundred thousand Scousers lined the road from Speke airport to Liverpool city centre for the hometown premiere. But its cultural impact was enormous too, as Lester remarked in Andrew Yule's biography: 'I think they were the first to give a confidence to the youth of the country which lead to the disappearance of the Angry Young Man with the defensive mien. The Beatles sent the class thing sky high … laughed it out of existence and I think introduced the tone of equality more successfully than any other single factor that I know.'

Unfortunately, if understandably given their now demigod status, Lester's next Beatles movie, *Help!*, just a year later, was much more plotted, much more glamorous and overtly comedic, and far less enjoyable. There are many reasons why *Help!*, though an underrated album, is a bad film. It finds The Beatles queasily following trends (Bond, Batman, comic book camp) rather than setting them. It has none of the charm or magical realism of *A Hard Day's Night*, neither its *Play for Today* graininess or Beckettian quirkiness. Then, of course, there's the racism. The portrayal of the Indian characters is a crude stereotype. But then everything in *Help!* is a crude stereotype and The Beatles were by this point presumably too stoned to realise or care.

Despite the exotic locations, alpine ski slopes and Barbadian beaches, all rendered in saturated Technicolor, *Help!* only really comes alive when The Beatles play, still so unforced and joyous even through the fug of marijuana they were living in. The Beatles never really warmed to the movie business again though Lester did cast Lennon in his satire, *How I Won the War*. He also went on before the end of the 1960s to direct *The Knack* with another Liverpudlian, Rita Tushingham, as well as the post-apocalyptic black comedy *The Bed Sitting Room*. He directed Buster Keaton in his last film, *A Funny*

Thing Happened on the Way to the Forum. Later he would enjoy hits with The Three Musketeers, Robin and Marian, and two *Superman* movies in the 1980s.

By the time I met him in a deserted Twickenham he was long retired to Sussex but still genially dry and sharp. On the award of an Honorary Fellowship from Liverpool John Moores University in 2010, cinema academic Neil Sinyard observed, 'In the history of pop music, no group has loomed larger in terms of talent than The Beatles; and in the history of the cinema, no pop personalities have ever been better served by their director.'

64. Alun Owen

'Grotty.'

For three months in late 1959, the protean Beatles were known as Johnny and The Moondogs, the name under which they auditioned for the *TV Star Search* talent show when it came to Liverpool. Later, flushed with success – they passed – we must assume that they went home to put their feet up in front of the telly that October night since Paul was struck by that evening's ITV play *No Trams to Lime Street*, a gritty homage to their hometown, written by Scouse/Welsh playwright Alun Owen. 'It was like an early Bleasdale or Willy Russell ... a sort of kitchen sink Liverpool thing.'

The only element that survives of *No Trams to Lime Street* today is a strangely bowdlerised musical version from 1970 featuring a truly terrible title song by Marty Wilde. But the energy of that original TV play was the key deciding factor when Alun Owen's name was offered as the potential writer of their debut movie. With typical suavity, Epstein wrote to Owen expressing their admiration and 'asking if a Beatles film is something you would like to be associated with'. Profitably for all, it was.

Owen had started life as an actor, appearing in *The Dick Lester Show*, occasioning a significant meeting between Owen and the rising star director, before carving a reputation as one of the new wave of social realist TV dramatists. While admiring Owen's work, producer Walter Shenson was unsure if he was nimble and witty enough for the project; he had found *No Trams to Lime Street* 'pretty heavy going'. Nonetheless, spurred by Shenson's idea that the film should be a vérité account of a day in The Beatles' increasingly crazy existence, Owen hung out with the group for several days in Dublin and Paris in hotels, cabs, trains and backstage. From this, he soaked up both a sense of their intense, absurdist, quick-witted rapport and repartee with each other and the notion that they were golden quarry, hunted men, prisoners (as Pattie Boyd's sole word in the film has it) of their own success.

Owen recalls: 'We went from the hotel to the theatre straight to a press reception and at no time were they allowed to enjoy what was supposed to be success … running from place to place doing things but at the same time being impelled and the only freedom they get is when they start to play the music and then you see their faces light up and they're happy.' Owen knew from these few days that a very different kind of pop movie was called for. 'We're not going to have a story that ends up at the Palladium,' he said, 'with the vicar smiling and giving the thumbs-up sign from the stalls.'

'He was a kind of street writer,' in Paul's words 'quite exciting, and so we knew enough to try and pump him full of every good story we could think of. The more we told him the more of us he'd get in it which is always a good thing. It would just reflect back.' He included some of these Beatle tales almost verbatim, such as an incident when a crusty old gent on a first-class train to London told the band that he had 'fought the war for them'. This was subsequently dramatised in the famous scene with Richard Vernon.* He also transformed real-life road managers Neil Aspinall and Mal Evans into Norm and Shake, played by another two British acting stalwarts Norman Rossington and John Junkin. The latter was a former East End primary school teacher turned respected comedy writer/performer while Rossington was a celebrated Liverpudlian actor whose autograph Paul McCartney had queued up for when he opened a local bowling alley. He is also the only person to have acted in films alongside The Beatles and Elvis.

So while much of *A Hard Day's Night* originates in The Beatles' and Liverpool's distinctive cultural micro-climate, some of Owen's contri-

---

* Remarkably, Vernon was only 39. He had though served with distinction in the Royal Navy in the Second World War.

butions were sheer invention. For instance, The Beatles had never heard the word 'grotty' which Owen claimed to have encountered on the streets of Liverpool but The Beatles were mildly embarrassed about having to say it. He inserted the line about Paul's grandfather, played by Wilfrid Brambell, being 'very clean', a sly running reference to the insult of 'you dirty old man', constantly aimed at him by his co-star Harry H. Corbett in the hit TV show *Steptoe and Son*.* As Dick Lester commented 'the script was very cleverly written so that there was never a time where any one person had too much to say before someone else said something. They were sound bites, one-line gags or a little speech which could be cut away from.' Despite the brilliance of the script, a United Artists executive in the States asked Lester to re-dub the dialogue from 'Scouse' to mid-Atlantic, to which Paul retorted, 'Look, if we can understand a fucking cowboy talking Texan, they can understand us talking Liverpool.'

Owen commented that 'in the film we see the boys in a world which has no future and no past'. But in truth The Beatles were at this point inventing the future with every minute. For his part, Owen received his £1,200 fee and, given the immediate success and acclaim for *A Hard Day's Night*, for which he was Oscar nominated for his script, he quite reasonably expected to be asked to write their next cinematic venture. Brian Epstein informed him, however, that Dick Lester already had American writers on board for what was clearly going to be a very different movie. Bear in mind that Lester's first choice for the writer of *A Hard Day's Night* was Johnny Speight of Alf Garnett fame, which would have made that a very different movie too.

The last day of filming on *A Hard Day's Night* was 24 April 1964. The very next day, the band were in rehearsals for their *Around The*

---

* Philip Norman misses this and instead declares it a 'steal' from a line in Gilbert and Sullivan's *Iolanthe*. It may also be a cheeky reference to Brambell's 1962 conviction for 'persistently importuning in two public lavatories in Shepherd's Bush'.

Beatles TV special. The day after that they played at the *New Musical Express* Poll-Winners concert at Wembley. On 27 and 28 April more rehearsals and then taping *Around The Beatles*. Then to Scotland for two nights of concerts and then 1 May saw them back in London recording an appearance for the BBC. And on and on it went now, the gilded travelling prison that Owen so vividly captured. Thanks in no small part to him, only twenty months on from their first single, The Beatles were now movie stars as well.

65. Dennis O'Dell

'I loved the idea of The Beatles
being small people in
Middle Earth.'

Dennis O'Dell, one of nine children of an Irish family in Kensington, grew up on film sets. He worked as a teaboy on the classic black and white whodunnit *The Arsenal Stadium Mystery* in 1939 and served his apprenticeship as assistant director and producer on Alastair Sim's *Scrooge*, the *Carry On* films and the Viking epic, *The Long Ships* before his association with The Beatles and perhaps the most tantalising 'what if' in their whole story.

For The Beatles' debut feature, *A Hard Day's Night*, United Artists wanted a quick, cheap but satisfying movie and, as 'fixer', O'Dell more than delivered'. The average feature film budget of the time was at least one and a half million pounds. O'Dell 'reckoned it could be done for £150,000. Eventually we got UA to push the budget up to about £180,000. It must be one of the cheapest films ever made ... The Beatles were paid £25,000 for the four of them, which was an extraordinarily small amount.' He said that the movie used 'top flight people for bottom flight money' adding knowingly, 'Early spring was traditionally a lean time for film freelancers.'

The initial idea of filming in Liverpool was abandoned as costly and impractical. 'There were no technicians of any major quality up in Liverpool at that time, these were very early filming days, and to take an entire crew from the South to the North and put them up for six or seven weeks would have been impossible ... We didn't have to pay anybody any subsistence allowances, accommodation, travel, etc.' Via a pal at British European Airways, (BEA) he got the helicopter used in the movie for an astonishing £25, The Beatles already having agreed to sport the now iconic 'BEAtle' bags in return for free air tickets. He also paid a bunch of navvies a few quid to use various holes in the ground for the scenes with chivalrous Ringo and the lady who disappears into the earth. 'When we did the scene with Ringo on the embankment, I think he overslept. Probably a late night at the Ad Lib, I should think, and I was responsible for a lot of it because I used to go with 'em!' He was always savvy enough to go through Neil Aspinall as he was 'the only one to have any control over them'.

After that he worked with Lennon on *How I Won the War* and *Magical Mystery Tour* which he felt was an opportunity missed. 'Paul had wanted to repay the BBC for their loyalty to The Beatles and they responded by showing it in black and white.' The scenes accompanying the 'Flying' instrumental were salvaged by O'Dell from Stanley Kubrick's 1963 *Doctor Strangelove* from hours of aerial shots over the Arctic for the climactic final scenes where the B52s bomb Russia. He told Paul 'I can get you some outtakes and he edited it together and tinted it to make it look very unlike Strangelove. Unfortunately, this didn't come over well in black and white.'

There is another Beatles Kubrick connection, or a near miss at least. After O'Dell was appointed a director of Apple Corps and head of Apple films, he had the idea for a Beatles version of *The Lord of The Rings*. When they (and he) embarked for their Rishikesh sojourn with the Maharishi, O'Dell took copies of the Tolkien epic with them, as well as Ringo's baked beans. According to O'Dell's memoir, *At the Apple's Core: The Beatles from the Inside*, The Beatles were keen on the project, with Paul as Frodo, Ringo as Sam, John as Gollum and George as Gandalf, with The Beatles' choice of director being Kubrick, fresh from his psychedelic masterpiece *2001: A Space Odyssey*. O'Dell later reflected 'I love the idea of The Beatles being small people in Middle Earth, but I wonder if they could have sustained the long period of shooting.' Also, Tolkien himself was less keen on a pop group getting their hands on the books and vetoed the project.*

An excellent judge of character it would appear, O'Dell quit Apple when Allen Klein arrived. In the early Seventies, he and Sean Connery set up a production company called Tantallon Films, named after a clifftop castle in East Lothian, although they only made one movie, the brilliant *The Offence*. In the downtime in early January before shooting began on *The Magic Christian* with Ringo and Peter Sellers, O'Dell suggested that if The Beatles couldn't agree where to hold the proposed concert for their next movie/TV special they could at least begin by filming rehearsals at Twickenham Studios. Thus was Michael Lindsay-Hogg's *Let It Be* and Peter Jackson's *Get Back*† conceived.

He was later a partner in Handmade Films and worked on The Concert for Bangladesh. But his influence in Beatledom lives on in song. On the infamously wacky final B side, 'You Know My Name, Look Up The Number' ('my favourite Beatles track,' Macca once bizarrely claimed to Mark Lewisohn), John introduces Paul as 'Dennis O Bell' instructing them to then follow the instruction of the song's title and give him a ring. Even with the slight misnomer, so many of them did, that it may have influenced O'Dell's decision to move to Almeria, Spain where he spent the last forty years of a full life.

---

* Seems like old JRR was not much of a pop culture maven. He also apparently didn't like Bo Hansson's brilliant, otherworldly cult prog album *Music Inspired by Lord of The Rings* though he did sanction a musical version of the quite dreary songs from the books by Flanders out of Flanders and Swann.

† Jackson of course did get his *Lord of The Rings* movies made. He remarked of The Beatles' abortive attempt, 'I've got two minds about it. I would have loved to hear that album, but I'm also glad I got the chance to do the films. But those songs would have been fascinating.'

66. Pattie Boyd

'Prisoners?'

The above being the single and only word of dialogue afforded to any of the chiefly decorative, problematically dressed 'schoolgirls' in the *A Hard Day's Night* movie. It is given, by a man of course, to a 19-year-old model called Pattie Boyd. In the film it's Paul who approaches her on that train trip to Cornwall; in reality it was George who asked Pattie to marry him almost immediately. When she, not unreasonably, refused, he modified this to a request for a dinner date, which she still turned down as she had a boyfriend. By the time the pair met again though, ten days later at a photo shoot for the movie's publicity, the boyfriend had been dumped* and the dinner went ahead, albeit a decidedly chaste affair at the fustian Garrick Club, chaperoned by Brian Epstein, who chose the young couple's food and wine.

Previously, George had briefly dated Hayley Mills, picking her up in his black E type and taking her to a charity film premiere in Henley. Openings were auspicious as the 17-year-old recorded in her diary; 'As soon as I walked down the stairs and saw him standing there in the hall with his black corduroy coat and hands thrust deep into the pockets and all that shining hair, my carefully cultivated calm vanished, my knees started to tremble.' On arrival though, she was horrified to be confronted by 'a snake-pit of shrieking, scratch-ing, maniacal girls. One of them nearly took my eye out with a jabbing Biro pen. Somehow, we managed to fight our way into the cinema, clinging to our clothes for fear they'd be torn off our backs

---

* The jettisoned boyfriend, who'd been living with her for two years, was photographer Eric Swain whose portrait of Pattie adorns her illustrated memoir *A Life in Pictures*.

... we were surrounded – people were leaning on our heads, their sharp elbows and grumbling stomachs in our faces. One woman actually knelt in my lap to get at him!'

Romance did not ensue. Then a few months later, George found himself on that train to Cornwall and thence into a serious relationship with Boyd. (According to a 1965 edition of *Fabulous* magazine though, she didn't like The Beatles till she met them. The Beatles probably already knew her from her appearance in a Smiths crisps TV commercial directed by Dick Lester.) As their relationship deepened Harrison spoke of the education in the finer things in life, like avocados, that the privately educated Boyd gave him. In turn, she recalled, not unaffectionately, that the Harrison family 'held their knives like pens and tea consisted of cold ham or pork pie, tomatoes cut in half, pickled beetroot and salad cream with white sliced bread'.*

Boyd was famously with Harrison (and John and Cynthia) when they took their first acid trip surreptitiously administered in coffee by Beatle dentist John Riley at a dinner party. Boyd wondered if Riley, who hadn't 'drunk' any himself 'had given it to us hoping there was going to be an orgy' and that, as George put it, 'he was going to get to shag everybody'. Perhaps because of this pretty creepy introduction to LSD, it never became the obsession for her that it did with some Beatles. 'It's boring ... it's irritating really because it lasts for so long and quite frankly I've got lots to do during the day.'

Soon after this infamous night out – Boyd had to be prevented from smashing a shop window and all believed the club they were in was on fire – George and Pattie became engaged. They were perhaps the most glamorous of all Swinging London's glitterati couples. 'I don't remember ever seeing a plane ticket or showing my passport.' They married in January 1966 at Epsom register office with Paul McCartney as best man. 'I wore a red fox-fur coat that Mary Quant

---

* Which sounds way nicer than avocado.

made for me, and she made a black Mongolian lamb coat for George. I thought, "This is it. We are sealing a declaration of love together for ever and we are going to live happily ever after."'

Things didn't turn out quite that way. Instead, they became part of rock's most celebrated, knotty *ménage à trois*. George's friend Eric Clapton was a regular visitor to Friar Park and had become besotted with Boyd. With George often away for recording Clapton 'sneaked in' in Boyd's words and they became lovers. He wrote the aching, desperate love song, 'Layla', for her, begging her to leave Harrison. Boyd said she felt confused and conflicted and Clapton disappeared from her life for the next four years.

During one of the increasingly frequent bad patches between Boyd and Harrison, she left Friar Park to spend time with her sister Jenny in LA and thence on to a tour with Clapton where romantic matters developed. When she eventually told George she was leaving him, he replied 'Well, I'm glad you're going off with Eric instead of some idiot.' Later George would jokingly refer to himself as 'the husband-in-law' in their presence. The trio even celebrated Christmas together. 'When I left him for Eric, he had said that if things didn't work out, I could always come back to him. It was such a selfless, loving thing to say.'

The notion of a 'muse' is fraught with difficulties these days, but whatever the dubious status it confers on women, there's no doubt that few muses have been as effective in the role as Pattie Boyd, 'Pop's Helen of Troy'. She inspired Eric Clapton's 'Layla', 'Bell Bottom Blues' and 'Wonderful Tonight' as well as George's 'I Need You', 'For You Blue' and, of course, the exquisite 'Something', described by Frank Sinatra as 'the greatest love song of the last fifty years', a compliment loaded with heavy backhand since Sinatra assumed it was written by Lennon and McCartney.

Also, it was Boyd who can claim with some justification to have changed The Beatles' lives and music irrevocably by introducing them to Indian philosophy and religion. At a time when most of

London's beautiful people were seeking some kind of instant enlightenment or spiritual 'fix', an advertisement for Transcendental Meditation courses held in central London caught her eye. She found the classes 'life changing. I couldn't wait to tell George. As soon as he came home I bombarded him with what I had been doing and he was really interested. Then, joy of joys, I discovered the Maharishi was coming to London in August to give a lecture at the Hilton Hotel. I was desperate to go and George said he would come too. Paul had already heard of him, was interested, and in the end we all went, John, Paul, George, Ringo, Jane (Asher) … we were spellbound.'

By now all charmed devotees of TM and the Maharishi, Boyd was part of The Beatles' retreat in Rishikesh the next year. On their return, she also sang backing vocals on the *White Album*'s 'Birthday'; 'I cannot sing, but the invitation was too delicious.' She isn't present on the roof of Apple for the famous valedictory performance because 'I think we'd had a bit of a domestic. I would have loved to have been there but I asked could I come and George said no.'

Now in her eighties, writing books and helming podcasts, she seems refreshingly free of the cant that dogged the utterances of her Sixties peers, including her former husband. It was Boyd who first noted that, paradoxically, George became more crabby and sullen after he had learned to meditate. 'Meditating lightens my day, but George didn't like the day. He preferred to be meditating. He was quite complicated really.'

67. Victor Spinetti

'I fell in love with them.'

Vittorio Giorgio Andre Spinetti's grandfather walked from Italy to the Welsh valleys to work in a coal mine and hopefully earn enough money to buy a plough. This was how, with characteristic elan, Vittorio, later Victor, described his origin story; co-star, friend and confidant of the Fab Four, he is the only person apart from The Beatles themselves to appear in all three of their dramatic movies.

The Spinettis, mum, dad and six kids of which Victor was the eldest, lived above the chip shop they ran in the tiny mining village of Cwm, near Ebbw Vale. The advent of the Second World War proved traumatic for them with Italy now our enemy. 'One day I'm Welsh, the next day I'm a spy.' His father was snatched by the authorities in the small hours and interned on the Isle of Man. Victor was shunned as an 'Italian bastard' and clubbed on the side of the head with a brick resulting in permanent deafness in one ear. Boarding school in Monmouth was a sanctuary and then, via local 'am dram', to Cardiff School of Music and Drama where he met his partner, the actor Graham Curnow who he lived with in an openly gay and gaily open relationship until Curnow's death in 1997. Via an apprenticeship in revues, concert parties, air bases and variety, Spinetti became part of a generation of British acting talent assembled by Joan Littlewood at Stratford East; Barbara Windsor, Harry H. Corbett, Murray Melvin and more. When he was 'resting' as actors often were and are, he cheerfully admitted having 'spanked old gentlemen for money … My dear old mother told me that, if she'd known at the time, she would have come along and given me a hand!'

Success in *Fings Ain't Wot They Used T'Be* and *Oh! What a Lovely War* brought him theatrical fame. John and George saw him in the latter, visited him backstage and thus he was cast in *A Hard Day's Night* where his angst-ridden, frazzled TV director is a highlight. 'You've got to be in all our films,' George Harrison said after *A Hard Day's Night*. 'If you're not in them, me Mum won't come and see them because she fancies you.' And so, seven months later, he was cast in *Help!* as a risibly mad doctor. Despite the glamorous location shoots in The Bahamas and in Austria 'the spirit of invention ... had gone. Tiredness and sullenness permeated the shoot.'

In his Beatles biography Hunter Davies states that The Beatles only have three real friends and Spinetti is one of them. The feeling was mutual; 'I fell in love with them.' He was closest to John, perhaps, whose two books he adapted for the stage. 'They were amazing people. And they were curious, they wanted to learn. They didn't have the laddishness which you get now, this wanting to be ignorant. I mean, we really were sitting there and talking about things like Beethoven. Not all the time, you know, but the tenor of their conversation was they wanted to find out. John would ring up and say, "We've never been to the theatre, let's go look at something ..."'

Richard Burton called Spinetti 'the most underrated actor in Britain' and he remained a constant in British culture for decades, and one with a wildly varied CV. His later work included a cameo in *The Krays* movie and a memorable interpretation of a Mexican thief with a sweet tooth in adverts for McVitie's Jaffa cakes. ('There's Orangey!') Fittingly, his last on-screen performance was in the DVD of Seth Swirsky's engaging interview compilation, *Beatles Stories*.

I once spent a happy evening with Victor and the great Barry Cryer in a pub by the BBC in Portland Place, a man of warm, roguish charm and evident love of The Beatles who lit up conventions in his later years. His joy and gratitude for being part of their story was so palpable and sweetly worn that Paul's description of him as 'the man who makes clouds disappear' seems the perfect epitaph.

68. Jimmie Nicol

'You're a Beatle till we put you on the plane.'

The Feast of Fools, sometimes known as Topsy Turvey, was cele-brated across Europe during the Middle Ages. Some say it's the basis of April Fool's Day. A lowly, subordinate peasant, sometimes a jester or 'fool', was elevated for one day to a position of nobility, feted and indulged like a king before being abruptly returned to obscurity and drudgery. Jimmie Nicol is the Fab Four's King for a Day. Or rather, a Beatle for thirteen days. Two weeks of fame and glory that bent his life out of shape forever.

On the eve of their first world tour on 3 June 1964, Ringo Starr was hospitalised with tonsillitis and pharyngitis presenting The Beatles and Brian Epstein with a pressing dilemma; to either cancel a major tour, disappointing thousands and triggering a colossal financial hit, or find a replacement. George Martin suggested Nicol, a peripatetic drummer on the London scene who he'd used on a recent Tommy Quickly session. Epstein, John and Paul were amena-ble with George initially hostile ('If Ringo's not going, then neither am I. You can find two replacements.') until informed just how much money was at stake. The next day Nicol was phoned at home in Barnes by George Martin asking him to become a (temporary) Beatle. 'I was having a bit of a lie down after lunch when the phone rang' he said. And, according to one report, 'I nearly shit my pants.'

He rehearsed with them in Copenhagen the following day prior to their appearance at the Tivoli Gardens. Ahead of this, he was given a speedy moptop crop and Ringo's suit although the trousers were too short for him; one unkind critic said he looked like 'Frankenstein without the bolt'. Nicol also took part in various press conferences, a little awkwardly. (There's a particularly excruciating Dutch TV appearance in which he performatively slaps the table and guffaws at some off-colour remarks from Lennon about buying his wife for fifty quid from Nairobi.)

The next week was to change Jimmie Nicol's life. After Denmark, Holland and Hong Kong, they took a thirty-hour flight to Australia. Even at 2.30 a.m., four hundred fans had gathered on a remote airstrip in Darwin, Northern Territory where the band made an unscheduled refuelling stop. For the two Adelaide shows, fifty thousand people applied for the twelve thousand available tickets. A third of a million people, half the state's population, lined the Anzac highway to catch a glimpse of them.

Back home in Britain, Ringo was feeling glum and confused – 'I thought they didn't love me anymore' – while down under, Nicol was reeling and not just from the musical highs. 'The day before I was a Beatle, not one girl would even look at me. The day after when I was suited up and riding in the back of a limo with John Lennon and Paul McCartney, they were just dying to get a touch of me.'

Nicol was having the time of his life. He hooked up with his cousin, Gladys Richardson and jammed in a jazz club with cabaret artist Francis Faye. But it was all over as quickly as it had begun. Two nights in Adelaide, eight shows in total. On the night before Ringo rejoined the fold, while the other Beatles partied in their suite imprisoned in a luxury Sydney hotel, Nicol slipped out despite Epstein's orders. Mal Evans and Derek Taylor later found him in a local bar and berated him. 'You're a Beatle until we put you on the plane.' At Melbourne's Essendon airport, the next morning, there was no media scrum nor fans to see him off. Seek out a fabulously melancholic, easily Googleable photograph of him in the deserted departure lounge; a study in bafflement and desolation. But before saying goodbye, Epstein did give him a gold commemorative watch plus an envelope stuffed with five hundred pounds.

A year later, in April 1965, after several attempts to relaunch his career including stints in Swedish novelty act The Spotnicks and as part of a duo in Mexico, the *Daily Mail* reported that he was bankrupt. Nicol was quoted 'standing in for Ringo was the worst thing that ever happened to me … the future? Nothing … there's nothing for me now.' He became increasingly and surely deludedly convinced that Epstein was sabotaging his career as punishment for that minor pub jaunt indiscretion on his final night as a Beatle. His wife said that his two weeks as a Beatle haunted him and blighted his mental health. Having surfaced briefly at a Dutch fan convention promising that the whole story would be told 'in the book when it comes out' (it never did), nothing has been seen of Jimmie Nicol since the early Noughties. In a strange coincidence, his son Howie, a sound recordist, worked on *Anthology* and won a Bafta for his contribution.

In an interview with The Ringer website Tom Hanks said that his 1998 directorial debut, the pop comedy *That Thing You Do* was partly based on Nicol's story. 'That had definitely stuck in my craw because I thought, "What was that guy's life like for a while?"' More directly, the film rights to a book on Nicol's story *The Beatle Who Vanished* by Jim Berkenstadt have been sold, on news of which Howie Nicol commented, 'He will be mortified if there is a film which will define him, that will be terrible. It is just two weeks in a person's life. I can understand why historians and fans are interested and I am interested myself, but it is an enormous thing to cope with.'

But Nicol's legacy is curiously enduring. His stock answer, whenever his brief Beatle bandmates asked him how things were, was 'It's getting better,' inspiring the McCartney song of that name on *Sgt. Pepper*. And Jimmie Nicol's thirteen days as a Beatle didn't just shape the rest of his life. It changed a continent. Mark Lewisohn thinks that of all the influence The Beatles wielded across the globe, their biggest social and cultural impact was in Australia. They influenced the style and mores of a generation of youth, especially young men, in what was still a highly conservative and macho culture. Australian historian Glenn A. Baker claims that the visit of The Beatles was 'singularly the most exciting thing that ever happened in Australia ... the impact was as instant as it was revolutionary.'

According to the website The Beatles and Their Watches (no, really) the watch Epstein gave Jimmie as his parting gift was a Swiss-made gold Eternamatic. A 1964 vintage model is now worth anything between four hundred pounds and eight thousand. Jimmie's would presumably fetch a good deal more. Unfortunately, one turbulent night in Mexico, Jimmie smashed his in despair, a reminder of his time as king for a day. The inscription read 'To Jimmy with appreciation and gratitude – Brian Epstein and The Beatles'. They had spelt his name wrong.

69. Alf Bicknell

'Would you be interested in working for a pop group?'

When Alf Bicknell became The Beatles' chauffeur in 1964, he looked rather like a plumper Eric Morecambe. Now see him in Alf Bicknell's Beatles Diary DVD of 1996, a collection of endearingly wonky pieces to camera and punchline-free anecdotes (bought by the author second-hand in Computer Exchange, Bearwood). His hair is now luxuriantly long and ash grey and he sports a collarless shirt and flamboyant jacket. Jewellery flashes about his person. He looks like Gandalf on the red carpet. The Beatles didn't just change music; they changed blokes like Alf Bicknell.

Alf had a rich and varied CV. He was 34 when he joined The Beatles' retinue as their chauffeur, having previously been an apprentice butcher and a circus clown. In the late 1950s, he began working as a driver with a car hire company whose clients were 'actors and film stars, among them Charles Boyer, David Niven, those sorts of people. I'd just finished working on a film as a driver and various things. I was at home when I lived at Number 28 Devonshire Mews, which is just off the back of the BBC, near Regent's Park. A knock on the door came … I go down and this man said he was from NEMS offices and he said, "would you be interested in working for a pop group?" I said, "Yeah. It sounds interesting … By the way, what's the band?" So he said, "It's The Beatles."'

He joined them in October 1964 at £30 a week (about £500 today) at the height of Beatlemania and was there till their final concert on 29 August 1966 at Candlestick Park, San Francisco. Through the madness of those years, Alf chauffeured them in a rather unglamorous Austin Princess (registration SST 626) since its doors opened wider than any other on the market and could be dived into at speed when making hasty getaways from fans.* When he began, Bicknell wore a peaked cap, but after only a few days Lennon tossed it out of the window saying 'You don't need that, Alf.'

'They didn't treat me as an employee,' he recalled, 'but as one of their mates.' Alf's mews cottage was just around the corner from Wimpole Street and so he would often pick up Paul as he finished one of Mrs Asher's cooked breakfasts. As for The Beatles as motorists themselves, while Ringo apparently was a superb driver and George something of a 'petrol head', 'I had to close my eyes with John.' As his time with The Beatles went on, so Alf Bicknell began his transformation, growing his hair and wearing shades.

When his memoir, *Baby You Can Drive My Car*, was published, George Harrison provided a foreword: 'Alf Bicknell lived moment to moment with The Beatles through those years … Anyone who was beaten up by Imelda Marcos's bully squad is a friend of mine.' A big teddy bear of a man, he became a regular sight at fan conventions; many of those fans will have understood just what he meant when he said 'I love talking about them. It makes me feel warm inside.'

---

* It was said to be one of only two cars in London to have blacked-out windows, the other belonging to Peter Sellers.

70. Robert Freeman

'Why are they looking so grim?'

Sitting on their twin beds in the Turk's Head hotel on Grey Street, Newcastle, John and Paul began to compose 'She Loves You'. At the Mitre in Carlisle, they gate-crashed the hunt ball. At Holdsworth House, Bradford, they ate turtle soup, cold duckling and steak tartare to celebrate John's 24th birthday while he did an impersonation of a Yorkshire mill owner. Before Beatlemania and their travels around the globe, The Beatles stayed in hundreds of provincial UK hotels; visits commemorated in plaques and publicity marketing still, emblazoned on the memories of locals and hoteliers and sometimes even the group for ever after.

Remarkably, The Beatles played in the genteel Dorset seaside resort of Bournemouth eighteen times, and, in August 1964, were making their third visit, staying at the art deco Palace Court Hotel on the seafront. It was to that a young broadsheet and fashion photographer called Robert Freeman was summoned by Brian Epstein. He'd shot Kruschev in Moscow and the girls of the fashionably glamorous Pirelli calendar, but it was his moody studies of US jazz legends like John Coltrane that attracted the interest of The Beatles, leading to a commission to take the pictures for their second album, *With The Beatles*.

In black polo necks against the heavy maroon velvet curtains, Freeman posed them full face in the shadows of the hotel's dining room, the only light falling from a huge window to one side. They stand in a line with Ringo, the new boy, demoted to a lower rank which, before the days of Photoshop, meant him kneeling on a stool for the duration of the shoot. The result was stunning; gravely monochrome, classical and almost eerie, building on Freeman's previous jazz portraits and Astrid Kirchherr's atmospheric Hamburg shots. 'The picture had a mood and directness that was the antithesis of the way groups usually appeared in the media' said Freeman in his later book, *A Private View*. 'George Martin deserves credit for supporting this approach because colour was the norm for pop albums at the time.'

Artistically and emotionally, it was a world away from the image of the cheeky moptops who had peeked down from the balcony at EMI's Manchester Square HQ on their debut album. The top brass inside that office, however, were dismayed. 'Shockingly humourless' they decreed, 'Why are they looking so grim?' and a nervous Epstein was unconvinced. But by now The Beatles wielded considerable agency and power. They had their way and Freeman's mise-en-scène has become one of the most iconic, even parodied, images of the rock era.* He was paid £75 for his work, three times the usual fee.

Beatledom had many court photographers during its different phases; Astrid in Hamburg; Deso Hoffman; Harry Benson who snapped/staged the Presidents Hotel pillowfight; Bob Whittaker of 'Butcher sleeve' fame; Linda, of course, and special mention should go to Albert Marrion of Wallasey who took the famous leather-clad *Mersey Beat* cover and, being bald, was of course called 'Curly' by John. But Bob Freeman was 'their' photographer at a crucial stage in the burgeoning Beatlemania, their visual stylist even. For the dazzling end titles of the *A Hard Day's Night* movie, he established a snapshot technique and clean 'new wave' style that fed into the album's cover with its 'contact sheet' approach and using the same pictures from the film. *Beatles For Sale*'s autumnal cover shot of the four weary, contemplative young superstars was shot in an hour and a half in Hyde Park. For *Help!*, inspired by a sequence in the Austrian snow in the movie, he had them spell semaphore in his London

---

* See The Residents' sinister and hilarious seafood/surrealist take for *Meet The Residents*.

studio against a white background.* When he was showing them his plans for the *Rubber Soul* cover, projecting a slide on to an LP sleeve-sized card as was his fashion, the card slipped resulting in that distorted, vaguely psychedelic sense of unreality that the band loved. George said it reflected their transition into 'fully fledged potheads'. Philip Norman described Lennon's expression in the picture as having a 'Saurian' disdain bordering on cruelty. In three years, Freeman shot the covers of five Beatles' albums. Illustrations each, of how rapidly they and the culture were moving.

Paul remembers that 'Robert was much more one of us than any of the other photographers.' But after a few years in their inner circle Freeman seems to have drifted away from them. At the time of his *A Private View* book, he toured with a stage presentation that was reasonably cordial. But later interviews suggest a certain calcification of his feelings. 'There was no input on *A Hard Day's Night* or *Help!* All the ideas for the covers were mine,' he said of their contributions to the famous sleeves adding, somewhat sadly, 'I have no contact with The Beatles … We live separate and distant lives.' Sadder still was the fact that a month after his passing from pneumonia in the winter of 2019, an unknown thief stole his entire photographic archive just as negotiations were taking place to mount a major V&A retrospective exhibition, presumably now on permanent display on the walls of some rich and unscrupulous people around the world.

---

* Contrary to popular belief, they aren't spelling HELP. That didn't look so good. They are actually spelling NUJV. Or NVUJ if you have the US pressing.

1965

71. Eleanor Bron

'Ola Na Tungy!'

Aside from Paul's outfit in the Salisbury plain 'The Night Before' sequence – grey Italian woollen suit with matching polo neck – Eleanor Bron is the best thing about *Help!* She is marvellous as the enigmatic and alluring High Priestess Ahme, even though it's a reductive, silly cypher of Eastern mysticism. But as a key player in the early 1960s satire boom, she was, for The Beatles, another fascinating emissary (of a kind that they were now encountering more and more often) from a seductive world beyond rock and roll and the proletarian north.

Eleanor Bron was spotted by fellow satire boomer John Bird at Newnham College, Cambridge. It's not hard to see why. Smart, talented, witty and beautiful, she became the first woman to join the celebrated poshos comedy revue, the Cambridge Footlights. She appeared in the pilot for pioneering 1960s TV satire show *That Was the Week That Was* but missed out on a regular berth as she was touring America for a year with Peter Cook's Establishment Club show. On her return though, she became part of another David Frost-fronted, Ned Sherrin-produced show, *Not So Much a Programme, More a Way of Life* alongside the aforementioned Bird, John Fortune, Roy Hudd and Willie Rushton and was already a familiar face to British audiences when she was cast in The Beatles' second movie and her first.

She wasn't entirely a stranger to the music world. Her father ran an orchestral services company and her older brother Gerry managed Uriah Heep, the Bonzo Dog Doo-Dah Band among others and had his own label, Bronze. But when she moved into the orbit of The Beatles, she was quite unprepared for what she encountered; 'a strange kerfuffle' as she put it. At Heathrow airport she thought she heard 'the sound of millions of starlings startled into the air but the starlings were girls, when I looked back, very young ones who covered the airport buildings ... a high sighing hopeless poignant sound.'

Initially she and The Beatles regarded each warily across the class, gender and cultural divide. One sniffy columnist said of Bron in *Help!* that she was 'a television intellectual thrust upon the four mop-headed millionaires'. But Bron harboured no such snobbery. She described her earlier time at Cambridge as 'three years of unparalleled pampering and privilege' and at a Nassau party during the *Help!* shoot, was horrified at how The Beatles were treated by 'the swells of the island ... if they could thrust themselves close enough to insult them personally, down their noses with snide remarks, requesting autographs for "demented" granddaughters'.

The Beatles were rather taken with her too, Paul loved her euphonious first name which he used for the title character of a ditty originally called 'Ola Na Tungy' ('blowing his mind in the dark with a pipe full of clay') sketched out one woozy afternoon round at Donovan's Maida Vale pad. Ola Na Tungy became Daisy Hawkins and then, after meeting Ms Bron, Eleanor Rigby with the addition of a surname from a Bristol wine merchant Paul liked.* So, from a scrap of doggerel came the piece that prompted Jerry Lieber (of Lieber and Stoller fame) to say 'I don't think there has ever been a better song written than Eleanor Rigby.'†

While filming in Salzburg, Bron and Lennon would often talk philosophy in the hotel bar till the small hours and she once visited him alone in Benedict Canyon, Beverly Hills prior to the band's Hollywood Bowl shows. But she always denied the oft rumoured 'fling'. In her autobiographical *The Pillow Book of Eleanor Bron*, she does however refer to all of her lovers as 'John'. Make of that what you will. In the Noughties though, she teasingly told *Varsity* magazine that she could not divulge her favourite moment of the *Help!* shoot, nor who her favourite Beatle was. But added 'Paul was much more sociable.'

She was on *Desert Island Discs* before she was 30 and is still acting in her eighties, making the occasional appearance in *The Archers*, maintaining an enigma that affects successive generations, such as the US indie band Yo La Tengo who speak for many when they sing 'I spent so much time, dreaming of Eleanor Bron.'

---

* There is a grave marked Eleanor Rigby in Woolton Church whose fête Lennon and McCartney met at, but Paul did not know this so assumes any influence was subconscious.

† The right-wing commentator Peter Hitchens, however, bemoaned in his *Daily Mail* online column 'the dismissal of faith and the mockery of quiet lives' in "Eleanor Rigby" which, in the face of stiff competition, maybe the most barmy and wrongheaded opinion he has ever expressed.

72. Barry Miles

'You don't do that in front of the birds.'

A genial Boswell to Paul McCartney's Dr Johnson, Barry Miles offers us a vital, necessary corrective to the narrative peddled by Jann Wenner of *Rolling Stone* and other male rock 'scribes' in the aftermath of The Beatles' split, namely that John was the edgy, and authentic genius of the band while Paul merely a slick vaudevillian. Miles has in his gently understated way, helped dispel that corny slighting myth. But he is more than just confidant, spokesperson and PR man; along with John Dunbar and the Ashers, he helped ignite Macca's fierce native intelligence and artistic hunger. Bluntly, while Lennon was nodding out in front of the telly in the stockbroker belt, Paul was immersing himself in avant-garde art, cinema, philosophy and music in the ferment of Sixties London, usually accompanied by Miles.

Miles worked at the achingly hip countercultural hub, Better Books and brought Allen Ginsberg to London which occasioned his first contact with The Beatles. 'The trouble was that by the time John and George arrived, with their wives, Allen had taken all his clothes off and had his underpants on his head and a "No Waiting" sign hanging round his dick. John was very upset at finding Allen completely naked. First of all, he and George instinctively looked around to check that there were no photographers, then John told me, "You don't do that in front of the birds."'

Soon after, Miles launched *International Times*, Europe's first underground paper, before setting up the Indica Gallery with Dunbar, partly with a loan from Peter Asher and later with very hands-on help from Paul. 'I think he put in more than anybody; I think a couple of thousand, maybe even three … But he also helped us put the place together. I mean, he helped with the walls in Indica.

He did a lot of work on them, you know? He helped put up shelves, paint the walls, and just generally helped out. Except, of course, if you've got a Beatle working on the place – I mean, the crowds were gathering outside. It's at the height of Beatlemania … It's late '65.'

Miles and Paul became firm friends, hanging out together in heady mid-Sixties London with Paul often in disguise: 'He went to the BBC, which had a very good make-up department, and they got him a perfect little moustache; this is before The Beatles had moustaches … And he had a different way of combing his hair, and just looked completely different. He wore a different kind of clothes – looked really nerdy.'

Miles ran the short-lived Apple spoken word and experimental imprint Zapple and in recent decades has become one of the most entertaining authorities on the Sixties, a period he described as 'a supermarket of ideas'. Indeed, *The Guardian* adapted the old saw in tribute to him: 'If you don't remember Miles in the Sixties, you weren't really there.' While Miles has become one of the best Beatle chroniclers, especially of Paul, he still regrets not being more assiduous at the time with recordings and documentation. But this is surely forgivable given the nature of those times; heady, hedonistic and long before every passing phase and fancy was digitally captured, processed and pored over.

'Had I been smart I would have made a note after each Beatles' session. It never occurred to me I might forget what I'd seen. I just assumed it would keep on going forever.'

73. Harold Wilson

'I thought you had to drive tanks and
win wars to win the MBE.'

With his Gannex mac, pipe and air of Yorkshire stolidity, Harold
Wilson may not now seem like a vibrant, youth-oriented, future-
facing moderniser. But this is a fossilised image, not helped by years
of bad impressions by Mike Yarwood and his Seventies peers. Back
in the early 1960s, cast against the costive, grouse-bothering manda-
rins at the helm of the governing Conservative party, he was freshness
and vigour itself. Indeed, unlikely as it may seem now, he was regularly compared to the USA's youthful young president John F
Kennedy. After JFK was tragically murdered, that New Frontier
spirit still seemed to live on in the Britain of 1964, and Huddersfield
born Harold Wilson was thought to exemplify it, along with The
Beatles. They were grammar school rock and rollers, he'd been an
Oxford PPE graduate and a brilliant young don, but all were driven,
smart, talented working-class northern lads. A year after JFK's death,
Wilson was Prime Minister.

Whereas his predecessor, the cadaverous toff Alec Douglas-Home
had been indifferent to The Beatles, Wilson courted them. He
included all four on the Queen's birthday honours list of 1965
alongside the usual roll call of party donors, captains of industry and
no less than 182 military officers. The ten million dollars of exports
The Beatles generated to the US alone in the previous year probably
influenced Wilson's decision but it was surely also shrewd populism
intended to strengthen their relationship and fix Labour as the party
of the lively arts and the new pop culture. Wilson was the first to
embrace this tactic, one which successors in his party like Tony Blair
and Gordon Brown deployed with varying degrees of success, as in
Blair's famous Downing Street 'Cool Britannia' reception and

Gordon Brown's inability to name one song by his purported 'favourite' band Arctic Monkeys.

By brown envelope, to the Twickenham Studios where they were filming *Help!*, came a series of forms delivered by a delighted Brian Epstein offering all four Beatles the award Member of The British Empire, a gong given, according to YouGov for 'achievement or service in and to the community which is outstanding in its field and has delivered sustained and real impact which stands out as an example to others'.

John Lennon commented 'I thought you had to drive tanks and win wars to win the MBE' while George claimed 'I thought they were calling us up for the army.' He also later commented on the *Anthology* documentary, somewhat peevishly, that what they were being offered, the MBE or Member of The British Empire, was 'the lowest honour that you can possibly get'.* Nonetheless, some were scandalised. Peers, wartime firewatchers and several retired Colonels in the shires returned their MBEs spluttering about declining standards and Britain's moral decay. People wrote horrified letters to the press, even the *NME*.† Princess Margaret sniped, in an utterance caught by the *Birmingham Evening Mail* 'I think MBE must stand for Mr. Brian Epstein.' which is breathtakingly rich, rather like she was.‡

---

* Two years later, George delivered a backhanded 'thank you' to Wilson and his Tory counterpart Mr Heath when he namechecked them on his song 'Taxman', the opening track on *Revolver*, written just after Wilson and Labour's 1966 election landslide. George, always the most fiscally 'canny' of the group, was bemoaning the amount of income tax he was now paying.

† Interestingly, there was no such objections to the awarding, the same year, of OBEs to Jack Warner and Violet Carson, 'Dixon of Dock Green' and 'Ena Sharples'.

‡ Someone I know was backstage at a charity concert when Princess Margaret came back to chance upon Paul McCartney playing the ukulele. Unable to say anything pleasant, she snarked 'Is that a poor man's guitar?' Macca replied deadpan 'No ma'am. It's a rich man's ukulele.'

'A formal occasion at Buckingham Palace on a foggy October morning! … The ceremony of bestowing awards of honour, a ceremony hallowed by a tradition going back over the centuries! After the investiture, Mr George Harrison, Mr John Lennon, Mr Paul McCartney and Mr Ringo Starr … Members of the Most Excellent Order of the British Empire … Mr Lennon, the famous author, had his hair specially cut before meeting the queen. Not even Victory Day or The Coronation produced such a scene of frenzied acclaim … now back to mundane affairs like Rhodesia and all that jazz …!'

This black and white Pathé newsreel coverage, shown in cinemas across Britain in the last week of October 1965, has that curious mixture of the excitable, the patronising and the wryly camp, which still attends many attempts by the 'serious' news media to capture the froth of pop. But this was more than frothy, man. This was the first time that the 'establishment' (as much as we can call the Labour party that, now or then) acknowledged the puissance of the new young pop culture.

The young, in their turn, were watching the establishment too. At the end of the ITN coverage of The Beatles' investiture, reporter Peter Linley records some vox pops, presumably far from Liverpool since the responses are chilly, the contributors patrician and the accents clipped, but one young man,* mildly bemused, asks 'Well, this medal of the British Empire raises a question … where is the British Empire … it's purely an honorary thing, you can give it to anyone you like. I don't think the thing's got any value at all.'

The wind of change, one begun with John Osborne's Jimmy Porter and the Angry Young Men, and now being fanned by The Beatles, was beginning to drift from young dissenters like this, through the country and out to the world.

---

* According to one YouTube commenter, this is their father Stefan Youngs. The setting appears to be Oxford.

74. Tara Browne

'A gentleman to the very end ...'

The Beatles came from that generation that read a newspaper every day, a comforting quotidian routine with cuppa and fag. On 16 January 1967, two stories in the *Daily Mail* caught the eye of John Lennon. One appealed to his sense of the absurd; a squib in the 'Far and Near' section about the four thousand potholes that Blackburn council had identified in their town. The other chimed with his love of the macabre. Lennon said after Epstein's death that 'there is a sort of little hysterical, sort of hee, hee, I'm glad it's not me or something ...' That winter morning, he must have been in that kind of mood when he read about the death in a car crash of Tara Browne, youngest son of the 4th Baron Oranmore and Browne, also the 2nd Baron Mereworth.*

In everything written about him, Tara Browne is described as a 'socialite', the coyly polite translation of exuberantly unemployed. Brown's lifestyle of parties and fine living was funded by his family's wealth, being the son of a double Baronet and long-standing Anglo-Irish peer and Oonagh Guinness, heir to the fortune amassed on British drinkers' love of 'the black custard'. After meeting one night at the Bag O'Nails, Tara and Paul McCartney became close friends, often hanging out at each other's London 'pads' with Paul describing him as 'a sensitive guy'. At Christmas 1965, Paul took Tara to Liverpool to meet his family, a visit infamous for Paul crashing his

---

* This may have been Lennon's initial inspiration, but in 1967 McCartney has said of the co-written lyric 'A Day in The Life'. 'In John's head it might have been. In my head I was imagining a politician bombed out on drugs who'd stopped at some traffic lights and didn't notice that the lights had changed.' However, in his 2021 book *The Lyrics* McCartney then confirmed that the lyrics were about the death of Tara Browne.

moped on the way to his aunty's and chipping a tooth. For his 21st birthday, Browne flew Paul, Mick Jagger, Brian Jones, Anita Pallenberg and a couple of hundred others out to a lavish party at his family's Luggala Estate in the Wicklow Mountains. There were boat races on Lough Tay and entertainment was provided by the Lovin' Spoonful. Lashings of acid were also available, a refreshment which Paul first tried at Browne's flat in Belgravia.

Eight months later, in the small hours of 18 December 1967, Browne's blue Lotus Elan broadsided a parked van in South Kensington. The circumstances are unclear; Browne's passenger Suki Potier, 19, said he swerved to avoid a white Jaguar (Barry Miles says a Volkswagen) emerging abruptly from a junction. Browne died of head injuries later that night in hospital. He was 21. At the time of his death, Browne was embroiled in a toxic divorce and custody battle with his estranged wife Nicky. She told the *Daily Mail* in an interview decades later that John Lennon had never warmed to Browne – 'I think he really sneered at people from Tara's background' – which perhaps explains how Lennon had the sangfroid to turn his death into a song, 'A Day in The Life', written immediately and recorded just three days after reading the newspaper stories.

Marianne Faithfull said the news of Browne's fatal crash was 'like a death knell sounding over London'. Speaking of his final act, swerving to protect Potier from the worst of the impact, Anita Pallenberg remarked, 'A gentleman to the very end.'

1966

75. Luciano Berio

'Paul McCartney Goes Too Far.'

Hand in hand with being one of popular art's most imperishable talents, Paul McCartney is also one of the most misunderstood. Or at least was. Until relatively recently, the received and erroneous wisdom had it that John Lennon was the radical and experimental Beatle, with Paul McCartney merely the congenial balladeer and musical comfort blanket. Nothing could be further from the truth; while John was becalmed in his drug habit, zonked on his sofa in front of sitcoms in suburban Surrey, McCartney lived in central London and was a very visible participant in its thriving, vibrant underground arts scene. He hung out with William Burroughs, Harold Pinter, Kenneth Tynan and Michelangelo Antonioni and made his own abstract Super 8 movies. He discussed the Vietnam war with philosopher Bertrand Russell. He was listening to the free jazz of Sun Ra, John Coltrane, Albert Ayler as well as the modern electronic music of Stockhausen. He was a regular at concerts of

John Cage and Morton Feldman and met with Delia Derbyshire at the BBC Radiophonic Workshop, encouraging her to make an all-electronic version of 'Yesterday'.

On 24 February 1966, Paul attended a lecture and taped performance at the Italian Cultural Institute in London's Belgrave Square by the Italian avant-garde composer Luciano Berio. The two men talked afterwards but excitable attention from embassy staff and other audience members made conversation difficult. Luciano must have been impressed though. He later arranged several Beatles songs such as 'Michelle' and 'Ticket To Ride' in delightful, surprisingly accessible baroque-style settings and his wife Cathy Berberian released an album called *Beatles Arias*, recasting the Fab Four in glorious operatic excess.

'I used to go to concerts like Stockhausen. That was me, all that shit in The Beatles. I'd play it to them: "Listen to this, man!" I went to this guy Luciano Berio, who's now an electronic classical kind of guy. "Pepper" came out of that ... That's my thing, really. I'd once said to John – I was talking about Stockhausen, Berio, Cage and these far-out composers – "I should do an album called Paul McCartney Goes Too Far." He said, "That's a great idea, man, you should do it." Of course, I never did.'

At home, Paul's restless musical curiosity was leading him to experiment with tape loops and electronic music in his home studio. Perhaps it was faintly galling then that 'Revolution 9' on the *White Album*, described by Ian MacDonald as the most widely distributed piece of avant-garde art ever, is most associated with John, especially since Paul's most famous work in this vein, 'Carnival Of Light', remains unreleased due to George's tetchy refusal to allow it on to *Anthology*.*

---

* Backstage at the Roundhouse at the Electric Proms of 2017, I said to Paul that, as it was a 'happening' at this very venue that 'Carnival Of Light' was composed for, perhaps he would let me give it its first public broadcast on my radio show that night. 'Nice try' he laughed.

The Beatles, however, did act as artistic sponsors for another piece of late Sixties contemporary experimental music, releasing John Tavener's *The Whale* on Apple thanks to Ringo's enthusiasm. Give it a listen. Also, seek out the third movement of Luciano Berio's *Sinfonia* of 1968, an attempt to encapsulate in music the turbulence of that febrile year. It's a thrilling and crazy piece of music. It is also very, very like 'Revolution 9'.

76. Kevin Harrington

'I don't really understand The Beatles phenomenon.'

In a bleak midwinter in the middle of the 1960s, Kevin Harrington was working as an electrician's mate on a 'cold and horrible' London building site when his brother pointed out an advertisement in the Situations Vacant pages of the *Evening Standard*. 'It was for an office boy at NEMS … which my brother told me was Brian Epstein's company … so I applied and I got it.' So, in January 1966, he began work at NEMS and started a life with The Beatles.

He was 15.

Perhaps it's the brightness, clarity and colour that Peter Jackson has brought to the original, far murkier *Let It Be* movie, but Kevin Harrington and his incendiary hair are emblazoned on The Beatles' story now. 'Who's the redhead on the roof?' asked one viewer on a Beatles reddit, giving Harrington the perfect title for his memoir. As for Peter Jackson's magisterial epic, Kevin has watched some of it but with no great enthusiasm. 'I thought it was tedious. I know it was fascinating for everybody else and it brought back some lovely memories but it's a thing I don't particularly want to go through again … but I'm glad everybody else enjoyed it.'

Initially he was the post boy, delivering mail and press releases around London, then became Epstein's personal office assistant. One day, receptionist Laurie whispered to him excitedly that 'Mal and Neil are coming in today.' 'Who are Mal and Neil?' he asked. When he was told they worked with the boys, he then asked '"Who are the boys?" … and then these two guys just wafted in … most impressive … an aura of confidence just followed them in the room.'

When Neil Aspinall took over Apple, Kev, restless as an office boy and encouraged by Epstein, started to work alongside Mal handling the equipment during the making of the *White Album*. On his first proper meeting with Mal, he visited the flat he shared with Neil on Sloane Street to deliver their visas and was invited in for a drink where he found Mal 'at the coffee table with a big pile of pot rolling joint after joint and putting them in cigarette packets and resealing them cos they were just going to America and didn't trust anyone to get them any pot in case it was a set-up.'

Harrington soon became indispensable. He would arrive first ahead of an evening session and set the gear up. He would be ever present, wandering from studio to control room to lobby waiting for the music to stop and 'go running to get them fish and chips or whatever ... or several dozen cups of tea ... most of my life with The Beatles was hanging around.' Kevin was standing next to George when the latter announced he was leaving during the *Get Back* sessions, but his notable discretion meant it failed to register. 'I heard lots of things ... but I never listened.'

He lugged the gear largely solo, 'five or six trips' up to the roof of Apple for what became their final gig, needing Mal's help only for Paul's giant bass amp 'The Coffin' and Billy Preston's organ. Harrington had always been closest to George – they had ridden the same make of bike when errand boys – and after The Beatles split, he moved into the then overgrown and derelict Friar Park; 'As gothic and as mad as ... Hammer House of Horrors ...' George just said 'it's a bit lonely ... do you wanna come in an make up the numbers for a bit?' He also handled the 'back line' of onstage amps and instruments for the Concert for Bangladesh.

His post Beatles CV as a tour manager is, frankly, ridiculous, Derek and The Dominoes, Wishbone Ash, Motorhead and Petula Clark. On the cabaret circuit in the Middle East, he worked with Tina Turner, Matt Munro, Chas and Dave, and, his personal favourite, Tommy Cooper.* 'He was a hero of mine ... that was up there

---

* It's a treat hearing Kevin on various US podcasts trying to explain exactly what the hapless comedy magician and fez aficionado Cooper actually did as an act.

with working with The Beatles for me … I don't really understand The Beatles phenomena, but I don't want to sound blasé about it. It was just a job, but an amazing job.'

77. Michael Lindsay-Hogg

'It's four people who love each other.'

He was the last person ever to film them. The first though was Leslie Woodhead, a young filmmaker for Granada TV in Manchester who in early 1962 became aware of the ferment The Beatles were creating locally. The next summer, he filmed a lunchtime session at The Cavern Club, the first film ever made of The Beatles. It affected him enormously; something hugely powerful and significant was happening here, and he felt it deeply. 'Driving back to Manchester down the East Lancashire Road I felt glutted with the overload of stuff The Beatles had served up in The Cavern. Abruptly I had to stop the car and be sick in a ditch.'

There were no such indignities awaiting Sir Michael Lindsay-Hogg, son of the 4th Baron of Rotherfield Hall, East Sussex.* That is a matter of record, though it's long been rumoured that Lindsay-Hogg was actually the son of Orson Welles who had a relationship with his mother, the Irish actress Geraldine Fitzgerald. Perhaps then, there was celluloid in the blood of a young man who was a teenage floor manager on *Ready Steady Go!* and by the mid-1960s much in demand as a director, especially by rock bands of the same generation.

He first worked with The Beatles on the promo film for 'Paperback Writer' and its B side, 'Rain', filmed at Abbey Road and on location at Chiswick House in May 1966. But it was his work on 'Hey Jude' that was the genesis for the *Let It Be* movie. For that film, Lindsay-Hogg surrounded the band with an audience of three hundred people. 'We wanted all ages and sexes, we wanted brown and black

---

* Though he never moved in this world really, he did recreate it when he directed *Brideshead Revisited* in the 1980s.

people to show how British society had changed since their Liverpool childhood.' In between takes, playing Motown and rock and roll oldies, he saw their easy rapport and delight at being back in front of an audience, 'They loved it and thought that a concert could work.'

And it did, in a way, though not before the capricious Beatles had changed their minds several times with many plans and schemes mooted and rejected. 'First it was going to be in a field, then Ringo wanted The Cavern but that would have been too small.' Most infamous and spectacular of all was Lindsay-Hogg's plan to film it at an amphitheatre near Tripoli. 'I had this idea that we start when the sun rose and Mal would start to lay out the instruments. We'd see it slowly build … The Beatles would come out and start to play and gradually the music would start to float across the desert … like musical notes floating into the sky and then landing in whatever community I wanted them to land in, whether it was a small village or an American service base. Gradually and slowly all the people would start to come across the desert and into the amphitheatre … and so by the time we're doing "Long and Winding Road" or "Let It Be" at midnight with torches, the amphitheatre would be filled by The Beatles and the world.'

The idea soon foundered though, and Lindsay-Hogg realised that what he was making was a documentary, not a concert special; 'I didn't even know what it was I was shooting … I just knew it had The Beatles in the frame.' Even so, it was unique. No one had ever seen The Beatles rehearse before or talk so candidly, though some of George's more negative interchanges and his abrupt walk-out were excised on Neil Aspinall's request. In the end, something rather more prosaic than a gig in a torchlit Libyan amphitheatre, but just as memorable, took place. It was Lindsay-Hogg's idea to play on the roof of Apple but even this was almost vetoed by Ringo ('too cold') and George ('what's the point?') before John exclaimed 'fuck it, let's do it'. It was also his idea, a brilliant move, to place the hidden camera in the lobby which afford us the wonderful interactions with the policemen, and to place some of the eleven cameras – without permission – on the roof of an adjoining building and to capture the reaction in the streets. Lindsay-Hogg's original cut ran to 210 minutes and Paul, George and Ringo felt it had too much of John and Yoko being intimate and exclusive. Allen Klein asked for it to be pared back, losing much of the chats and interactions and creating a claustrophobic, murky version of the sessions. The timing was unfortunate too; the movie came out just a month after they broke up, giving *Let It Be* the feel of a requiem although, as Lindsay-Hogg has always been keen to point out 'they weren't breaking up there ... it's four people who love each other ... and still do in life and death.'

After quickly disappearing from circulation, *Let It Be* was, for several decades, available only on poor-quality bootlegs, casting a further pall over the project. This was all redressed though, fabulously, by Peter Jackson's recasting and restoring of Lindsay-Hogg's original footage into the *Get Back* docuseries. They corresponded regularly through this process and Peter Jackson has repeatedly praised Lindsay-Hogg for tremendous work under difficult circumstances. In the interviews he's given in the last few years, Lindsay-Hogg exudes grace and modesty, referring to himself in *Get Back* as comic relief and a 'fat little porky pig'. But he is so much more than that. His enthusiasm and calm while trying to manage these four, volcanic ungovernable talents is admirable, lovable even. If *Get Back* gave us vindication via a new, positive view of the last days of The Beatles, it's also a vindication of the talent of Michael Lindsay-Hogg.

'The Beatles, I think, do represent a kind of joy,' he says. 'They represent a connection with each other, but they also represent wanting to connect with us. They know what an extraordinary thing has happened to them, but also, they know they deserved it, insofar as anyone ever deserved anything. But, most of all, I think they came along at a certain time when the world was waiting for them.'

78. Iannis Alexis 'Magic Alex' Mardas

'He was a fucking TV repairman.'

Number 94 Baker Street, Marylebone, on the thoroughfare made famous variously by Sherlock Holmes and Gerry Rafferty, is now Marsh & Parsons, an upscale estate agents. Next door is The Everyman cinema where, on the morning I pass by, the new *Bridget Jones* is playing. Across the road is a Rosa's Thai and a Franco Manco, chains offering exotic fare like Pad Thai and Sourdough Pizza that presumably wouldn't have been a part of The Beatles' London when, as the blue plaque high on Marsh & Parsons' wall informs 'John Lennon, MBE, 1940–1980, and George Harrison, MBE, 1943–2001, worked here', back in the days when 94 Baker Street was the heart of The Beatles' maddest venture, Apple.

For a man famed and feared for his sarcasm, scepticism and corrosive cynicism towards everyone from Jesus to the Maharishi, the former could sometimes be a sucker for whatever bunkum swam into his ken. Primal Scream therapy, Allen Klein and Maoism all seduced him at various times and nothing and no one more completely than Iannis Alexis Mardas, a Greek bearing decidedly dodgy gifts who rejoiced in the entirely undeserved nickname of 'Magic'.

Mardas came to London on a student visa in 1965 and fell in with arty London bohemia including such scenesters as John Dunbar at the Indica Gallery and The Rolling Stones, while his day job found him fixing tellies in the basement of Olympic Electronics. His creative CV at this point was thin; he had designed some underwhelming lights for a Stones tour but John Lennon was more impressed by his 'Nothing Box', a cuboid festooned with random lights that flashed on and off, ideal to be gawped at during John's increasingly frequent

LSD binges.* Soon John was introducing Mardas to Paul as 'my new guru ... Magic Alex!'

While Paul was less enthusiastic, Mardas seems to have been generally plausible and entertaining enough to rise through The Beatles' chaotic structures during the madness of the Apple era.

Put on the payroll in August 1967, by Christmas he was director of Apple Electronics. Among the bold new inventions he promised for The Beatles, and by extension, a grateful humanity, were force fields that would protect their houses (which could also hover), musical wallpaper and invisible paint, an innovation of limited use one would have thought. For the opening of the Apple boutique, he said he would create an artificial sun to illuminate the London night sky (he didn't). For the new Savile Row Apple offices, he promised a seventy-eight-track studio in the basement. Not only did he not manage to do this, he forgot to drill holes in the walls for the cables and leads, and failed to install an intercom between studio floor and control room. (The pained eye roll that George Martin gives in *Get Back* when he surveys Mardas' 'handiwork' is priceless.) What equipment did arrive was plastered with the names of the German manufacturers, somewhat undermining Mardas' claim to have built them all himself. In any case, the basement intended as the studio was full of unsold and unwanted Nothing Boxes, mainstream high street shoppers being less easily amused than a tripping John Lennon.

Other aspects of Mardas' time with The Beatles are darker and weirder. An enthusiast for trepanning, he tried to convince Ringo to let him drill a hole in the drummer's head to reveal his inner third eye. Turning up in Rishikesh, and jealous of the Maharishi's hold over them, especially John, he poisoned their minds with largely unsubstantiated tales of the older guru's sexual impropriety with the female adherents, although he may have had a point that an ashram

---

* Many sources claim that Mardas invented these, when they were in fact US novelty items made in 1962 by New York company Hammacher Schlemmer.

with four-poster beds, chefs and accountants is a bit 'materialistic' to say the least.*

Peter Brown says that 'Magic Alex made Cynthia Lennon's skin crawl the moment she met him.' Nonetheless, also according to Brown, Lennon had Mardas seduce Cynthia, so John could file for adultery and threaten to ask for custody of their son Julian and 'send her back to Hoylake'. Cynthia agreed to an uncontested divorce and a settlement of £100,000. As a reward, John gave Mardas an Italian sports car. Then there was the time he tried to get The Beatles to buy a Mediterranean island. Several islands in fact. Bored of their celebrity and looking for a haven to get quietly stoned together, The Beatles dispatched Mardas and Alistair Taylor to Greece to find an island where they could escape London. A mere forty-eight hours later Mardas had found just the place; a little archipelago way out in the Aegean where The Beatles could chill in peace with their entourage in their hovering, force field protected houses. As Derek Taylor trilled in his autobiography; 'We were all going to live together now, in a huge estate. The four Beatles and Brian would have their network at the centre of the compound: a dome of glass and iron tracery (not unlike the old Crystal Palace) above the mutual creative/ play area, from which arbours and avenues would lead off like spokes from a wheel to the four vast and incredibly beautiful separate living units.'

Even better, the main island had sixteen acres of olive groves which, according to Mardas' 'calculations', would pay for the island's purchase in under a decade. What he had neglected to mention was that the newly installed military junta in Greece, of which his father was a member apparently, loathed lefties and long hairs. That said,

---

* In a rare interview Mardas told Peter Brown and Steven Gaines that the Maharishi 'tried to flatter me. He knew my interest in electronics and he was starting to discuss with me a big project to put up in the Himalayan hills … the strongest radio station to broadcast his message around the world.'

the junta may have been willing to relax their ideological hostility to hippies for the PR coup of a Beatles endorsement. Alex struck a deal with the Ministry of Tourism in which he would share details of the band's movements affording various PR opportunities.

Partly because of the ensuing constant attention from press and fans, the island purchase scheme came to nothing. Still, George enjoyed it. 'It was a great trip. John and I were on acid all the time sitting on the front of the ship playing ukuleles.' Also, the nature of the ruthlessly totalitarian Greek regime didn't seem to disturb John. 'I'm not worried about the political situation in Greece as long as it doesn't affect us. I don't care if the government is all fascist or communist. I don't care.'

Once Allen Klein arrived at Apple, Mardas' magical kingdom was doomed. Klein estimated that Alex had lost the company millions in today's money. A hundred patents had been applied for and every one turned down on the grounds that they were not inventions at all but variations on existing devices. In the 1970s, Mardas moved into the world of security where he failed to supply a fleet of armoured cars to King Hussein of Jordan. (Later he gave his name to a band formed by actor John Simm who made one album entitled *Dated and Sexist*.)

The Beatles' story ran concurrently with the white heat of the Wilsonian technological revolutions and featured innovations that would transform the nature of everyday life; the jets they flew on, the LPs they sold in such profusion, the TV sets where they were viewed adoringly by millions. All of these things – useful, practical, necessary things – would change the lives of The Beatles and the world, unlike musical wallpaper and invisible paints and the fantasies of Alexis Mardas to whom history has not been kind. George Harrison recalled 'Alex's recording studio was the biggest disaster of all time. He was walking around with a white coat on like some sort of chemist, but he didn't have a clue what he was doing … it was awful. The whole thing was a disaster.'

John Dunbar was even blunter. 'He was a fucking TV repairman. Yannis Mardas, none of this "Magic Alex" shit!'

79. Imelda Marcos

'If I go back, it will be with an H Bomb to drop on it.'

The Philippines is a republic of some seven thousand islands on Asia's Pacific fringe. In 1966, it presented itself to the world as a modern, cosmopolitan nation of thirty-two million people, a tourist paradise of blue ocean and golden sands. Twenty years on from independence from the USA, they'd just elected a new youthful president, Ferdinand Marcos whom *Life* magazine dubbed, along with his regal wife Imelda, 'the John and Jackie Kennedy of the Pacific'. The Beatles' nightmarish experience in Manila in 1966 was perhaps the first hint to the wider world that there might be trouble in this corner of paradise and that the golden couple of pacific politics had more than a little tarnish to their gilding too. It would also change The Beatles' personal and artistic journey irrevocably.

Imelda Marcos arrived in Manila in 1952 aged 23 with five pesos in her purse. Thirty years later she was the world's richest woman, worth ten billion dollars. She amassed this huge fortune in the intervening years largely at the expense of the Filipino people, who nevertheless seemed to have loved her even as she passed through their ragged and dirt-poor communities and shanty towns dripping in diamonds, 'a star and a slave to my people'.

By the mid-1960s many of those people were also besotted with The Beatles thanks chiefly to DJ Ramon Jacinto on Station DZRJ. Their appearance in front of eighty thousand people for two shows at the Rizal Memorial Football Stadium was a PR coup for the Marcos regime and they were determined to make political capital from it. Unbeknownst to the band, as they rested up listening to Dylan and Ravi Shankar on a yacht in the bay (before being forced to a hotel by a seasick Epstein at 4 a.m.), Imelda Marcos was expecting them to play at a private reception the next morning to three hundred invited military families at the Presidential Palace. Here, details get sketchy. Had The Beatles received the telegram inviting/ ordering them to the palace? Did they ignore it? Did they politely but firmly decline such invitations, as has been suggested, as a matter of policy after the nastiness at the Washington Embassy in 1964? Whatever, when the escort turned up the next morning, The Beatles, or rather Brian Epstein, turned them down.

Some have argued that this was culturally insensitive, others that it was merely a misunderstanding, yet more (including this writer) that it was a perfectly reasonable (if brisk) decision by some weary young Englishmen sick of travel and forelock-tugging. But to the Marcos' and some, if by no means all, of the Filipino people, it was a personal and national snub. Client journalists fumed and railed. IMELDA STOOD UP: FIRST FAMILY WAITS IN VAIN FOR MOPHEADS ran one headline while a palace spokesperson said The Beatles had 'spit in the eye of the First Family'. While the shows themselves were triumphs – this was the biggest audience the band would ever play to in a single day – by the next day, things had soured. Literally. Neil Aspinall remembered grimly that 'They would bring up food that was terrible. Even if it was cornflakes for breakfast you'd pour the milk out and it would come out in lumps.'

Staff at the Hotel Manila refused to provide room service or to handle their baggage. At the airport the next day, there was no assistance for The Beatles' party. Airport manager Guillermo Jurado ordered the escalators to be switched off forcing them to lug amps, instruments and luggage* up several flights of steps. Armed heavies and a belligerent mob chanting 'Beatles Alis Dyan' ('Beatles Go Home') arranged by Imelda's brother, roughed up The Beatles' entourage with cudgels and coshes and waving weapons. Epstein was

---

* The Beatles were anxious that their stash of grass would be found in their suitcases. They needn't have worried; marijuana was only made illegal in the Philippines in 1972.

kicked in the groin and punched. Driver Alf Bicknell and Mal Evans sustained broken ribs. Mal later wrote in his diary 'I would give my right arm for any of those boys but under these circumstances it was most inadvisable to retaliate in any way whatsoever but to stand there and see my beloved Beatles treated so roughly was heart break-ing to me.' Someone shouted in English that The Beatles were not special and should be treated just like ordinary passengers prompt-ing Lennon to say in a TV interview 'Ordinary passengers? They don't get kicked and thumped, do they?' NEMS employee Vic Lewis dashed across the tarmac to their plane fully expecting a sniper's bullet.

Even once aboard their KLM flight, an announcement went out that 'passengers Barrow, Evans and Epstein must exit the plane'. George Harrison remembered, 'They were ordered to get off and they looked terrified. Mal went past me down the aisle of the plane breaking out in tears and turned to me and said "Tell Lil I love her." He thought that was it. The plane was going to go and he would be stuck in Manila. The whole feeling was ... fucking hell what's going to happen?' In the end, after some forty minutes of tension on the tarmac, and with the payment of some entirely spurious 'taxes', the flight took off with all The Beatles' entourage onboard.

The Beatles of course wanted nothing more than to 'alis dyan'. Once safely back in the UK, they pulled no punches of their own. Ringo stated that he hated the Philippines. Paul swore never to return and George, always the grouchiest, declared 'If I go back, it will be with an H Bomb to drop on it.' Many young Filipinos were ashamed and horrified at the Marcos' action. It had been a sinister hint at the ruling couple's true nature and what they were capable of, something that would be proved as they systematically exploited their people, hoarded gold and instituted martial law. As Paul later said 'It was an unfortunate little trip but the nice thing about it was that in the end when we found out what Marcos and Imelda had been doing to the people and the rip-off that the whole thing allegedly was, we were glad to have done what we did. Great. We must have been the only people who'd ever dared to snub Marcos.'

Most significantly of all, the unpleasantness in Manila would convince them to quit touring and concentrate on studio work. Without imperious Imelda – a woman who once spent $2,000 on chewing gum, forced a plane to perform a mid-air U turn because she had forgotten to buy some cheese in Rome, a woman whose enormous shoe hoard is now kept in not one but two museums – there may never have been a *Sgt. Pepper*. For this at least, she maybe deserves a word of grudging thanks. Salamat Po, Imelda!

80. Ravi Shankar

'If you appreciate the tuning so much,
I hope you'll enjoy the music more.'

Social historian Dominic Sandbrook has speculated that had Britain still possessed an empire in the early 1960s, the world may not have fallen quite so utterly in love with The Beatles. As it was, our colonising days were all but over, we were no longer an imposing martial force and, without this complicated 'baggage', the world was ready to be charmed by these charismatic, talented young men drawn not from the milieu of Sandhurst and stiff upper lips but the streets of Liverpool.*

Over two centuries of colonial domination and the days of the Raj, Britain's ruling class had been both seduced and repelled by India, finding it both seductive and inhospitable and developing along the way a taste for Darjeeling, Kedgeree and Bombay Sapphire gin and tonics. But among working-class people, the culture, art and religion of the Indian sub-continent were opaque and alien, if, to curious autodidacts like The Beatles, mysterious and alluring.

The sweet but unlikely story has it that George Harrison's mum, Louise, would listen to Indian music on shortwave radio when she was pregnant with him, the foetal Beatle being thus bathed in vitro in the sounds of the tabla, sitar and tambura. When he first heard them again as an adult, they felt comforting and familiar. That was in early April 1965, when traditional music was played in the Indian restaurant scene of *Help!* at Twickenham Studios. 'The first time I heard Indian music I felt as though I knew it ... it was just so strong,

---

* Paul McCartney has remarked 'It didn't worry me that the empire was crumbling. I thought it was a good thing. I was very pleased to see that old regime get out.'

so overwhelmingly positive ... I went and bought a sitar from a little shop at the top of Oxford Street called Indiacraft – it stocked little carvings, and incense. It was a real crummy quality one, actually, but I bought it and mucked about with it a bit.' Harrison's subsequent untutored but deft and perfect sitar line in 'Norwegian Wood' was the first use of the instrument by a western musician on a commercial recording.

On the way back from their ill-fated Philippines trip in July 1966, The Beatles had a two-day layover in Delhi, their first visit to India. Assuming they were unknown there, they were amazed to find six hundred fans and journalists waiting for them in the middle of the night at Palam airport. 'Delhi was a really funny feeling,' recalled George later. 'There were little kids coming up to us with flies all over them and asking for money: "Baksheesh! Baksheesh!" Our cameras were worth more money than the whole village would earn in a lifetime. It was a very strange feeling seeing this: Cadillacs and Poverty.' The Cadillacs being the ones The Beatles were being ferried around in.

Hysteria notwithstanding, The Beatles found time to stroll and shop in the airy lanes of Connaught Place in the Lahore Music Store and Rikh Ramh music shop who brought various Indian instruments for them to try in their suite at the Oberoi hotel. Harrison was much impressed by the proprietor Mr Sharma's proficiency in the sitar. When he asked who had taught him to play, the reply was the first time he had heard the name of the man who would become his lifelong friend; Pandit Ravi Shankar.

Shankar, son of a high-ranking politician, had been a dancer and musician since his teens, had travelled widely in America and Europe and become recognised as a virtuoso ambassador for the music of the sub-continent. Harrison first met Shankar at a dinner given by the Asian Music Circle in London. In either case, the connection between the two men was genuine and immediate, like 'wildfire' as Ravi said. He gave George sitar lessons and Harrison was a dedicated and industrious student, practising sometimes eight hours a day.

The next year he and Pattie Boyd made a further trip to India to visit Shankar, drawn not just by the new sonic possibilities of the music but a growing spiritual calling. 'Ravi and the sitar were excuses … although they were an important part of it, it was a search for a spiritual connection.' George's commitment to finding inner peace was sincere, but it didn't entirely placate the grumpiest Beatle. He told All India Radio that he was not happy at having to be a Beatle 'on his holiday' and told super fan, Pat Rekhi, 'Tell your friends if they like me to keep away from me.' One can only imagine the culture shock, especially for Boyd, a 22-year-old model who had been whisked from the boutiques of the Kings Road to watching funeral pyres blaze on the banks of the Ganges in Benares.

Shankar and Harrison remained close for the rest of his life; so much so that Ravi felt that they must have had some connection in a previous life. Through Harrison he became well known to western pop and rock audiences. In 1966 he provided the music to Jonathan Miller's exquisite, psychedelic BBC TV adaptation of *Alice In Wonderland* and in 1967 he shone at the Monterey Pop festival though was horrified to watch Hendrix set fire to his guitar: 'That was too much for me. In our culture, we have such respect for musical instruments. They are like part of God.' After the dissolution of The Beatles, the plight of flood-ravaged Bangladesh moved him to ask Harrison for help. The result was the Concert for Bangladesh, rock's first major charity mega-gig. Shankar and his ensemble opened proceedings and he gently chided the well-meaning hippies in the audience who greeted the first brief section with rapturous applause: 'If you appreciate the tuning so much, I hope you'll enjoy the music more.'

By his death in San Diego in 2012, Shankar had been awarded India's highest honour the Bharat Ratna (Jewel of India), the Légion d'Honneur and, ironically, was a Knight of The British Empire, that hugely loaded notion. The Indian actor, Monica Dogra, says The Beatles helped remove 'the post-colonial culture of apology in India. The most powerful cultural force in the world revered Indian culture.' Ajoy Bose, director of the excellent documentary *The Beatles In India* makes a similar point. 'It wasn't just a fad or something exotic, it was a genuine feeling … Similarly, The Beatles were our introduction to a new kind of westerner and specifically, a new Britain. They made the Indian westernised middle class realise the value of their own culture and Hindustani classic music. The world has changed now, and there isn't such a vast chasm between West and East anymore. But The Beatles were the pioneers in building a cultural bridge and the global culture we have today.'

More flippantly but just as powerfully, Prabha Dutt, who became India's first female war correspondent and a top reporter on the *Hindustani Times* said that of all the things she saw and did in her career nothing compared to 'Oh my god, to have been sitting between John and Paul.' Musician Neil Mukherjee is even more heartfelt and accurate about The Beatles' impact on India and beyond. 'The world would have been, like, so shit without them.'

81. Leslie Cavendish

'My first day I saw Shirley Bassey.'

It was the hair they noticed first, the old order with their short back and sides and crew cuts. Not the songs, not the primal energy, not the charisma or sex or wit. It was the hair.

When Astrid Kirchherr washes the grease out of The Beatles' hair in Hamburg and Jurgen Volmer styles John and Paul's fringes in Paris, these are hugely symbolic moments of transition, of generational and cultural shift. No more brilliantine, no more quiffs, no more of the slicked, oleaginous look of Teddy Boy, spiv and Sgt Major. The Beatles' hair was clean, lustrous, abundant and above all modern. The shock of the new Beatles' hair would completely change the way men and boys looked in Britain. Like 16-year-old Thomas Charnock, an apprentice at the K.W.K. engineering factory in Birkenhead, suspended, along with other apprentices by boss William Kaminski who said Beatle haircuts were 'unsightly, unsafe, unruly and unclean'. In the end though, Thomas won the day. 'I think my hair is perfectly all right, but I have had it trimmed and hope there will be no more trouble.' His grandmother, Mrs Elizabeth Charnock added, 'I do not understand what all the fuss is about. He has a lovely head of hair.'

Generally, after their German friends' intervention, The Beatles had great hair, at least until the infamous (to me at least) 1969 photo shoot at Tittenhurst Park in which, as John Higgs has pointed out, 'Lennon has objectively bad hair. When a Beatle was photographed with bad hair we were suddenly in uncharted waters. There had never been a photo of The Beatles with truly terrible hair before. Usually, they had great hair. Sometimes their hair was just OK and there had been questionable moustache choices along the way, but never before had their hair made you wince.'

Up to this point, The Beatles' great hair was testament to the tonsorial skills of Leslie Cavendish at the Vidal Sassoon salon. His was not quite a spiritual calling. Picking his mum up from a hairdressing salon in the London suburb of Burnt Oak, the teenage Cavendish noticed a Chevrolet belonging to the hair stylist. 'You don't see many Chevrolets in Burnt Oak ... and I was sitting there and I thought ... he comes to work every day in his nice car and he's surrounded by women ... how nice is that?' Abandoning his dreams of being a footballer, he instead went to work for Sassoon at his 171 New Bond Street salon; 'My first day I saw Shirley Bassey ... it was terrific ... Cilla Black ... Lulu ... Peter O'Toole going upstairs to get his hair highlighted.'

He became Jane Asher's hairdresser and it was her who, one Saturday morning in 1966, asked him if he could cut her boyfriend's hair. Despite knowing full well who Jane Asher's boyfriend was, Cavendish asserted that it would have to wait till 6.30 p.m. when he'd got back from the QPR v. Swindon glamour clash at Loftus Road. Later that day then, he made his first visit to 7 Cavendish Avenue ('My surname ... it was meant to be'). It was September, and The Beatles had played their last concert the previous month.

From this point until their dissolution, Cavendish was to become court hairdresser to The Beatles (although naturally Ringo, being married to a hairdresser, required his services less). He first cut Lennon's hair during a meeting and gave Ringo a trim on the set of *The Magic Christian*. Eventually, The Beatles opened a Kings Road salon for him under the Apple auspices that George would 'float up to'. He became the on-the-road hairstylist on the *Magical Mystery Tour*. 'The camaraderie between all four of them was nice ... but it didn't take long for me to realise that McCartney was the director of The Beatles.' In an interview with *Disc* magazine, Cavendish mentioned that John's hair was slightly less rich and lustrous than his bandmates. 'The next thing I knew, Derek Taylor rang me late at night. "Did you tell the press that Lennon's going bald?" John phoned and I grovelled, crying, "I'm so sorry, she's taken me out of context and I never said that …"' Lennon cut him short 'You don't need to explain what the press is like. Look what happened to me. I said we were bigger than Jesus and America wanted my head on a plate.'

His Beatle crops attracted the attention of other 1960s glitterati and soon Cavendish was also shampooing and snipping the locks of Keith Moon, The Bee Gees, The Dave Clark Five, Terence Stamp, James Taylor, Graham Nash and Bob Weir of The Grateful Dead (presumably the only member of the shaggy San Franciscans to regularly visit the barbers). History does not record whether he offered his clientele 'something for the weekend'. He cut The Beatles' hair till the mid-1970s, never using gel but occasionally a little conditioner. His memoir is called, with the hairdresser's traditional delight in the pun, *The Cutting Edge*. At the premiere of the remastered *Magical Mystery Tour* and meeting Paul for the first time in many years, Cavendish pointed out that, despite Macca's prediction in 'When I'm Sixty-four', now that he had got older, he was not in fact losing his hair, or even its auburn lustre, it seemed.

82. Yoko Ono

*'If he'd fallen in love with Petula Clark,
no one would have cared.'*

I'm at an exhibition at the Tate Modern Art Gallery on the South Bank of the river Thames, wondering exactly how self-conscious I would feel if I, as urged by various signage, were to obey their exhortations to climb inside the large black bag lying before me. In the end, British reserve wins and, rather than enter belatedly into the spirit of 'Bagism', I do what most of the visitors are doing and hammer a nail into a piece of plywood, again, as encouraged by the exhibition's subject, Yoko Ono.* As I look around her works, the dryly witty conceptual and surreal poetry, the slow-mo films of burning matches and exposed bums, the portentous sculptures such as suspended helmets filled with jigsaw puzzle pieces, I am aware of the buzz in my head that is the endless competing, conflicting assessments that have dominated the Yoko 'discourse'; that she is a purveyor of humbug who derailed The Beatles or that she is a genuinely fascinating and thought-provoking artist who has been the victim of racism, sexism and philistinism. In the end, the only sensible conclusion is that Yoko, enigmatic, exasperating, electrifying, may be a little of both.

Yoko Ono didn't break up The Beatles, but she probably didn't help them stay together. On a very basic level, as *Get Back* showed, taking your girlfriend (or boyfriend) to work every day, a baleful, silent presence at your elbow to the evident annoyance of your workmates is no more a sensible or productive notion for a rock musician than it would be for a teacher or plumber. Whether it was this,

---

* Like much else about her, we get her name wrong. The Japanese is Ono Yoko or 'Ocean child'.

eating his digestive biscuits or perching on his amplifier that so aggrieved George is unclear. But aggrieved he was. Macca was characteristically diplomatic and generous, 'Ok, they're going overboard, but then John always does … but it's none of our business, even when it comes into our business.' He adds, with extraordinary prescience, 'It's going to be such a comical thing in fifty years' time, you know, they broke up because Yoko sat on an amp.'

On the other hand, in an essay in *The New York Times* entitled 'The Sublime Spectacle of Yoko Ono Disrupting The Beatles', Amanda Hess celebrates her 'obtrusive' presence, claiming Ono was 'staging a marathon performance piece' for Lindsay-Hogg's cameras. 'She refuses to decamp to the sidelines, but she also resists acting out stereotypes; she appears as neither a doting naïf nor a needling busybody. Instead, she seems engaged in a kind of passive resistance, defying all expectations of women who enter the realm of rock genius.' You pay your money and you take your analytical choice.

Ono grew up in a defeated, starving post-war Tokyo; developing fantasy dinner menus with her brother was, she said, her first piece of conceptual art. In her twenties, she moved to Manhattan and became part of the Fluxus art movement, who also included musician Beck's granddad, Al Hanssen. Fluxus was heavily influenced by the work and theories of John Cage and it was collecting material for a Cage tribute that first took her to Paul McCartney's door and thence to John Lennon. When he climbed the ladder at Yoko's exhibition at the Indica Gallery to look through a magnifying glass at the word 'Yes' on a suspended canvas, a seismic change, for him, his group and the wider world, was begun.

Ono haters claim she hunted Lennon as her celebrity quarry, inserting herself between him and Cynthia with manic persistence. Others think this is sheer prejudice. What is not in doubt is that Lennon was smitten with her. When Lennon sang 'I'm in love for the first time' on 'Don't Let Me Down' he may well have meant it, but one can only guess at how Cynthia must have felt. The rest of

John and Yoko's courtship, marriage, break up, reunion and eventual bloody severance, is so well known as to be almost colourless now, even though the events are sometimes lurid. I interviewed Yoko in the Noughties. Physically tiny, she had enormous presence. I told her that I loved some of her albums like *Fly*, *Approximately Infinite Universe* and *Yes I Am A Witch* (I even like some of her tracks on the reviled John & Yoko set *Sometime in New York City*) and she seemed genuinely charmed and intrigued. I didn't mention that for me some of her aphorisms ('Smile in the mirror. Do that every morning and you'll start to see a big difference in your life') make the slogans on Cotswolds gift shop fridge magnets seem like Wittgenstein. Looking back at her recent tweets in the winter of 2024 one stands out as strange and mildly heartbreaking; 'The world was really hating me and sending hatred vibes toward me very overtly for I don't know how many years … It was sort of fashionable to put me down. You don't hurt me though, because I know you and I love you. I can take hatred because I don't believe that people are capable of real hate. We are too lonely for that. We vanish too quickly for that.'*

A 1970 interview with Ono was published in *Esquire* under the appalling headline 'John Rennon's Excrusive Gloopie'. So we can all now see much of that hostility to her for what it was, racism and sexism, pure, patriarchal and poisonous. But for all her fame and candour (putting the bloodstained spectacles John was murdered in on an album sleeve was pretty breathtaking) she remains a complex, unknowable person, forever condemned to be both lionised and misunderstood not for herself but for the man she married, like Jackie O or Mrs Lincoln. In the end, as Beatle podcaster Robert Rodriguez has said 'If he'd fallen in love with Petula Clark, no one would have cared.'

---

* Tennis star Andy Murray's mother Judy went through an unedifying phase of replying sarcastically to Yoko's drippier tweets.

83. David Christian

'A collection of Beatles Oldies.'

In those long, penurious, purchase-free Saturday afternoons of my early teens, browsing Wigan's record racks with little hope of buying, a handful of albums languished unloved and unbought in the racks at Roy Hurst's Records, Wigan. There was *Terrapin Station* by The Grateful Dead, a Harry Secombe album and that Barclay James Harvest LP with the cover of a baby in a plant pot. But I was always surprised that there was a Beatles album in among them, until at least I flipped it over and looked at the track listing. It was a Greatest Hits of sorts, not a very interesting one, and there was one of those old rock and roll reworkings on there that for some of us were the only duff moments on the early albums. And so I went back to seeing if there were any cheap Gentle Giant or Wire albums on offer (I was a weird kid).

For those of us who weren't around to buy Beatles records as they were released, compilations offered a gateway drug into their impossibly thrilling world. A generation of 1970s youth were introduced to them via 1973's 'Red' and 'Blue' career spanning double albums, ubiquitous in every record collection of the day. The motivation here may have been venal – Allen Klein wanted to squeeze every last cent from the now estranged Beatles – but the legacy of those four discs was joyful in the main. Three decades later, the *1* album, corralling all their singles, was a global phenomenon, especially timely in the UK with New Labour, Britpop and Cool Britannia chiming with a very Sixties mood of Beatle-adjacent optimism and vigour.

1966's *A Collection of Beatles Oldies But Goldies* is, as its extended tenure in Roy Hurst's Records attests, less well loved, but it too has its own story. It was essentially a stop-gap release for the Christmas market, which had featured a Beatles album for the past three years. EMI were also fearful that ravenous Fab Four fans might be seduced by new sensations like The Monkees during the (what was for them, protracted) radio silence as The Beatles assembled *Sgt. Pepper*. It was their first compilation, consisting of sixteen songs recorded between 1963 and 1966, with, as noted above, one previously unreleased cover, the undistinguished 'Bad Boy', included to tempt diehards. It was hard to see why else they would buy it, and to a significant degree, they didn't. '*Oldies*' was the first Beatles' album not to reach Number 1, partly because *Revolver* was still in the shops and selling well and partly because of the staggering success of *The Sound of Music* soundtrack, the best-selling album of the past two years.

It was also the only Beatles album to date to not feature The Beatles on its cover. They wanted nothing to do with the project but were nevertheless bound to two albums a year for Parlophone. Epstein, then, commissioned a young Australian illustrator called David Christian, now based in London. His daughter Nicola told *Beatlefan* magazine, 'They had apparently been let down by someone else and needed artwork done quickly … I don't know how much my father was paid for it, but it can't have been a huge amount – he was no millionaire! … My dad was very proud of the work he did with The Beatles and had fond memories of those times. I think he was rather pleased with how the artwork and lettering turned out.'

With no Beatle available, Christian's illustration echoed the prevalent militaria chic and the vogue for Edwardiana of modish boutiques like I Was Lord Kitchener's Valet and songs like 'Winchester Cathedral'. Foregrounded is a groovy figure garbed in migraine-inducing, flamboyant, psychedelic style that The Beatles were in the process of assuming, but most of their fans would not have been aware of this until the promo clips for 'Penny Lane' and 'Strawberry Fields Forever' emerged a few months later. Though it courts the clichéd today, Christian captured the aesthetic of the times, perhaps even encouraged it.*

Not helped by a decidedly lame title – 'oldies but goldies' would hardly seem to apply to tracks like 'Paperback Writer' and 'Eleanor Rigby' that had been huge hits just months previously – the record did little to endear itself to UK fans. Its real significance, though, lay further afield. Beatles albums to this point had not been released behind the Iron Curtain where the authorities feared their seditious hedonism would sap the revolutionary zeal of socialist youth.† But with the dawn of the 'Prague Spring' and Alexander Dubcek's 'communism with a human face', *A Collection of Oldies But Goldies* became the first Beatles album available, on the state owned Supraphon label, in the former Czechoslovakia and thus on throughout the Soviet bloc.

Its impact was enormous. Though Dubcek's Prague Spring was ruthlessly put down as tanks rolled into Wenceslas Square, the spirit embodied in The Beatles' music – youth, hope, freedom – had been set free across Eastern Europe. 'The Beatles brought us the idea of democracy. For many of us, it was the first hole in the iron curtain', Russian musician Sasha Lipniski told *The Guardian* in 2013. A collection of Beatles oldies but goldies, that naff Christmas cash-in, disowned and unloved, was heard and seen very differently by teenagers in Kyiv, Magdeburg and Bratislava. David Christian's artwork, and of course the music within, evoked a dayglo world of long hair, garish ties, crazy colours that may have been becoming commonplace and even corny here but that behind the Iron Curtain, meant freedom.

---

* Christian also designed the vibrant lettering for the sides of the Magical Mystery Tour coach and front cover of the album and EP.

† Angela Merkel would have to wait to 1969 to travel for her copy of *Yellow Submarine.*

1967

84. Pablo Fanque

'I want to smell the sawdust.'

I've never liked circuses. It's not just the now obligatory disquietude around clowns, or any moral revulsion at watching animals perform. I just think they're really boring. So many Easter Monday TV teatimes of my childhood were ruined by Billy Smart and Charlie Cairoli when what I really wanted was *Marine Boy* and *Joe 90*. The only version of the Big Top I've ever enjoyed is the one that ends Side One of The Beatles' summer of love masterpiece.

A few months before *Sgt. Pepper* was released The Beatles filmed the promotional video for 'Strawberry Fields Forever' over two days in late January 1967 in Sevenoaks, Kent. During a break, John Lennon wandered into an antique shop near to their hotel where his eye was caught by an elaborate, detailed poster advertising a Victorian circus benefit performance by Pablo Fanque in Rochdale in 1843. Lennon had always been attracted to prolix, ornate, nonsensical prose, the verbal spaghetti of Stanley Unwin, the absurdities of Lewis Carroll, Edward Lear and The Goons. The poster charmed and intrigued him with its mixture of mystery and grandstanding, the excitable claim that this would be 'positively the last night but three!' and the promise of 'somersets', 'hoops' and 'garters', hogsheads of real fire, horses, trampolines and the acrobatics of the Henderson's ('late of Pablo Fanques fair') and all 'Being for The Benefit of Mr Kite'.*

Lennon bought the poster and put it above his piano at home where the heady psychedelic soup of phrases and images fed, of course, into the lyrics of one of *Sgt. Pepper*'s most aurally stunning songs. But there's a great story lurking behind the whirl of colour and images. 'Being for The Benefit of Mr Kite' stands as a powerful if accidental tribute to a man who was not just an exceptional showman but a pioneer of black entrepreneurialism, creativity and artistic endeavour in Britain.

Pablo Fanque was born William Darby in 1796 in Norwich, the son of a black father and a white mother. Though details are vague, he seems to have been a physical prodigy, a gifted acrobat, tightrope walker and horse trainer who joined a travelling circus as 'Pablo Fanque'. After three decades of life in the ring, Fanque formed his own circus in 1841 where he was joined by the acrobat, Mr William Kite, and Mr John Henderson, a high wire walker. By the middle of the century, Pablo Fanque's circus was one of the biggest entertainment draws in Northern England. Much of its success was down to astute and grandiose self-promotion such as driving a 'twelve-in-hand' of horses through the streets of Bolton and employing the pioneering poster designer Edward Sheldon when he was just 17. It was one of Sheldon's dazzling creations that ended up on John Lennon's wall via the Sevenoaks antique shop.

---

* Fanque seems to have been a generous man. In 1857, he performed a benefit in Bradford for the family of a recently deceased clown.

Though Fanque was enormously popular and seems to have encountered little in the way of overt or institutional racism, there was real sadness in his story. On 18 March 1848, when his circus was playing in Leeds, a section of wooden seating collapsed. Hundreds of people were buried in falling timber but there was one single fatality; Pablo Fanque's wife, Susannah Darby, who was in the pay office below the gallery. In the chaos, someone stole her watch and the evening's takings of fifty pounds.

Fanque remarried and later in life changed his circus to an entirely family oriented show, recognising that it would appeal to a broader range of customers. Bringing in a more middle-class audience allowed Fanque to charge the then dizzying price of a shilling for a box seat and sixpence for the pit. Nevertheless, by the time of his death in a rented room in a Stockport pub aged 76 he was 'in great poverty', according to former colleagues. But he remained rich in public affection. A huge crowd lined the route of his funeral procession in Leeds where he is buried. After Fanque's death, the chaplain of the Showman's Guild remarked: 'In the great brotherhood of the equestrian world there is no colour line, for, although Pablo was of African extraction, he speedily made his way to the top of his profession. The camaraderie of the Ring has but one test, ability.'

He lives on in an echo on one of the famous albums of all time. Lennon, according to Ian MacDonald, sat staring at the poster and 'playing his piano, sang phrases from it until he had a song'. But 'Being for The Benefit of Mr Kite' only really bloomed into mesmerising life thanks to the genius of George Martin's eerie, intoxicating melange of wobbling tape loops, calliopes, harmoniums, and other assorted arcana, a response to Lennon's demand for a 'fairground' production, saying to Martin 'I want to smell the sawdust'. The result is one of the greatest examples of the later period Beatles' uncanny ability (see also 'The Fool on The Hill', 'Cry Baby Cry', 'Strawberry Fields Forever,' etc.) to combine the enchanting and the disquieting in a single song.

One of the few items on the poster that Lennon changed was the name of the horse from Zanthus to Henry. Because of this, it was one of three songs from the *Sgt. Pepper* album that were banned on the BBC who thought it was a drug song because it combined two words 'Horse' and 'Henry' that were individually known as slang for heroin. They were, of course, wrong.

85. Meta Davies

'She was slightly military looking.'

Former Chief Constable of Nottingham, Captain Athelstan Horn Popkess is memorable not merely for his splendid name. He was the man who proposed in 1957 'a body of men, eager for police work, but barred by height or age to deal with trifling motoring offences like illegal parking and obstruction'. Thus was born the Traffic Warden.

By 1967, women had joined this much maligned and misunderstood body. Meta Davies had a beat that took in Paul McCartney's St John's Wood 'manor', which is how, according to her, she came to give him a parking ticket one spring day in that year. 'He was on a meter showing excess, so I gave him a ten-shilling ticket ... I'd just put it on the windscreen when Paul came along and took it off. He looked at it and read my signature which was in full, because there was another M. Davies on the same unit. As he was walking away, he turned to me and said, "Oh, is your name really Meta?", I told him that it was. We chatted for a few minutes and he said, "That would be a good name for a song. Would you mind if I use it?" And that was that. Off he went.'

Off he went to write 'Lovely Rita'. That's the lovely story anyway. In fact, Macca had probably already written that charming *Sgt. Pepper* track, inspired by a walk near brother Mike's house on the Wirral around the time that parking meters were becoming a fixture on British streets. 'Meter Maid' is what the American's called female traffic wardens, a fact which caught McCartney's ear for the mellifluous and memorable. 'I thought, God, that's so American! Also to me "maid" had sexual connotations, like a French maid or a milkmaid, there's something good about "maid", and "meter" made it a bit more official, like the meter in a cab; the meter is running, meter maid.'

288

So he told Barry Miles in *Many Years from Now*. But later in his *Lyrics* book, he claims 'There was one particular meter maid in Portland Place on whom I based "Rita". She was slightly "military" looking. I know it's a terrible thing to say, but those meter maids were never good-looking. You never heard anybody say, "God, that's one stunning parking attendant." In any case, "I caught a glimpse of Rita" opposite the Chinese embassy in Portland Place. She was "filling in a ticket in her little white book". The "cap", the "bag across her shoulder". It's sheer observation.'

Was that Meta Davies? Portland Place is 2.3 miles from St John's Wood according to Google Maps. What is certain is that by the time Meta gave Paul his ticket in the spring of 1967, 'Lovely Rita' had already been recorded, on 23 and 24 February. John Lennon certainly didn't think Rita was real. 'Nah … He makes 'em up like a novelist. You hear lots of McCartney-influenced songs on the radio now. These stories about boring people doing boring things: being postmen and secretaries and writing home … I'm not interested in writing third-party songs' he stated, adding perhaps unnecessarily, 'I like to write about me.'

86. David Mason

'Why are you all in fancy dress?'

The Beatles' ravenous musical appetite and insatiable curiosity led them to search out new, exciting sonic adventures in much the same way that some Roman emperors sought out ever more extreme 'pleasures' to excite their jaded sensual palettes. The results inside Abbey Road though were generally more edifying than the goings on within Caligula's palace. The Beatles' encounters with the worlds of classical music, jazz and the music of other cultures were unprecedented delights for them and their listeners.

Just five session musicians are named on Beatles recordings. Alan Civil performs the plaintive French horn solo on 'For No One', Anil Bhagwat plays tabla on 'Love You To', while Hariprasad Chaurasia contributes the lovely Bansuri bamboo flute on 'The Inner Light'. Billy Preston ('Don't Let Me Down'), George Martin ('Not A Second Time') and Mal 'Organ' Evans contribution of Hammond on 'You Won't See Me' complete a short list ideal for a Beatles nerd quiz night.

Sheila Bromberg provided the exquisite intro and harp accompaniment on 'She's Leaving Home', as well as the equally fabulous intro to Heatwave's brit funk classic 'Boogie Nights' (and appeared in a Monty Python sketch playing the harp in a wheelbarrow). As 'She's Leaving Home' is one of a very few Beatles' songs on which none of them play an instrument,* she had never even met Ringo until an appearance on the BBC's *One Show* under the excitable auspices of Chris Evans. (Ringo was pleased that her fee of £8 was more than she usually received.) Jason Kruppa's superb *Producing The Beatles* podcast has a whole episode devoted to the clarinet trio

---

* See also 'Eleanor Rigby', 'Good Night' and 'The Inner Light'.

arrangement on 'When I'm Sixty-four'. From this, I learned the pleasing fact that one of the three players, Frank Reidy, later went on to play the sax in The Muppets' resident rockers, Dr Teeth and The Electric Mayhem.

Most notable of all perhaps is David Mason. One night, Paul McCartney was watching a performance on TV of Bach's *Brandenburg Concerto* by the English Chamber Orchestra when he realises that the bright, piercing sound of the piccolo trumpet is just what he needs to replace the somewhat dreary existing cor anglais line on his new song, 'Penny Lane'. Finding out that the player was David Mason, George Martin hires him for the next day's session where Mason is surprised that all The Beatles turn up in their new psychedelic finery. 'I said "Why are you all in fancy dress? Have you come from a film set?" They said "Oh no, we dress like this all the time now."'

Mason played the demanding line with flair, eventually 'nailing it' according to engineer Geoff Emerick and, though Paul suggested another take, Martin wisely knew a tiring Mason would never surpass it. When he asked what the track was intended for, he was surprised to learn it was to be the B side of another song they were working on, 'Strawberry Fields Forever'. 'I said, quite innocently, this is much better than Strawberry Fields. John Lennon who was sitting in the corner said "Thanks a lot, mate, I wrote that."'

Thus, Mason was instrumental (sorry) in the decision to release what became the greatest double A side, possibly the greatest pop single ever. He left the session £27. 10 shillings the richer and told the BBC many years later 'a lot of people have said to me that they think my solo makes the record … and I think they're probably right.'

87. Linda McCartney

'I was impressed to see his Magrittes.'

Locals say that Calderstones Park is the most beautiful in Liverpool. It looks its best, all ornamental gardens and sparkling water, on a warm spring day, when the swings and climbing frames ring to the sound of children's warm Scouse laughter. The Linda McCartney Play Area was opened on 19 July 1999 by her husband, Paul, who unveiled a plaque and planted a Cypress oak. A happy, safe place for children and families is an appropriate memorial to the late Lady McCartney. Linda, muse, animal lover, supportive wife and devoted mum, significantly blonde and sweet and undeniably Caucasian, would seem on this evidence to have avoided the suspicion and hostility that came Yoko's way.

But this wasn't always the case. For periods of her too short life, Linda too suffered from the kind of nasty, casual sexism that was rife in the 1970s rock culture. She had a hard time from the Apple Scruffs that haunted the offices on Savile Row and the fans that ringed Paul's home on Cavendish Avenue. She was routinely mocked during her time in Wings for her supposed musical shortcomings. She was slighted in interviews by condescending males; John Lennon once said, 'She got the same kind of insults, hatred, absolute garbage thrown at her (as Yoko) for no reason whatsoever other than she fell in love with Paul McCartney.'

But, as Danny Fields says in his biography of her,* by the time of her passing, 'She had managed to win everyone round and, unless you were a meat-packer or a furrier, she wasn't even vaguely controversial ... in fact she was beloved.' Those two provisos are there

---

* British journalist Leslie Ann Jones was also in discussions with her to write a biography. The proposed title, which Linda loved, was *Mac The Wife*.

because she probably did more to advance the cause of vegetarianism than any other human being, and certainly any other musician, even Morrissey. For it is one thing to wag an admonishing finger through dreary songs about meat being murder, but quite another, more useful thing to produce some actually half decent sausages and burgers so 'the veggies' have something to scoff at the barbecue.

The daughter of a wealthy showbiz lawyer, Lee Eastman,* she grew up in fine houses in the Hamptons and Scarsdale in Upstate New York, where film stars and musicians would often drop by. Aged six, she had a song, 'Linda', written about her by one of her father's clients, Jack Lawrence, a hit for Buddy Clark in 1947 and also covered by Perry Como, Jan and Dean, Jimmy Young and, coincidentally, Dick James. (Sadly, it's terrible.) Her Scarsdale High Yearbook entry described her as 'a strawberry blonde with a yen for men'. Her mother was killed in the terrible 1962 crash of American Airlines Flight 1 in Jamaica Bay, New York when she was just 18 and, in an apparent daze, she married. 'My mother died in a plane crash and I got married. It was a mistake.'

After the marriage broke down, she moved to New York as a single mum with four-year-old Heather, bought a Pentax and through sheer effort of will became a celebrated (and favoured) rock photographer. In May 1967 researching a book called *Rock and Other Four Letter Words*, she dropped in to the Bag O'Nails club on Kingly Street, London to see Georgie Fame and The Blue Flames, a favourite band and haunt of Paul McCartney (as well as Frank McClintock and many Arsenal players of the day). Paul recalled, 'I saw this blonde across the room and I fancied her. So, when she passed my table I said something stupid like "Hello. How are you. Let me take you away from all this."' He then delivered what he referred to as 'my big pulling line' asking her on to The Speakeasy

---

* He changed it to Eastman from the family name, which was, ironically, Epstein.

293

where, along with Chas Chandler and Eric Burdon, they enjoyed chef Enzo's special; steak and chips with mushy peas alla nonno (with fried onion).* Later still they repaired to Cavendish Avenue, Linda remarking afterwards 'I was impressed to see his Magrittes.'†

Exactly a year later Paul and John went to America to appear on *The Tonight Show* and to publicise their new Apple venture and Paul and Linda met again. She slipped him a note with her phone number and they spent the next few days together, Paul even babysitting for Heather while Linda went out snapping bands at the Fillmore East. They were married at Marylebone registry office on 11 March 1969. Paul forgot to buy a ring and had to persuade a local jeweller to reopen his shop to buy one for £12. Once married, they did not spend one night apart for the rest of her life, aside from Paul's incarceration in Japan.

Without Linda, Paul may not have made it through the dark postscript to The Beatles, a period when he was drinking heavily and spending most of his day in bed in a woebegone fugue. The suggestion to buy the dilapidated High Park Farm in Scotland was Jane Asher's but renovations didn't begin until after Paul and Linda married. He thought it was 'a dump' but she embraced it as a potential family home, refuge and place of inspiration. 'She said, "Could we go up there?" And then with Linda, and with raising the family there, I saw things I'd never seen before in the countryside and scenery. It became really special.' 'Mull of Kintyre', the 1977 Christmas Number 1 and the first single to sell over two million copies nationwide, was his love song to the area. Less well known is that 'The Long and Winding Road' was inspired by the view of the nearby country road 'stretching into the hills'.

---

* Paul is apparently still keen on the dish. On tour recently in Uruguay, his catering team served him Fish (battered tofu) and Chips with mushy peas.

† She had an ear for a good line; she once said 'If slaughterhouses had glass walls, the whole world would be vegetarian.'

'My father would like me to have married a commuter and drink Martinis in the evening' Linda once said. Instead, she married a small-time Scottish farmer and musician, never happier than when riding his Massey Ferguson 315 around his isolated homestead, not far from Campbeltown, where there is a statue and memorial to Linda McCartney nee Eastman 'girlfriend, lover, wife and the mother of my children'.

88. Peter Blake

'Even the people that did the flowers were paid more!'

When *The Guardian* came to interview the about-to-become nonagenarian artist Peter Blake in 2022, his wife Chrissy pleaded 'Let this be the only article in the last fifty-five years that doesn't mention The Beatles.' There was, naturally, no chance of that. For all his widely admired body of work, his pivotal influence on UK art, his twenty-odd other album covers from Ian Dury to Paul Weller, Oasis to Band Aid, one commission from 1967 defines him, though it certainly didn't make him rich, something he has always been keen to point out.

Peter Blake studied graphic design at Gravesend Technical College, then after National Service studied at the Royal College painting course during which he developed his distinctive warm and playful vernacular rooted in the pop culture he loved; badges, comics, amusement arcades, tattoos, wrestling, records, the Union Jack. He was part of that pop art movement that brought freshness and vitality to British painting. His friendship with The Beatles began when, via a director friend who'd enthused to him about the band, he sat in on a Beatles London TV appearance when they performed 'Please Please Me'. After the show, 'We went back to the hotel with George and John and Ringo, but no Paul … then John said: "Do you know any nightclubs? We don't really know London and we've never been clubbing here." The week before I had been taken to a place called The Crazy Elephant … But the doorman said: "No, sorry mate, you're not a member." They were playing a Beatles song and John said: "Well that's our song, I'm a Beatle." He didn't believe him. But a voice from around the corner said: "Can you let them in? They're friends of mine." We went in, and it was Paul. He was already there with Jane Asher.'

Four years later, with Paul in the meantime having commissioned him to 'paint something good' for his newly purchased Scottish farmhouse, The Beatles asked him to work on the *Sgt. Pepper* cover, having rejected a design by Dutch art collective The Fool. 'The album name was already decided. They were having the uniforms made. They had a vague idea of it being like a brass band, Black Dyke Mills Band or something like that ... I did it with my first wife, Jann Haworth. It slowly evolved into the idea that they had just done a gig, they were in a park and a group of their fans were getting behind them for a photograph. Various ideas came from The Beatles, and others from us.' Blake and Haworth blew up the various collaged figures to life-size and posed the band in front, with a real flower arrangement. The Beatles chose most of the personnel – Lennon wanted Hitler, naturally – but some were Blake's own suggestions such as Simon Rodia, the Italian 'outsider artist' who flanks Bob Dylan.

The result of course is the most famous, beloved, widely aped and most parodied album sleeve ever (with the possible exception of *Abbey Road*). Blake, though, in recent interviews has exhibited a certain ambivalence towards his most famous work: 'I always say it's been a mixed blessing ... It's a cross I bear, it's an albatross I have to deal with ... What vaguely depresses me still is that I'm known pretty much as "Peter Blake – who did the cover of *Sgt. Pepper*" when I've done so much else ... Every so often I manage to forget it but it comes back all the time.' One imagines this lack of enthusiasm is partly due to a mild and mildly nurtured sense of grievance over his fee. Blake and Haworth were paid £200. 'Even the people that did the flowers were paid more', he has grumbled. But there is of course the sense of artistic satisfaction. 'If you bought the record, you also bought a piece of art on exactly the level that I was aiming for.'

Just as 'Revolution 9' is the most widely distributed avant-garde musical composition ever, so the *Sgt. Pepper* sleeve is the most loved and owned 'pop art' artefact in the world. It far exceeds what must be its nearest rival, Warhol's soup cans and Marilyn prints because of course it features on a Beatles' record rather than one by The Velvet Underground. But it might also be because Blake's work has a warmth, charm and lack of cynicism that Warhol's lacks. He is a fan, and remains one, even if he is still a little peeved about the two hundred quid.

89. Maharishi Mahesh Yogi

'A Spiritual Butlin's.'

In the mid-1980s I was a young teacher in the Liverpool overspill new town of Skelmersdale. I loved my job and the people but 'Skem' was reeling from the tender mercies of Thatcherite economics. Feral dogs roamed the grim shopping concourse or 'connie', drugs were as plentiful as jobs were scarce. But there was one good news story. The town had become an unlikely base for a thriving Transcendental Meditation community. They founded an excellent school and a factory making 'Mountain Breeze' Ionisers that employed many locals. Essentially, 'trannies' and 'scallies' rubbed along genially, meaning that twenty years after he'd charmed The Beatles, the Maharishi was still winning the hearts and minds of Scousers.

Is the Maharishi, along with Yoko, the most unjustly maligned figure in The Beatles' story? And like Yoko, is that suspicion and hostility a toxic mix of xenophobia and the persistent whiff of char-latanry? Critics who know about these things allege that his teachings were a very westernised version of Vedic philosophy, simplified to be palatable to rich foreigners. He was close to a number of right-wing Indian politicians, since his doctrine that it is better to accept life's travails rather than question them suited their purposes well. But, again as with Yoko, much of the mockery directed his way was clearly simply down to good old-fashioned racism. A long-haired, perma-grinning brown man in flowing robes was still an affront to the sensibilities of many westerners, even at the height of the summer of love.

Mahesh Prasad Varma was born in either 1911, 1917 or 1918 ('My earthly age is of no importance' he once declared) in the Chhattisgarh province of the British Raj. After studying physics at university, he developed his theories of Transcendental Meditation following studies with various gurus in the 1950s. 'We'd seen Maharishi up north when we were kids' said Paul. 'He was on the telly every few years on Granada's *People and Places* programme, the local current affairs show. We'd all say, "Hey, did you see that crazy guy last night?" So we knew all about him: he was the giggly little guy going round the globe seven times to heal the world.'

In early 1967, by now a Beatle and a superstar of course, McCartney's interest was piqued by news that the same Maharishi was coming to England to give a series of talks. According to Pattie Boyd, 'In those days if one Beatle did something, they all did it,' and thus three of the four Beatles (Ringo was visiting Maureen who'd just given birth) attended his lecture in the ballroom of the Hilton Hotel in Park Lane. The Maharishi's serene and simple message of inner peace, reflection and abandonment of ego was spiritual catnip to tired minds fried with pressure, drugs and a growing disillusionment with stardom.

Which is how, on 25 August 1967, what seemed like most of the UK media clustered on a platform at Euston station to watch four blokes and their celebrity mates get a train to North Wales for the Marahishi's Bank Holiday retreat in Bangor. In *Anthology*, McCartney recalls 'I remember Cynthia not making the train, which was terrible and very symbolic. She was the only one of our party not to get there. There's a bit of film of her not making it. That was the end of her and John, really, weirdly enough. There was a big crowd at the train station, and there was another to meet us in Bangor. We all wandered through in our psychedelic gear. It was like a summer camp.' Everyone slept in student accommodation at the standard rate for lodging: £1.50 per night, including breakfast.

While in Bangor, news reached The Beatles that Brian Epstein had died. More symbolism. Orphaned and stunned, the mantle of mentor and father figure seemed to be passing on to the tiny shoulders of the Maharishi. In Bangor, they had been given personal mantras. Now meditation and the Maharishi seemed to be replacing

Epstein's discrete elegance as their handrail. Lennon and Harrison were particularly smitten, the former saying of Brian's death, admittedly in the immediate devastating aftermath to TV reporters, 'We all feel it, but these talks on Transcendental Meditation have helped us to stand up to it so much better. You don't get upset when a young kid becomes a teenager, or a teenager becomes an adult, or when an adult gets old. Well, Brian is just passing into the next phase.'

Not everyone thought this a happy turn of events. Writing in the *New Statesman*, John Mortimer worried that 'the unfortunate Beatles like many of us it seems are in grave danger of coming into contact with the spirit of universal truth, an unhelpful tipple which has in the past turned the ground mind of Aldous Huxley to mystical blotting paper'.* The Beatles though were drinking deep. They now planned to spend three months in early 1968 at the Maharishi's ashram in Rishikesh, Uttar Pradesh, India; a devotional retreat in a compound of spartan barbed wire fenced 'chalets' (as Paul called them, or a 'barracks' according to Cynthia) on a hillside overlooking the holy Ganges reached by the infamous Lakshman Jhula swinging suspension bridge. Cows and monkeys roamed in what one visitor called 'a collision of magnificence and wretchedness' and Ringo Starr dubbed 'a spiritual Butlin's'.

There was initial awkwardness, an iciness broken when Lennon patted the Maharishi on the head saying 'There's a good little guru.' Soon The Beatles and other celebrity acolytes settled into a daily pattern of lengthy meditation, roughly eight hours a day in Lennon's case, sunbathing down by the river, chatting, reading and music. They would sometimes nip out at night for a verboten glass of wine at Nagoli's café but they were also intensely musically productive, writing about forty songs that would go on to comprise much of

---

* Mortimer also baits Harrison and Lennon about TM, unpleasantly, during their joint appearance on the Frost programme in September 1970.

the *White Album* as well as 'Polythene Pam', 'Mean Mr Mustard', 'Across The Universe' and what became 'Jealous Guy'. 'Bungalow Bill' came from Lennon's revulsion at two wealthy ashram dwellers Richard A. Cooke III and his socialite mum, Nancy Cooke De Herrera taking a break from meditation to pop out and shoot some tigers.

Starr hated the food – though the cook was English and had worked in a Nottingham hotel, Starr famously took a consignment of Heinz baked beans – and Maureen the insects. Paul had never been as sold on TM as Harrison and Lennon, and was there as a supportive pal essentially. Both Paul and Ringo left early. John was beginning to get bored and was missing Yoko, collecting daily postcards from her at the local post office even with Cynthia in situ. The breaking point came when his new chum 'Magic' Alex Mardas, a superannuated TV repairman discussed elsewhere, arrived and began to spread rumours of the Maharishi's sexual impropriety with the camp's young women. The Maharishi always denied this and asserted his celibacy but Lennon, hoodwinked generally by Mardas and perhaps looking for a way out and back to London and Yoko, broke up the party in typical style. The remaining two Beatles and their retinue bolted in cars rented by Mardas leaving the Maharishi desolate and baffled. 'Why, why?' he asked, to which Lennon replied, 'If you're so cosmically conscious, you'll know why.' On the way home he wrote a brilliant if slightly vindictive song called 'Maharishi', later changed to 'Sexy Sadie', a good song but possibly rooted in spite and half truths.

Lennon had once said of the Maharishi, 'So what if he's commercial? We're the most commercial group in the world!' but he also told Barry Miles, 'Ain't no ethnic bastard gonna get no golden castles out of me.' And he didn't. He was left devastated by Lennon's rejection of him. One adherent said he was 'visibly frail, and without his usual effervescence. His beautiful yogic radiance was reduced to grey and ashen.'

But time has been kinder to the Maharishi than Lennon was. Even John softened in later years, saying his time with him was one of the happiest times of his life. Ringo never acquired a taste for the food – this remember is a man who has apparently never eaten an onion – but he speaks positively of Indian spirituality and meditation. Paul had never believed the accusations against him, saying immediately, 'I think they are completely untrue'. In the wake of the estrangement from the Maharishi he explained 'He's still a nice fella and everybody's fine but … we don't go out with him anymore.' In a later interview, he said 'He wasn't one of the fakes. He wasn't into Rolls-Royce and chicks …' George continued to visit him for the rest of his life, at one point, apologising for their brusque dismissal. The Maharishi replied that he believed The Beatles were angels on earth and had nothing to feel guilty for. George said he felt cleansed.

When the Maharishi died in 2008, the Ganges flooded and a huge storm engulfed the former Rishikesh. For years it was a graffitied ruin, abandoned and overgrown, frequented by leopards and tigers. Now it has been restored and is the most far-flung stop on The Beatles tourist trail.

90. Hunter Davies

'Would you like to see Paul McCartney's underpants?'

10.30 a.m. on a chilly, bright North London morning in March 2019 and Hunter Davies answers the door to me in shorts, beaming and clutching a huge goblet of wine. I had got to know Hunter through our shared love of the Lake District, being (sort of) Cumbrian neighbours and fellow writers and we've shared a glass of wine and a lamb Tatie Pot at his former local The Kirkstile Inn, Loweswater, and today he had invited me to see his 'treasures'. 'Come in ... fancy a drink ... you're not teetotal are you?' As I enter, he points to a picture of an Old English Sheepdog in the hallway. He turns briskly to me, waving the goblet at the picture. 'What's that dog's name?' 'Martha', I answered and he smiles again. 'Good ... you've passed.'*

There are far more Beatle books than there are Beatles songs, and the range is even wider and more bewildering. The Beatles' canon encompasses both the apocalyptic hard rock of 'Helter Skelter' and the chamber melancholy of 'Eleanor Rigby', the arch vaudeville of 'Honey Pie' and the Indian ragas of 'Within You, Without You'. Similarly, as discussed in the introduction, you can find Beatle books on every element and aspect of their history. However, there is, has only ever been and will only ever be, one authorised biographer of The Beatles and that is Hunter Davies. Over eighteen months from the middle of 1966, he was given unfettered, unparalleled access to the band at their artistic zenith, even holidaying with the McCartneys. His subsequent authorised biography appeared not

---

* As in, as many of you will know, Paul McCartney's long-time pet, an Old English Sheepdog, immortalised in the song 'Martha My Dear'. He has also had two dogs called Jet.

long before the band split up, thus ensuring that his singular and unique status can never be usurped.

He first broached the subject of a 'big, definitive, serious book' about the band when he interviewed Paul for the *Sunday Times* early in 1967. A bright, northern working-class lad making a name for himself in the London media, there was an obvious kinship. His pitch to Epstein was brilliantly barmy; 'As Truman Capote put together a murder, I'm sure there's a need for a full anatomy of The Beatle phenomenon' he wrote, referencing Capote's current hit *In Cold Blood*. The deal was signed on 25 January 1967 for an advance of £3,000, 'nothing startling' as Davies puts it; one of the Heinemann directors told him that 'The Beatles bubble would soon burst'. Over the next year and a half, he spent hours with them in the studios, visited their homes, met their old school friends and stayed with their parents, also tracking down Lennon's estranged father Freddie. He was in the invited throng for their performance of 'All You Need Is Love' on the *Our World* satellite broadcast and accompanied them to the Transcendental Meditation seminar they attended in Bangor when they learned of Epstein's death.

'I wanted the research to go on forever' he says in the 1996 edition. 'I had worked on it for eighteen months and I thought I had to call it a halt. The reason was that it was changing all the time. Every day I met The Beatles they always disowned what they said yesterday ... The Beatles were always changing in their views.' These days, he wishes he had put more in about how the group made their music which he was a privileged witness to. But 'most of the time, I must admit I was at Abbey Road, I was bored out of my skull cos they were going over and over things and I couldn't see the difference between one version and another.'

Hunter was infuriated by Lennon's claim in the notorious 'Lennon Remembers' *Rolling Stone* interview that his book was 'bullshit' and a whitewash, phoning him in New York to berate him. 'Oh, you know me, Hunter,' pleaded Lennon 'I just say the first thing that comes into my head.' What Hunter did soft-pedal on was tales of groupies and drunkenness, some references to John's childhood family background (at the insistence of Aunt Mimi) and Epstein's sexuality which Brian's mother Queenie wanted removed. 'I couldn't spell it out. I did use the phrase "gay bachelor".'

The book appeared with 'Hey Jude' in the charts and *Yellow Submarine* in the cinemas and nearly sixty years on is still a terrifically engaging, illuminating read and a much valued 'primary source'. Hunter is a fan but not, like some of us, a Beatles nerd, and thus he can be dismissive of geekery, as when he writes that there are newspaper files full of their touring itineraries 'for those mad enough to want them'. It is neither hagiography nor hatchet job, which is why it has lasted while other 'period' works (and many more recent ones) have been forgotten.

Appropriately, Hunter is a gatherer. On the day I visited him in North London, he showed me all his many and various collections; first editions of Wainwright's guide books to the Lakeland fells, Carlisle United football programmes, launch issues of any new magazine. But mainly The Beatles. At one point, he took a Ziploc bag from a filing cabinet with what appeared to be a pair of Y fronts in it, 'Would you like to see Paul McCartney's underpants? He left them behind in the villa when him and Linda stayed with us in Portugal.'

A few years later, and a few months back as I write this, we sat by each other at the *Let It Be* premiere and Hunter, a little deaf these days, grumbled about the sound and left early. A robbery at his London home deprived him of many of his 'treasures' such as a signed copy of *Sgt. Pepper** but, in his will, all the memorabilia and artefacts of The Beatles that this inveterate hoarder kept will be bequeathed to the nation. He loves the thought that it will be kept

---

* He claimed £3.50 insurance for a replacement copy. In 2013, one was sold for $290,500 in Texas.

and treasured 'alongside Shakespeare and Magna Carta'. He ends the introduction to a recent edition of his authorised biography thus: 'Perhaps its virtue is that it is of its time, a first-hand account of an unusual period, an eyewitness report on the rise of a phenomenon then at its height, soon to fall apart.'

Hunter would never claim to be above the other Beatle historians: what sets him apart is that he was there.

91. John Mustard

'Scotsman's Meanness "Was Cruel".'

Since their mendacious coverage of the Hillsborough tragedy, *The Sun* newspaper is hardly read or bought on Merseyside. But even back in the Sixties, it was unlikely The Beatles could be found with their noses in it, since, before Rupert Murdoch's takeover in 1969, it had a small circulation and was, in the words of journalist Patrick Brogan, 'a worthy, boring, leftish broadsheet'. It was more usually the *Daily Mirror*, paper of choice for working-class Labour voting Northerners, that The Beatles would dip into. It was in these pages that Paul McCartney read the story of Melanie Coe that inspired 'She's Leaving Home', and it was in the *Mirror* of 7 June 1967 that John Lennon's eye was caught by a headline 'Scotsman's Meanness "Was Cruel".*

Elgin born John Alexander Mustard was a 65-year-old civil servant living with his wife in Enfield, or was until headteacher Freda divorced him on the grounds of his exceptional stinginess. The judge was told that he had given his wife just one pound in the year before the split, would shave, go to bed and even listen to the radio in darkness since 'it was not necessary to see in order to listen'. In his defence, Mustard 'was at pains to explain that he came from north of the border where carefulness was part of the upbringing'. The judge said that he did not believe he was 'unpleasant or vicious' to his wife but there was 'a menacing quality about him'.

That certainly emerges, along with surreal dark humour, in the song John finished about him in India. Originally called Shirley, his

---

* The story also appeared that day in the *Mirror*'s Scottish sister paper the *Daily Record* under the headline 'A Mean Husband Shaved in the Dark' but it's much more likely Lennon saw the English paper.

sister in the song becomes Pam to tie in with 'Polythene Pam', another song in the *Abbey Road* medley. 'I changed it to Pam to make it sound like it had something to do with it ... I'd read somewhere in the newspaper about this mean guy who hid five-pound notes, not up his nose but somewhere else. No, it had nothing to do with cocaine.'

The song was performed in one take with its *Abbey Road* predecessor, 'Sun King'. Originally it led into 'Her Majesty' but that was moved to the medley and album's close. However, the final D major chord of 'Mean Mr Mustard' can still be heard at the start of 'Her Majesty', and Macca plays this when he performs the latter song live.

92. Ivor Cutler

'I'm going in a field.'

In the late 1990s I hosted a weekly BBC radio show called *The Treatment* recorded in front of a live audience in Bush House on the Strand in London. One day, producer Chris Wilson told me that a friend of his would be coming to the show, one Ivor Cutler. Perhaps I was aware of him. I certainly was. One night in the late Seventies, listening to the John Peel Show, I had heard Cutler read one of his poems, 'Egg Meat' – funny, sinister, deeply odd – and had never forgotten it. Ivor in person though was a quirky delight. We chatted before the show and I spotted him in the front row when we began the recording. He gave me a little wave. But as soon as the theme music began – Fatboy Slim's 'Going Out of My Head', if memory serves – he leapt up with his hands over his ears and ran for the exit, never to return.

Cutler – poet, musician, broadcaster, eccentric comedian, absurdist philosopher – was born into a Jewish family in the Ibrox district of Glasgow in 1923. Having flunked his RAF navigator training, he built aeroplanes during World War II before drifting south into teaching, some of it at the experimental Summerhill School in Suffolk which he loved. He took to performing his own strange little songs and poems, accompanied by himself at the wheezing harmonium, after realising that no one else was likely to. He became a fixture on the 'Home Service' and 'Third Programme' and, in the late 1950s, producer Ned Sherrin booked him to appear on Cliff Michelmore's *Tonight* show on TV where he was received with equal parts bafflement and enchantment. In 1966, he and his trio entered Abbey Road studios to record the charming *Ludo* album with George Martin, an album that brought him to the ears of Paul McCartney who was particularly taken with the track 'I'm Going in a Field'. 'That's a big hit in my mind' he said on a BBC documentary about Cutler. McCartney had also been intrigued by a TV appearance on *Late Night Line Up*. 'I saw him on television and was impressed and amused by his laconic sense of humour and his Scottish wit and I actually just rang him up ... I just thought he's the kind of bloke I wouldn't mind going out to dinner with so I said "Hello Mr Cutler ... this is Paul McCartney and I'd like to take you out to dinner" ... and he thought about it for a little while and eventually accepted the invitation so we went out to dinner and we became friends ... We kind of like people who just sort of say "this is me, this is what I do" and he certainly was one of them.'

Cutler was cast as the tour guide on The Beatles' next project, *Magical Mystery Tour*, the silly, sweet, exasperating TV fantasia involving the band driving a coach around the West Country with a motley gang of passengers and a minimum of plot or camera crew. Cutler, who named his character Buster Bloodvessel, invests his role with a kind of menacing yet touching melancholy. *Magical Mystery Tour* aired on BBC 1 at 8.30 p.m. on Boxing Day to almost universal bewilderment. Twenty million people watched it, among them Mrs H. Murray of Walthamstow who found it 'too stupid for words' and Mary Grant of Walton On Thames who thought it 'a load of old codswallop'. Of their peers, Pete Townshend thought it was 'a great film' but Scott Walker 'got bored frankly'. Tony Hicks of The Hollies felt 'fed up with seeing people running across fields in slow motion'. Queen Elizabeth observed 'The Beatles are turning awfully funny, aren't they?'

So herewith a few words in defence of *Magical Mystery Tour*. It didn't help that the BBC screened what is essentially a psychedelic seaside postcard in black and white and cut some of the most interesting sections such as Cutler's Buster Bloodvessel romancing Ringo's Aunt Jessie on the beach to a delicate orchestral version of 'All My Loving'.* But the film does at least show artistic ambition if a certain

---

* This seems to have been excised on the orders of BBC TV chief Paul Fox who, weirdly, thought this sweet segment was 'insulting to old people'.

hubris. A good time seems to have been had by all, including large sections of the population of the West Country who enjoyed seeing The Beatles in various seasides, hotels,* pubs, on Plymouth Hoe and getting stuck under a bridge near Widecombe.

Cutler remained a fascinating, beloved outlier of British cultural life until his death in 2006. While he may not have introduced The Beatles to the surreal and absurd – LSD and Edward Lear got there first – he surely skewed their imagination, especially Paul's and his influence crept into the later lyrics. Not the rock settings though. A staunch member of the Noise Abatement Society, he loathed loud music, hence his swift exit from my studio on hearing Fatboy Slim. It was nothing personal, Norman. And 'Eggmeat' is still terrifying.

---

* Ted O'Dell delivered food to pubs and hotels in the Newquay area. Calling at the Atlantic hotel, the kitchen porter said 'The Beatles just got off the bus and they're taking photos of your van.' Painted on the side was the slogan 'the Eggman'.

1968

93. Prudence Farrow

'Hi Prudence, we all love you ... you're wonderful!'

The assorted celebrities, devotees and hangers on who accompanied The Beatles on the Rishikesh ashram sojourn brought different things to the meditation 'after party'. Magic Alex attempted (and of course failed) to build an elaborate and powerful transmitter. Beach Boy Mike Love was, one imagines, 'problematic' if his reputation is to be believed. Mia Farrow, initially dismayed at The Beatles disrupting the contemplative calm, later reflected in her memoir that 'nevertheless with cheerful chatter and guitars and singing the new arrivals brought an element of normalcy to the ashram a sort of contemporary reality which at first seemed jarringly out of place.'

Scottish troubadour Donovan turned up in hot pursuit of Mia's 19-year-old sister Prudence and, having met Donovan several times, I can suggest that his arrival would definitely have brought some levity to proceedings. More practically, Donovan taught John

Lennon how to play fingerstyle guitar which is how he came to write one of his very finest songs, a song of love and support to Donovan's potential paramour.*

Prudence Farrow was by far and away the most committed TM disciple. She spent most of the day locked in her tiny room, failing to appear for meals. 'Prudence meditated and hibernated,' Ringo remembered. 'We saw her twice in the two weeks I was there. Everyone would be banging on the door: "Are you still alive?"' Lennon told *Playboy* magazine, 'Mia Farrow's sister, who seemed to go slightly barmy, meditating too long, wouldn't come out of the little hut we were living in. They selected me and George to try and bring her out because she would trust us. She went completely mental. If she'd been in the West they would have put her away. We got her out of the house. She'd been locked in for three weeks and wouldn't come out, trying to reach God quicker than anybody else.' Paul recalled to Barry Miles 'Prudence Farrow got an attack of the horrors, paranoia, what you'd call these days an identity crisis, and wouldn't come out. We all got a bit worried about her so we went up there and knocked. "Hi, Prudence, we all love you. You're wonderful!" But nobody could persuade her out. So John wrote "Dear Prudence, won't you come out and play?"'

Using the fingerpicking style Donovan had taught him, Lennon had composed a beautiful psychedelic Indian inflected serenade that would eventually make its way, as did many Rishikesh songs, on to the *White Album* where it emerges serenely from the screaming jet engine coda of 'Back in The USSR' at the album's outset. On the Esher demo version, John contributes a spoken outro that is both sardonic and heartfelt, 'No one was to know that sooner or later she was to go completely berserk under the care of Maharishi Mahesh

---

* It would be around this time that Allen Ginsberg earnestly petitioned Queen Elizabeth II to make Donovan the new poet laureate after the death of John Masefield. Disappointingly, she went with the safer bet of Cecil Day Lewis, dad of actor Daniel, instead.

Yogi. All the people around her were very worried about the girl because she was going insane. So we sang to her.'

'It epitomised what the Sixties were about in many ways' Prudence later mused. 'What it's saying is very beautiful; it's very positive. I think it's an important song.' Farrow returned to the United States where she earned a BA, an MA, and a PhD from Berkeley studying Sanskrit and Asian studies. Her doctoral dissertation concerned 'Nadivijnana, the Crest-Jewel of Ayurveda: A Translation of Six Central Texts and an Examination of the Sources, Influences and Development of Indian Pulse-Diagnosis'. She remains an adherent of Transcendental Meditation.

94. Francie Schwartz

'Oh I remember her! How could I forget?'

As London commutes go, it's quite pleasant. I know. I've done it. A nine minute or so stroll along the wooded, peaceful avenue, past the blue plaque to another famous resident, Billy Fury, left and past the handsome villas, period townhouses and apartments of Circus Road, then right at the lights and up to where Grove End Road meets Abbey Road. Then over the famed zebra crossing and through the gates, past reception with a nod to the doorman and the secretaries and into Studio 2. It's a journey Paul McCartney made many times in the mid to late Sixties and it began at his house at 7 Cavendish Avenue.

He bought the three-storey Regency townhouse from a physician named Desmond O'Neill for £40,000 in April 1965 and he and Jane Asher moved in the following March. But when the couple split up, as he later told Barry Miles in 1997, it 'became what I used to think of as my bachelor pad'. Back in 1967, he told Miles, then just his friend rather than his biographer, 'It's terrible. The birds are always quarrelling about something. There's three living here at the moment … and there's another one, an American groupie, flying in this evening. I've thrown her out once. I had to throw her suitcase over the wall. But it's no good; she keeps coming back.'

This, one assumes, was Francie Schwartz, a 23-year-old New York scriptwriter who had travelled to London to try and interest Apple Corps (and Paul McCartney specifically) in a movie script about a New York street musician. The film never happened but she secured a gig with Derek Taylor writing press releases for various Apple acts like James Taylor, Mary Hopkin and Badfinger. More significantly, she and Paul became an item of sorts and she moved into Cavendish Square. Finding her there in bed with Paul on an unexpectedly early return from her US acting tour in *Romeo and Juliet*, Jane Asher moved out. Schwartz described the scene the next day when Margaret Asher came to collect her daughter's belongings as 'cold'.

It certainly can't have been comfortable for anyone; neither we imagine was the moment when Schwartz, Paul and his dad Jim were watching the Simon Dee show and Jane Asher announced to the world that she and Paul were no more. Schwartz was also around for some of the *White Album* sessions and claims that she sang backing vocals on 'Revolution 1' as well as choosing some of the photo locations on the famous Mad Day Out photographic spree around London in July 1968. Like so much Beatles lore, the truth would seem to depend on who you speak to and what you read. Memory is always mutable and malleable, particularly if you were a participant in the heady summers of the late 1960s.

In the book *All You Need Is Love*, Steven Gaines asks Paul if he remembers Francie Schwartz ('Oh I remember her, how could I forget?') and suggests that she 'has made a career out of those three weeks'. This sounds harsh, though she did later write a melancholic, faintly lurid memoir called *Body Count* which has less Paul in it than more prurient readers would probably like. On the cover, Schwartz states: 'Women are likely to gobble up the Paul McCartney chapter and then say "boy, is she a groupie" ...' You can pick the book up on eBay and Amazon for several hundred pounds if you want to delve deeper into this brief period and judge for yourself if Steven Gaines was fair in his assessment. As for Paul, the bachelor period did not last long. He and Linda married the next March.

95. Shyamasundar Das

'Who's that little old man?'

Early in Peter Jackson's epic *Get Back*, the camera finds a man with shaven head and red beads seated cross-legged in a corner of the cavernous Twickenham Studios. We will become used to all manner of tangential extras hanging out at these sessions, from Peter Sellers and Dick James to, well, Yoko Ono. But this one is especially intriguing, certainly to John. 'Who's that little old man?' he asks, 'Clean though', Macca replies, both referencing their opening gag about Wilfrid Brambell in *A Hard Day's Night*.

Shyamasundar Das was neither little nor old though. In fact, he was two years younger than Lennon. 'Born in the body of Samuel Speerstra in Salem, Oregon', as he puts it on his website, the newly rechristened Das was one of six young disciples who'd ventured to London in December 1968 to set up a Krishna Consciousness centre, ideally with the help of some eminent benefactors ripe for enlightenment and with substantial bank balances. Basing themselves in a derelict warehouse in Covent Garden, and via the intercession of various Hell's Angels and Ken Kesey, they wangled an invite to Apple HQ, then the epicentre of freebooting hippy chaos in London, if not the world.

Das evokes the scene vividly. 'The place is crowded with about fifty people drinking and talking – rock stars, elegant women, Carnaby Street hippies, guys in suits, and our motley San Francisco crew spread out among them ... Hours pass. No Beatles ... Finally, one by one, Paul, John, and Ringo each stick their head out of one of the doors and then bolt for the exit, not pausing to speak to anyone. A few minutes later, George pokes his head out too, and those famous, intense dark eyes scan the room and light on me. Before anyone can react, George shoots out the door, crosses the room, and comes straight at me, grinning. "Hare Krishna! Where have you been? I've been waiting to meet you! Please come down here to Twickenham Studios. I want you to explain Krishna consciousness to the boys.'"

This he apparently did over the lunch break. Over the next year or so, the London-based Krishna adherents lived on the fringes of The Beatles' court. With The Beatles' help, they set up their first Radha Krishna Temple on Bury Place by the British Museum and, as Radha Krishna Temple, released 'Hare Krishna Mantra' with George on harmonium and Paul at the mixing desk. Initially rejected by Peter Asher as Apple A&R, it sold seventy thousand copies on the first day of its release and reached Number 12 on the UK chart. George remarked that sitting at home watching them on *Top of The Pops* was one of the happiest moments of his life. Later, both George and John invited the Temple folk to stay at their respective country piles, and help 'fix them up', suggesting that they had become, effectively, peripatetic transcendental painters and decorators to The Beatles 'spiritual' half.

For any readers finding this brief resume inadequate, Das, 82 at the time of writing, has produced a three-volume, 1,400-page memoir which he feels fills 'a huge and important missing gap in The Beatles' vast biography'.

He adds 'I'm not very good at selling stuff, but … I could really use the money!'

96. Dr Richard Beeching

'Stick to making records.'

At some point in the autumn of 1968, perhaps when the Hell's Angels had sequestered the Savile Row offices of Apple as their own personal crash pad or maybe when the stoned hacks of Fleet Street were in situ downing the contents of Derek Taylor's cocktail cabinet or possibly when random passers-by were walking in off the street and helping themselves to the furniture, The Beatles decided that enough was enough. Something was rotten in the state of Apple.

Stephen Maltz, The Beatles' accountant and financial adviser for nearly four years, resigned, sending a forensic, candid five-page letter to each member of the band, detailing the calamitous state of their finances. Long-time associate Alistair Taylor told them 'Apple is far too complicated a business to be run by Neil and me. We are not up to the job … this company needs a figurehead, a proven business-man. You need someone like Lord Beeching.' Clearly, Alistair was no trainspotter, nor The Beatles rail romantics, otherwise they would never even have uttered the name of the reviled axeman of Britain's beautiful branch lines.

In 1963, Conservative transport minister Ernest Marples asked the Chair of British Railways, Dr Richard Beeching, to investigate ways to cut the train network's losses. Never great enthusiasts for public transport and much fonder of the privatised (in all senses) world of the car, the Tories were delighted when Beeching delivered a breathtaking report – 'The Reshaping of British Railways' – that called for the closure of a third of the train network and the loss of hundreds of services, branch lines and stations. 'The Beeching Axe' became instantly notorious, loathed by the train-going public, hard-headed trade unionists and soppy romantics alike.*

More practically, it didn't work. While some small technical benefits to do with 'shunting' and such were achieved, a great many analysts (and not just the moist-eyed softies) thought the 'axe' was short-sighted, badly implemented and ineffective. By the time John Lennon went to meet him, Beeching's savage measures still hadn't made the railways profitable (they were haemorrhaging one hundred million pounds a year) and his approach was substantially deemed to have failed, especially by the incoming Labour government of Harold Wilson who promptly sacked him (though there is some dispute here). Wales was worst hit, losing nearly two hundred stations which devastated rural communities. Beeching's legacy was to make Britain the most car dependent, road-clogged country in Europe.

In the early Noughties, I made a TV documentary about the state of the North's transport systems. As part of it, I stood at Manchester's Piccadilly station and 'vox popped' rail travellers asking whether they had ever heard of Doctor Beeching, some younger ones hadn't, but most of the ones over forty knew the name; their faces curdled with anger, they spat the words Beeching out like something that tasted nasty. One kindly looking old rambler even called him a name I dare not repeat here.

Perhaps because of their Rolls-Royce Phantoms (John) and Austin Healey 3000s (Paul), it seems The Beatles didn't feel the same way. In November, at Paul's instigation, John Lennon consulted with Beeching. The meeting was unproductive, but Beeching did offer a nugget of sound advice; 'Stick to making records.'

By now though, the end was in sight. Another axeman called Klein was coming down the track, much to John's approval, but the light at the end of the tunnel were the lights of an oncoming train.

---

* I include myself among the latter. Flanders and Swann's lovely, melancholy song about the cuts, 'The Slow Train', always reduces me to a blubbing wreck.

1969

97. Tariq Ali

'Yes, John. The Politburo agrees. It can go out.'

Three men from the Indian sub-continent each left their mark on The Beatles, their music and their world of ideas. If Ravi Shankar brought new sounds, beauty and creativity, and the Maharishi offered solace, acceptance and serenity, Tariq Ali was the outlier. He was Pakistani, Muslim not Hindu (by birth if not practice), and he represented, to The Beatles and Britain, disruption, defiance, revolt.

'My name was a household curse' as the Oxford educated Trotskyist writer, filmmaker and activist described to *The Guardian* in 2011 of his Sixties infamy, acquired with his outspoken rhetoric and striking presence on the front lines of various marches. (The pictures of him and Vanessa Redgrave at the helm of the London 1968 Anti-Vietnam war march positively smoulder with revolutionary glamour.) Reputedly the inspiration for the Stones' 'Street Fighting Man', Ali found Jagger more committed to the cause than The Beatles. 'I attacked John Lennon for not coming on the Vietnam demonstrations whereas Mick Jagger did and he said that he was desperate to come. He said he had to be restrained almost by force by Brian Epstein who said "if you guys go on these Vietnam demos you realise, we might never play the States again". And he said "you know I should just have said, well that's crap and so what and joined you.'"

Given The Beatles had long given up playing anywhere, this seems an odd threat to say the least but let that pass. Ali edited an ultra-left magazine called *Black Dwarf* whose critic John Hoyland criticised The Beatles' songs 'Revolution 1' and 'Revolution 9', saying these were very weak songs. 'To our surprise, a letter to the editor from John Lennon arrived, which we published. I got our music critic to reply, Lennon replied back. And then he rang me up. "Hey Tariq, you know, are we going to carry on fighting in the letters pages of your paper. Why don't you come around and let's have a chat?"'

Ali wrote up and nicely edited the conversation and showed it to Lennon. 'He read it and said, "God, you make me sound so intelligent" and "are you sure I should be published in the magazine? Because it's very serious, and I don't want it to lose any prestige." And I said, don't be silly, it will just sell a few more copies … Then after some time, he rang and said, "Will you come to my home? Because I'm just finishing a new LP, and I want you to hear the songs." So we went over to his house and he had just written "Imagine". I had gone with Robin Blackburn, and Régis Debray (French Marxist philosopher) just released from a Bolivian prison. So we took Régis along and John said, "Ok, I'm going to sing it to you." So he sang "Imagine", and then he looked at me. So I said, "Let me think." I made some fake consultations with Robin and Régis, and I said, "Yes John, the politburo agrees. It can go out."'

With almost comedic predictability, the always fissile *Black Dwarf* split apart in 1970 into the Leninist and non-Leninist factions with Ali and his gang of the former going on to found *Red Mole*. In the week of the release of 'Power To The People', Lennon (and this time Yoko) gave another interview for *Red Mole* to Ali, a wide-ranging discussion covering items as diverse as Arthur Askey, women's liberation, folk music and Primal Scream (the therapy not the band) and simultaneously fascinating, boring, enlightening and occasionally excruciating. At the chat's conclusion, Ali asks the kind of goofy question whose period earnestness is positively quaint: 'How do you think we can destroy the capitalist system here in Britain, John?'

John's answer neatly avoids any need for sacrifice, sympathy or indeed activity on his part. 'I think only by making the workers aware of the really unhappy position they are in. We've got to start all this from where we ourselves are oppressed. I think it's false, shallow, to be giving to others when your own need is great. The idea is not to comfort people, not to make them feel better but to make them feel worse, to constantly put before them the degradations and humiliations they go through to get what they call a living wage.'

Which must have been very cheering if you were digging coal or cleaning toilets while Lennon drove around London in a psychedelic Rolls-Royce. While he may have annoyed the hard left of the day by not wanting to carry Chairman Mao's picture, he shared some of the old tyrant's grimly authoritarian outlook. 'If we took over Britain, then we'd have the job of cleaning up the bourgeoisie and keeping people in a revolutionary state of mind,' he once told Ali. But Lennon would later rethink all this, saying in a 1980 *Newsweek* interview, 'That radicalism was phony, really, because it was out of guilt. I'd always felt guilty that I made money, so I had to give it away or lose it. I don't mean I was a hypocrite. When I believe, I believe right down to the roots. But being a chameleon, I became whoever I was with.'

Unlike *Black Dwarf*, *Red Mole* and the other samizdat publications of that febrile age, Tariq Ali is still very much with us and active at 81. He is a staunch supporter of Julian Assange and, on the morning that I write, has tweeted twelve times about the war in Gaza. His latest book is a profile of Winston Churchill. Spoiler alert; he's not a fan.

98. Glyn Johns

'I look like a bloody clown.'

At the drinks reception at the premiere for the remastered *Let It Be* movie, I found myself at the canapé table with a handsome, silver-haired man of about 80 who, after fortifying myself with a slurp of buckshee plonk, I told that he was way cooler than any one of the musicians in *Get Back*. The goatskin Afghan coat, the neckerchiefs, the outsize Janis Joplin shades, the crocodile-skin Levi jacket gifted him by Keith Richards …

Glyn Johns smiled a little wearily, clinked my glass, said I was very kind then went off to get an artisanal sausage roll. Most people in these pages have exerted some shaping influence, major or minor, significant or trivial, on The Beatles' story. Glyn Johns is different. He is a brilliant, rightly revered producer for his work with The Stones, Steve Miller, The Eagles and more. But it's the influence he didn't have (and could and should have done) that marks him out in The Beatles' narrative. The *Let It Be* album as produced by him might have been much more than a 'cardboard tombstone', as the *NME* review described it, and if John Lennon had heeded his advice about a man called Allen Klein, the whole Beatle story might have ended a great deal happier ever after.

Just before Christmas 1968, Glyn Johns took a phone call from Paul McCartney inviting him to Twickenham where The Beatles would be working on a new project, a TV special and concert. Paul wanted Johns to be involved in the production of the accompanying album and came down to record them at work. 'I originally put together an album of rehearsals with chat and jokes and bits of general conversation in between the tracks which was the way I wanted *Let It Be* to be; breakdowns, false starts. That became an obsession with me and I got the bit between my teeth about it.

I mixed a bunch of stuff that they didn't even know I'd recorded half the time – I just whacked the recorder on for a lot of stuff that they did and gave them an acetate the following morning of what I'd done as a rough idea of what an album could be like … but they came back and said they didn't like it or each individual bloke came in and said he didn't like it and that was the end of that.'

Later though, 'because they were bored rigid with it', John and Paul did hand over to him the hundreds of hours of tape to produce as he saw fit. Lennon, enamoured of his work on his own 'Instant Karma', unwisely gave the tapes to Phil Spector which Johns 'always thought was a strange combination and he puked all over the tapes … awful record … I cannot bring myself to listen to the Phil Spector version of the album. I heard a few bars of it once, and was totally disgusted, and think it's an absolute load of garbage.'

Two of Johns' tracks did get released as singles; 'Get Back' and 'Let It Be'. 'I'd really appreciate the producer's credit. I don't want any royalties or any money, just the credit. All the others said that was perfectly alright, but Lennon couldn't understand why I didn't want any money.' And so 'Get Back' bears no producer credit while 'Let It Be's sleeve states 'produced by George Martin'. Neither is due acknowledgement given for the decision to stage the climactic concert on the roof of Apple. 'Paul wanted to go to Tunisia with a bunch of fans on a boat … Ringo said he wouldn't get on with the African food.' Ringo, though, took Glyn up to the roof and, inspired, Johns suggested to Paul they hold the concert there.*

If only John had been listening as sympathetically when Johns tries to warn him off potential manager Allen Klein. One of the most gripping moments in Peter Jackson's *Get Back* happens in the control room when Johns feels compelled to intervene –

---

* This is one of my favourite moments in *Get Back*. Though we cannot hear what Glyn whispers to Paul, you can see the look of interest and pleasure bloom across Macca's face.

diplomatically – when John is eulogising his new best friend, the accountant Allen Klein. 'He's a strange guy … really very strange … I don't know if he speaks to you the same way he speaks to other people. Not perhaps because of who you are but he left you a question and halfway through your answering if he doesn't like the answer or if it's not really what he wanted to hear he'll change the subject right in the middle of the sentence … that bugs me a bit actually.'* John and Ringo though think it might be cool to have a 'hustler' and a 'conman' on their side. As we know, they get their wish in spades.

Johns continues to be respected. Students of production are routinely taught many of the strategies he pioneered, such as his close individual drum miking technique that's a studio standard now. He feels other of his endeavours have aged less well. He now cringes at his outfits in *Get Back*. 'I look like a bloody clown … I'm fed up with it now, I'll tell you … I have 9,000 emails and texts from people from my past, all taking the mickey unmercifully.' They are wrong. Johns is the epitome of late Sixties chic in these frames and looks every inch the pop star that actually he nearly was. He recorded a handful of solo singles in the early and mid-1960s, one of which was his cover of 'I'll Follow The Sun' from *Beatles For Sale*. It's quite sweet, if a little drippy. Nicely weird oboe solo. Gossamer girly backing vocals. Produced, naturally, by Glyn Johns, who will surely have been the coolest looking dude at the session.

---

* At this point in *Get Back*, I, and literally millions of others, yell 'YES, TELL THEM GLYN!' at the screen.

99. PC Ray Dagg

'Millions of people don't get remembered at all.'

After The Beatles themselves, and maybe their girl fans, the single most visible group of people in any of their photographs must be the police force. No one gets so close, so often, and with such evident glee tempered with occasional mild professional consternation. Hundreds of images show them embedded in the mayhem in every town the band visited from 1963 on; coppers with hats askew, laughing and grimacing as they link arms against a tide of young womanhood. Or sometimes with the lads themselves, chortling with them in a theatre in Buxton, trying on their helmets in Birmingham, or smuggling them through an alley in Scarborough.

In America, relations with the cops were more fraught.* In September 1964 in Boston, local police had ridden their horses at and through the crowd to try to disperse the frenzied fans, treating them 'like bowling pins' according to accompanying journalist Ivor Davis. 'The police were truly awful', commented Derek Taylor, to the annoyance of the ever-emollient Epstein who thought it would alienate the cops. Sure enough, at the Cleveland show a few days later, after some of the usual fan frenzy, a bristling Deputy Inspector Carl Bare barged on stage midway through 'All My Loving' and waved the band to a halt, confronting George nose to nose and bellowing 'Get off!' When they didn't, he manhandled George and Paul off stage.

Relations with the copper on the UK beat were always more stiffly polite right until the very end. And when the very end came, the British bobby was there – morose, awkward, chewing on his chin

---

* Apart from with Buddy Dresner as discussed elsewhere.

strap – in the form of Police Constable 574C Raymond Dagg.*

Born in Chelsea, Ray followed his dad's size nine footsteps into the Metropolitan police as a teenager. As a young man working out of West End Central station, on 30 January 1969, he was dispatched by his sergeant to investigate the noise emanating from a building in Savile Row which was causing crowds to form and rubbernecking traffic to back up. Entering the Apple building, the hawkeyed young Dagg (19, nearly ten years younger than John and Ringo) smells a rat when he spots Michael Lindsay-Hogg's hidden recording equipment. 'I said, "Look I need to speak to somebody about this noise" and as I walked in I saw to my right one of those two-way mirrors and there was something moving behind it … my suspicions were confirmed when I got to the desk because there was a bunch of flowers there on the desk and in the flowers there was a microphone so I knew we had to be on our best behaviour.'

All of this is of course captured – vividly, delightfully – in Peter Jackson's *Get Back*. What follows is a fantastic pas de deux between Dagg, his colleague, Apple's mod doorman Jimmie Clark and receptionist Debbie Wellum, a culture clash of such wonderful feints and winks and stuffy policespeak that it would not be out of place in a sitcom of the day. Eventually, Dagg works his way up to the roof where he becomes a hilariously lugubrious presence haranguing 'Mr Malcolm Evans, the road manager' as he calls him while The Beatles continue to 'rock out' in their period peacock finery. It's a joy worth watching and re-watching. The long suffering Dagg eventually gets his way and the plugs are pulled but not until after The Beatles have completed a forty-two-minute set that was to prove their last ever.

---

* The notorious Norman Pilcher, long suspected of planting drugs in rock stars' houses, did bust George Harrison's house in 1969 and found 120 joints and some hash in a shoe, an amount and location that astonished George. But the whole business seems to have been reasonably cordial. Oh by the way, Pilcher, thought to be Semolina Pilchard in 'I Am the Walrus', later served four years in jail for perverting the course of justice.

Over half a century on, Jackson's epic documentary made Dagg a cult star. 'It's ridiculous, I just don't understand it. It was just work, and it's blown up into all this.' In the interview he gave to Canadian TV, 57 years later, PC Dagg, (72 and long retired) is a curious, not dislikeable mixture of bemused, wry indifference and sly wit ('I told them there were fifteen thousand people down there ... I just made it up.') Most of the responses to Dagg's brush with fame and destiny were cordial. Many acknowledged that he was 'just doing his job' and handled the situation, in which he was clearly being stalled while as much film as possible was recorded, with patience and equanimity. Sadly, a few nasty oddballs managed to contact Dagg; 'I hope karma visits you, you bastard, stopping a genius band like that', one wrote.

Asked if he regrets shutting down the last live show of one of the greatest cultural forces ever, Ray, sensibly and correctly points out that The Beatles didn't break up because of him. We shall come to that of course.

'They could have easily done many more concerts together ... responsibility I feel for it? ... none ... If that's my lasting image of life, if that's what people remember me for, that's not bad. Thousands, millions of people don't get remembered at all.'

100. Allen Klein

'The Demon King.'

All great myths need a great monster. Epic tales depend on an epic villain. In the saga of The Beatles, that beast is Allen Klein; he is its Sauron, its Moriarty, its Grendel, the bête noire that wreaks destruction on our heroes. In this case of course, that surely cannot be what he intended. But without the intervention of Allen Klein, hustler, huckster and accountant, would The Beatles have been forced to their own Crack of Doom, their Reichenbach Falls, entering the narrative just as The Beatles, jubilant from the Apple rooftop gig are embarking on a new project, *Abbey Road*? As Derek Taylor put it, 'Klein is essential in the Great Novel as the Demon King. Just as you think everything is going to be alright, here he is.' Beatle scholar Ken Womack's verdict is harsher. 'Allen Klein only had one end game, and that was to con The Beatles out of everything.'

Like Lennon, he was brought up by an aunt. Unlike Lennon, this was after a spell in an orphanage where his parents placed him because they were unable to support him, a chastening experience that forged his personality and outlook on the world. Bumping into Bobby Vinton at a wedding, Klein, now a rising accountant, told the singer he could make him a hundred thousand dollars for doing nothing. After going through the accounts, Klein did just that, finding unpaid royalties and unclaimed fees that led to a huge payday for Vinton and a boost in Klein's reputation. Buoyed, he moved into the world of business management, snapping up Sam Cooke, Neil Sedaka and a host of British invasion bands such as The Dave Clark Five, The Kinks, The Who and The Rolling Stones. He managed to negotiate a superb, lucrative mid contract rise for the latter from Decca by sheer pluck and will. But the band themselves do not seem to have ever warmed to him. Klein once asked Bill Wyman why he didn't like him and the bassist replied 'Because I don't trust you.' Mick Jagger said of Klein enigmatically 'He's alright … if you like that sort of thing.'

As soon as Brian Epstein died ('I heard the news on the radio as I drove over a bridge in New York. I thought "I got 'em."') Klein embarked on the long game to ensnare the biggest trophy of all. Shared Jewish heritage apart, he was the antithesis of Epstein, generally weak on the accountancy brief but charming and well mannered. Klein had no such qualities. He relied not on suavity and politesse but a gimlet eye for the small print and remorseless crunching of the numbers. He certainly never relied on charisma. Beatles assistant Alistair Taylor remarked that he 'possessed all the charm of a broken lavatory seat'. However, this (admittedly prevalent) view does not go uncontested. Andrew Loog Oldham said, 'He was not greasy; he did not have three chins; he did not swear like a trooper or a gangster. He spoke calmly, invitingly and warmly.' Alan Steckler, who worked for him, maintained 'Allen Klein could be the most charming, interesting person' but quickly added 'but he could be crude, rude and very uncaring … Working for Allen Klein had its benefits and its shit days. Some days he could be the greatest person in the world. Most days he was the biggest asshole you ever met.' Even Loog Oldham, who seems to have had some perverse grudging admiration for Klein, admits 'He started out representing us and ended up owning us.'

That's not how it panned out with The Beatles. But the outcome was equally calamitous. After an interview in which Lennon bemoaned that Apple was going to bankrupt The Beatles, Klein scented blood, even across two thousand miles of ocean. He flew to London and arranged to meet with John and Yoko on 27 January 1969 at the Dorchester Hotel. From this moment, the days of The Beatles are numbered. The next day, Lennon cheerleads for Klein in a truly embarrassing scene in *Get Back*. 'He's brilliant … he knows about everything … he knows me as well as you do' he splutters to

George, staggeringly given that he met Klein less than twelve hours ago and George has been at his side since their teens. But soon, Ringo and George too decide that they are more than happy to have a 'conman on our side'.

Paul was less easily taken in. He was naturally keener to use the services of his wife's family, the Eastmans, at that point The Beatles' legal representatives. In Glyn Johns' memoir, he recalls 'Paul and I were working together in Olympic that afternoon, and there was a noticeable sense of relief when he heard that Klein had left for the airport. However, Klein had second thoughts about leaving and decided to have one more attempt at changing Paul's mind face-to-face. Unannounced, Klein walked into the studio, and very quickly it became apparent that as voices were raised a private conversation was taking place. I turned off all the mics in the room and left them to it. The control room of a studio is isolated from the recording room where the musicians play, but even all that acoustic treatment was not enough to prevent me hearing Paul McCartney defend himself against Allen Klein's attempt at bullying him into submission. It was extremely unpleasant to witness.'

Unpleasant and doomed. It might be uncharitable to lay all the blame for what happened next at the door or desk of Allen Klein. Yes, he fired or tried to fire everyone at Apple, however close and important to The Beatles, even Neil Aspinall. Yes, he ended up alienating everyone, including the formerly besotted Lennon who eventually conceded, 'There were many reasons to finally give him the push, although I don't want to go into the details of it ... Let's say that possibly McCartney's suspicions were right.' Yes, he actually went to jail for irregularities over the proceeds from The Concert for Bangladesh.

But perhaps we have misunderstood him, the great villain of our piece, the sacred monster of our tale. Perhaps all he really wanted was to make a lot of money, possibly even some of it for The Beatles, and this is not against the law. But such a baldly unlovely motive, such bullying greed, feel antithetical to the essential spirit and ethos of The Beatles, that giant engine for human happiness, that hand-grenade of rainbows thrown into a tired world, that sunburst of joy that told us all we needed was love.

Within months, by the close of 1969, the end of a decade The Beatles invented, as 'Auld Lang Syne' was sung and champagne corks popped, Paul McCartney resolved to be free of Klein and his charges, the friends he had known since schooldays, the young men he had lived with, sung with, changed the world with.

The dream was over.

The Beatles were dead.

Long live The Beatles.

Part Three

BEYOND THE BEATLES

The Beatles are dead.
Long live The Beatles.

I write these words on a winter dusk in room 211 of The Hard Day's Night Hotel, North St John's Street, Liverpool, 'the bustling heart of The Beatles quarter' as TripAdvisor styles it. Unlike some Beatles-related endeavours and enterprises, The Hard Day's Night Hotel is actually quite tastefully done. The large watercolour above my bed of John Lennon, Bob Dylan and an ashtray was spectacularly poor to be frank but elsewhere there are nice touches; a video of Paul doing his incredibly self-possessed performance of 'Yesterday' on *The Ed Sullivan Show* plays by the lifts; in a display case is a tape recorder used by a Hull student on which he recorded a never before broadcast interview with John that the hotel had just bought at auction; the logo of the hotel is the guitar tablature for the fingering of the chord that opens 'A Hard Day's Night' (F add 9). The 'Do Not Disturb' sign for your door reads 'Let It Be' on one side and 'I Need You (to service this room)' on the other.

The Beatles Quarter itself or Cavern Quarter if you prefer, that raucous little web of lanes and alleys around Mathew Street was thronged. People were taking pictures of the various statues and plaques or enjoying a drink and a selfie in the sweaty, jostling noisy interior of The Grapes pub where The Beatles drank. On the corner is a store called Beatle News – it's a newsagent – and across the way are the Harrison apartments. There's a McCartney bar around the corner … and on it goes.

While I was pondering whether, as I think Hunter Davies was gently and chidingly wondering of me, the world really needed another Beatles book, I decided to see how 'relevant' they still were by counting the number of Beatle references I came across as I went about my business. I thought I might find a few each week, which I still thought pretty good for a northern pop group who split up over half a century ago.

I found one every hour.

Headed to London on the train I sat across from an American tourist in a Beatles t-shirt. As I reached the Northern Line, a busker was playing 'All You Need Is Love' on the saxophone. On a podcast I heard Linda Evangelista referring to herself, Heidi Klum, Naomi Campbell and Christy Turlington as 'The Beatles' of Supermodels, an epithet I also heard applied, somewhat differently, to a British terrorist quartet who had fought for the Taliban. On the tram in Manchester, I encountered a little girl called Lennon. In the paper was the preview of an upcoming *Doctor Who* episode 'The Devil's Chord', where the time lord travels back to the 1960s to meet The Beatles.*

Some Beatle events were major commercial endeavours, showing how they are still one of the world's biggest entertainment brands over half a century since they dissolved; the 'Red' and 'Blue' albums' historic release on vinyl, the final single, 'Now And Then', restored from a fragment of a Lennon demo and its attendant hoopla, played on all radio stations simultaneously at 4 p.m. to an

---

* This is the second time The Beatles have appeared on *Doctor Who*. During the 1965 1st Doctor (William Hartnell) serial 'The Chase', the Doctor and his assistants watched The Beatles playing 'Ticket To Ride' on a device called a Time-Space Visualiser. As the footage was not preserved by *Top of the Pops*, it only exists in this *Doctor Who* episode.

expectant world. There was the re-mastered *Let It Be* movie, the *Midas Man* movie about Epstein and Scorsese's *Beatles '64* documentary. Most extraordinary of all was news of Sam Mendes' projected four biopics of the individual Beatles. And then there was Macca live in London and Manchester at the end of his Got Back world tour, four shows of incredible emotional heft to tens of thousands of people still in love with the story that began a few miles down the East Lancs road from the Manchester Co-Op Arena just after the Second World War.

To those inexplicable few who remain unmoved and uninterested in The Beatles, all this must seem ridiculous, annoying even. They were just a pop group, who had some toe-tappers back in the benighted pre-Internet world of rationing and two TV channels when entertainment was thin on the ground. Claiming (and who knows, actually really meaning it) not to like The Beatles remains a fashionable pose among some, a statement of perverse individuality, of imagined coolness, usually attended by a preference for The Rolling Stones or The New York Dolls or some other hugely inferior group. There is less of this than there used to be, and it looks increasingly callow and 'studenty', but it persists. A very average Scottish 'new folk' artist once told me that he 'didn't really rate The Beatles' and I spat my tea in amused disbelief. When I told this to Blur guitarist Graham Coxon (a Beatles nut, obviously) he said, 'Pretending not to get The Beatles is sheer affectation.' I agree. And if you are still with me, I think you might feel the same.

Why do they continue to mean so much? Why do they still exert such a hold on the public imagination as well as individual hearts, still matter artistically, commercially, historically, even politically? And how come it was them rather than (sorry again Paul) Gerry and The Pacemakers? Their power, significance and longevity can be explained to a degree by the fact that the generation that grew up with them, electrified and galvanised, went on to become journalists and TV commissioners, prime ministers and pontiffs, entrepreneurs and editors, the most glittering elite of the much maligned 'boomer' cohort, that is only a tiny part of the truth. For millions of people around the world; like the young Italian girls I talked to at Abbey Road or Hannah, 20, who works with me at 6 Music with her Paul McCartney tattoo, adore them who were not born when they split up. They have found them of their own volition, via battered albums in parents' collections, or grainy YouTube videos, or school sing-alongs, or some mysterious conduit of magic that cannot be explained.

Undoubtedly, it's about talent. The Woolton Village Fête of 6 July 1957 just happened to be attended by two of the greatest songwriters of the twentieth century, not long out of short pants and not aware of each other till that hot afternoon. Later they would accrue a third young scruff who wrote what Frank Sinatra called the greatest love song of the twentieth century and later still a sickly kid from the Dingle who became one of the finest, most idiosyncratic if underrated drummers in the history of pop. That they should all end up in the same band suggests something that defies logic. Even an agnostic like me starts to think it feels very like destiny.

At the heart then is the music. The Beatles' canon is popular music's most extraordinary body of work. For variety, innovation, significance and popularity, nothing and no one can touch it, not Dylan, not Gershwin, not Joni Mitchell, definitely not The Rolling Stones and certainly not bloody Schubert, who always gets dragged in around now. I suggested once in a tweet – back in the days when it was there for silly, fun things of this nature – that Paul McCartney might be the most musical human being who has ever lived, certainly that we're aware of. I was buffeted by a small squall of harrumphing in which the name Mozart came up a lot. But I stand by my grandiloquent claim. In terms of sheer range of faculty and imagination, even if he'd been born in the right era with the right stuff around him, would Wolfgang have been able to come up with both 'Helter Skelter' and 'Yesterday'? More to the point, would he have wanted to?

For better or worse, The Beatles invented the trope of the rock group, which can feel reductive and restrictive, a gang of (usually white boys) showing off and acting cool to impress girls. But it has certainly served the culture well even if these days it's good to see other identities, formulations, genders, races breaking the mould of what a pop group can be. But if you have ever enjoyed a record by everyone from Black Sabbath to The Eagles, Radiohead to The Smiths, Fairport Convention to Girls Aloud, The Clash to The Cure, Arctic Monkeys to Wet Leg, you have, at a germinal, sub-atomic level, The Beatles to thank.

But, as this book has gently suggested I hope, there is more to it than music, however dazzling and sublime. The Beatles helped invent the modern world, the one we live in today. Writing in the *London Review of Books*, Ian Penman astutely pointed out that 'It's The Beatles's admixture of pop and art, commerce and experiment, which now seems to prefigure so much of the mass culture to come. The attempt to turn the Apple record label into a multi-tentacled brand, for instance, predicts a lot of what we now take for granted as consumers. The Apple Boutique, with its tingly visual environment, was part hipster Woolworths, part multimedia experience, part chill-out room: a space where the music you liked and who you worshipped and how you dressed weren't discrete entities but linked-up "lifestyle choices". It now looks like our current Goopy moment of wellness and crystals, beard care and curated playlists.'

Just as Shakespeare contributed some 1,700 words to the English language and gave us its first psychological novel, The Beatles were the first band to play a stadium, the first to include a lyric sheet, the first to use any number of studio techniques now taken for granted, the first to introduce non-western instruments into pop, as well as chamber arrangements, feedback, tape loops, music concrete. Their influence has been colossal and enduring. Mark Lewisohn has noted that by the autumn of 1963, The Beatles, like no other cultural phenomenon before or since, had become part of the daily national conversation. 'Whether you were five or eighty-five, you had heard of them, heard them, knew what they looked like.' Nothing has really changed in sixty years. They are still here, still changing the world. The fact remains that, as Philip Norman has remarked, when you say the word 'Beetle', a little black insect is the second thing everyone thinks of.

All the pieces in this book, all of the dramatic persona who I think shaped The Beatles' story in their different ways, enter this tale between the childhoods of the four Beatles and the dissolution of the band in 1970. Since then, there have been many others who have affected what we might call The Beatle narrative, and not all in a happy or beneficial way. Some have been what we might call in the modern parlance, bad actors, malign interventions ranging from the merely cloth-eared or annoying to the wicked. I have a list, you may have them too, from crappy writers to grifters to assassins. But I will not name them here. Because this is a book about love and joy, just like The Beatles were.

Instead, and in the absence of dedicatees, let me celebrate and mention some of the people who have helped progress and illuminate The Beatles' narrative in the years since 1970. From excellent biographers, historians and writers like Mark Lewisohn, Craig Brown, Dr Christine Feldman-Barrett, Erin Torkelson Weber, Bob Neaverson, and many more, podcasters and YouTubers (a media development that has been manna for Beatle nerds) such as Chris Shaw, Robert Rodriguez, Alison Boron and Erika White, Jason Carty & Steven Cockcroft, Chloe Walls & Daisy Cooper, Nick Anthony, Jason Krupa, Joe Wisbey and all the rest. But special mention must be made of Peter Jackson whose monumental *Get Back* achieved the impossible, and made us fall in love with The Beatles again and harder and deeper than ever. Paul McCartney said at the London premiere, 'It's lovely because it brings back to me my mates.' For the rest of us, it made The Beatles feel like our mates for a while, or at least gave us a new, better, happier understanding of their final days. They loved each other like we loved them. That was obvious.

Mention of Paul brings up something I must address. Clearly the origin story of The Beatles is magical and alchemical and took four magicians/alchemists to will it into being (plus the hundred in this book to varying degrees). But if you have got this far, you will have realised that I am, if we must indulge in the odious business of taking sides and on those rare occasions when sides have to be taken, unapologetically 'Team Paul'. I love them all. But just like the girls who screamed at The Cavern in 1961, you have to have a favourite.

As I was finishing this book I saw an interview with Paul McCartney on the Laura Kuenssberg current affairs show. He was talking passionately about Artificial Intelligence and machine learning, how it had been used on the *Get Back* film and the 'Now and Then' single, and the thrilling and frightening prospect it holds for art and humanity in the coming decades of the twenty-first century. Later that day I read about the fossilised remains of AL 288-1 or Dink'inesh, a female of the species Australopithecus Afarensis discovered in Hadar, Ethiopia in 1974 and sometimes thought to be the earliest known member of the human family. She is nicknamed Lucy; one of the archaeologists Pamela Alderman called her that because the team were listening to 'Lucy in the Sky with Diamonds' when she was found.

I could use this surely. It felt like something profound to end with; how The Beatles have a connection with our earliest history and maybe our final days or the far future. But whichever way I framed and phrased it, I couldn't make it sound anything other than bombastic and pretentious, something the young Beatles would have laughed at in The Grapes or Ye Cracke, said 'come ed, soft lad' as they drained their glass and took the mick out of this woolyback.

So here's a different end.

One day, while I was just embarking on this book, one of my little grandsons, Noah, then seven came up to my work room and, wide-eyed and slightly bemused at all The Beatles 'stuff', the posters on the wall and shelves of books and teetering piles of CDs and albums said, firstly, 'Wow, you really like The Beatles' and then asked me if I could play him 'Hello Goodbye', as it was one of his favourites. When I asked him how he knew it, he told me that his class sang it every time a new person joined or left their primary school class. I thought this was just wonderful, perfect, moving even. The Beatles are woven into the life and folklore of the world, there for the young and the old, when they are happy and when they are sad, when they are getting on and doing well or not getting on and not doing so well or are fed up with the whole rigmarole of getting on and doing well or not. At all those times, The Beatles will be there.

My mum would talk often about that October night when she took me to see the Beatles. Her review of the actual music would never have landed her a berth on the *NME* but she could recall every other detail; queuing for tickets on a foggy Lancashire morning, the screaming, the police kindly and baffled outside the hall, me bouncing up and down on the back of the seat in front to the music. So, when I look at that black and white shot, the one I'm sure is me and my mum captured in that moment at the Wigan ABC Cinema in 1964, I can't help but think of the difficult, unhappy person she could be during the latter years of her life and the wearying strain it put on our relationship. But then I see her there; transfixed, transformed, biting her nails with sheer excitement, a mum, yes, but a young woman too, caught up in something astonishing, something all her own and yet ecstatically communal. If Peter Jackson gave Paul McCartney his mates back, The Beatles, among a million other things, have given me my mum back.

As John Lennon once said on a freezing rooftop in Savile Row, I would like to say thank you on behalf of the group and ourselves and I hope we've passed the audition.

Long live The Beatles.

SOURCES

INTRO
Rolling Stone, July 2014

PROLOGUE
Bob Spitz, *The Beatles: The Biography*

JULIA LENNON
Craig Brown, *One Two Three Four*

MIMI BAIRD
Mark Lewisohn, *Tune In*
Erin Torkelson Weber, *The Historian and The Beatles*, blog

JULIA LENNON
Anthology, 2000

HARRY GRAVES
Anthology, 2000
Mark Lewisohn, *In Tune*

JIM MCCARTNEY
Barry Miles, *Many Years From Now*
Penthouse, September 1984

HARRY HARRISON
Barry Miles, *Many Years From Now*
Anthology, 2000

LOUISE HARRISON
Liverpool Echo, August 2002

PETE SHOTTON
Hunter Davies, *The Beatles*

ROYSTON ELLIS
Mail on Sunday, 12 November 2021
The Telegraph, 17 April 2023

ROD MURRAY
Mark Lewisohn, *Tune In*

STU SUTCLIFFE
New Yorker, March 2022
Phillip Norman, Shout

JOHNNY HUTCHINSON
David Bedford, *Finding The Fourth Beatle*

PETE BEST
Anthology, 2000
Financial Review, March 2018

ASTRID KIRRCHHER
Spitz, *The Beatles*
The Quietus, 21 September 2010

BILLY PRESTON
Anthology, 2000

CHAZ NEWBY
Spitz, *The Beatles*
Anthology, 2000

NEIL ASPINALL
MOJO, October 1996

GEORGE MARTIN
George Martin, *All You Need Is Ears*

NORMAN SMITH
Guardian, 11 March 2008
Sound On Sound, March 2008

FREDA KELLY
Good Old Freda, Documentary 2013

RORY STORM
Spitz, *The Beatles*
Robert Rodriguez, *Revolver: How the Beatles Reimagined Rock 'n' Roll*

GEOFF EMERICK
The Herald, October 2018

TONY BARROW
Spend 1963 With The Beatles, Omnibus Press, Substack

HELEN SHAPIRO
Ray Coleman, *Lennon*
Martin Creasy, *Beatlemania*

MAUREEN CLEAVE
Daily Mail, 19 December 2009

DEREK TAYLOR
GQ, May 2018
Derek Taylor, *As Time Goes By*

MAL EVANS
Philip Norman, *Shout*

DOUGIE MILLINGS
Square Mile, webzine, March 2022

JANE ASHER
Miles, *Many Years from Now*
The Paul McCartney Project, 28 August 2024

DICK JAMES
Martin, *All You Need Is Ears*
Miles, *Many Years From Now*
Rolling Stone, December 1970
Ray Coleman, *McCartney: Yesterday and Today*

MARSHA ALBERT
Rolling Stone, 16 February 1984

NICKY BYRNE
Spitz, *The Beatles*
Norman, *Shout*

MELANIE COE
Guardian, December 2008

PETER YOLLAND
Today I Found Out, Blog, April 2016
The Beatles Bible Website, *The Beatles Christmas Shows Begin*

THE MAYSLES BROTHERS
The Beatles: The First Us Visit, DVD Interview
New York Daily News, January 2004

ED SULLIVAN
Spend 1963 With The Beatles substack, 20 December
Washington Post, February 2004

MURRAY THE K
Martin A. Grove, *Beatle Madness*

DAVID ORMSBY GORE
Rolling Stone, December 1970
Spitz, *The Beatles*
Sunday Times, November 2021

BUDDY DRESNER
Paul McCartney, *Eyes of The Storm*, Exhibition Notes
Bob Kealing, *Good Day Sunshine State: How the Beatles Rocked Florida*

BOB DYLAN
Rolling Stone, 16 February 1984
Clinton Heylin, *Bob Dylan: Behind the Shades*, cited in *MOJO*, December 1993
Far Out, magazine, July 2024

ALUN OWEN
Miles, *Many Years From Now*
Bill Harry, *Beatles Browser*, February 2019

DENNIS O DELL
MOJO, November 2002
Guardian, 14 January 2022
Craig Brown, *One Two Three Four*
Daily Mail, 22 August 2021
The Beatles and the Krishnas: The Untold Story! Zoom session,
    Beatles Convention

VICTOR SPINETTI
The Dictionary of Welsh Biography
MOJO, November 2002

JIMMY NICOL
Barry Miles, *The Beatles Diary Volume 1*

ALF BICKNELL
Interview with Gary James, *Classicbands.com*

ROBERT NEWMAN
Rolling Stone, November 2019
Interview with Steve Matteo, *It's Psychedelic, Baby*, website

ELEANOR BRON
The Pillow Book of Eleanor Bron, quoted in Craig Brown, *One Two
    Three Four*

BARRY MILES

Jonathon Green, *Days in the Life*
Please Kill Me, website, January 2021
David Jones, *The Beatles and Wales*
Jan Wenner, *Lennon Remembers*
Paul du Noyer, *Conversations With McCartney*

KEVIN HARRINGTON

Something About The Beatles, podcast, August 2022
Leslie Woodhead, *How The Beatles Rocked The Kremlin*
I Am The Eggpod, podcast

MAGIC ALEX MARDAS

Anthology, 2000
Hunter Davies, *The Beatles*
Ken Womack, *Everything Fab Four: The Strange, Nefarious Life of Magic Alex*
Barry Miles, *Many Years From Now*

IMELDA MARCOS

Anthology, 2000

RAVI SHANKAR

Anthology, 2000
BBC News website, December 2012

META DAVIES

Keith Badman, *Beatles Off The Record*
Miles, *Many Years From Now*
Playboy, January 1981

DAVID MASON

The One Show, June 2009
Miles, *Many Years From Now*

LINDA MCCARTNEY

The Paul McCartney project website

PETER BLAKE

Guardian, June 2022
Anthology
Video interview with Moti Shefi's Transcendental Meditation
    YouTube Channel
Playboy, January 1981
Spitz, *The Beatles: The Biography*
The Beatles and the Krishnas: The Untold Story! Zoom presentation,
    Beatles Convention San Francisco, August 2024
Jacobin website, December 2020
Glyn Johns, *The Record Producers*, BBC Radio 2, 1982
New York Times, December 17, 2021

PC RAY DAGG

Sunday Times, December 17 2021

ALLEN KLEIN

Derek Taylor, interview w/ Peter Doggett for *Record Collector*,
    August 1988
Nothing Is Real Podcast January 2023
Peter Doggett, *You Never Give Me Your Money Nothing Is Real*
    Podcast January 2023
Alistair Taylor, *With The Beatles* 2011
Nothing Is Real Podcast January 2023
Meet The Beatles For Real Website February 2016
John Lennon Weekend World, ITV, April 1973

SELECT BIBLIOGRAPHY

Hunter Davies, *The Beatles*, 1968 (revised 1996)

Philip Norman, *Shout!*, 1993

Ian MacDonald, *Revolution in the Head*, 1994

Craig Brown, *One Two Three Four*, 2020

Barry Miles, *Paul McCartney Many Years From Now*, 1997

George Martin, *All You Need Is Ears*, 1982

Mark Lewisohn, *Complete Beatles Chronicle*, 1992

Mark Lewisohn, *Complete Beatles Recording Sessions*, 1989

Mark Lewisohn, *Tune In*, 2013

The Beatles, *Anthology*, 2000

Bill Harry, *The Beatles Encyclopaedia*, 2000

Bill Harry, *The Encyclopaedia of Beatle People*, 1997

Martin Creasey, *Beatlemania! The Real Stories Of The Beatles UK Tours 63–65*, 2011

Bob Neaverson, *The Beatles Movies*, 1999

Richard DeLillo, *The Longest Cocktail Party*, 2014

John Higgs, *Love and Let Die: Bond and The Beatles*, 2023

Geoff Emerick, *Here There And Everywhere*, 2007

David Bedford et al, *Fab Four Cities*, 2021

Sean Egan (ed), *The Mammoth Book Of The Beatles*, 2009

Alistair Taylor, *With The Beatles*, 2011

Erin Torkelson Weber, *The Beatles And The Historians*, 2021

Jonathan Gould, *Can't Buy Me Love*, 2007

Peter McCabe and Robert Schonfeld, *Apple to the Core*, 1972

Ray Coleman, *Lennon: The Definitive Biography*, 2000

Ray Coleman, *McCartney: Yesterday and Today*, 1997

Peter Doggett, *You Never Give Me Your Money*, 2010

Robert Freeman, *The Beatles: A Private View*, 1991

Jim O'Donnell, *The Day John Met Paul*, 1996

Peter H. Brown & Steven Gaines, *The Love You Make: An Insider's Story of the Beatles*, 1984

Glenn A. Baker, *The Beatles Down Under*, 1985

Kenneth Womack, *Living The Beatles Legend*, 2024

Ian Leslie, *John and Paul: A Love Story in Songs*, 2025

Cynthia Lennon, *A Twist of Lennon*, 1976

Avalon & Geoffery Guiliano, *Revolution: A Secret History of The Beatles*, 2019

Pete Shotton, *The Beatles, Lennon and Me*, 1984

Allan Williams, *The Man Who Gave The Beatles Away*, 1975

Michael Braun, *Love Me Do: The Beatles Progress*, 2019

Dierdre Kelly, *Fashioning The Beatles*, 2013

Leslie Cavendish, *The Cutting Edge*, 2017

Harper
North

BOOK CREDITS

HarperNorth would like to thank the following staff
and contributors for their involvement in making
this book a reality:

Sarah Allen-Sutter

Laura Amos

Fionnuala Barrett

Peter Borcsok

Sarah Burke

Alan Cracknell

Jonathan de Peyer

Anna Derkacz

Tom Dunstan

Kate Elton

Sarah Emsley

Simon Gerratt

Lydia Grainge

Monica Green

Natassa Hadjinicolaou

Emma Hatlen

Jess Haycox

Jo Ireson

Megan Jones

Jean-Marie Kelly

Taslima Khatun

Holly Kyte

Rachel McCarron

Dan Mogford

Alice Murphy-Pyle

Adam Murray

Genevieve Pegg

Amanda Percival

Dean Russell

Colleen Simpson

Eleanor Slater

Hilary Stein

Chris Stone

Emma Sullivan

Katrina Troy

Hannah Williamson

Ben Wright

For more unmissable reads,
sign up to the HarperNorth newsletter at
www.harpernorth.co.uk

or find us on X at
@HarperNorthUK

Harper
North